Where are the Women?

Where are the Women?

A GUIDE TO AN IMAGINED SCOTLAND

Sara Sheridan

Published in 2019 by Historic Environment Scotland
Enterprises Limited SC510997

HISTORIC   ÀRAINNEACHD
ENVIRONMENT   EACHDRAIDHEIL
SCOTLAND   ALBA

Historic Environment Scotland
Longmore House
Salisbury Place
Edinburgh EH9 1SH

Registered Charity SC045925

British Library Cataloguing-in-Publication Data. A catalogue
record for this book is available from the British Library.

ISBN 978 1 84917 273 8

Typeset in Adobe Caslon Pro and Trajan Pro by
Carol Twombly, PT Sans by Alexandra Korolkova
and Diotima by Gudrun Zapf von Hesse

Printed in the UK by Clays Ltd, Elcograf S.p.A.

MIX
Paper from
responsible sources
FSC
www.fsc.org   FSC® C018072

Contents

Introduction

I can't imagine how I might have conceived of myself and my possibilities if, in my formative years, I had moved through a city where most things were named after women.

Rebecca Solnit

In 2016, writer and activist Rebecca Solnit worked on a map which renamed the stops on the New York subway after women and, in one stroke, highlighted the gendering of our built heritage. It was a strange feeling to look at that remade map and wonder why I had never noticed that, in the normal run of things, all the stops were named after men. I had never heard of most of the women Solnit chose to memorialise. They had achieved amazing things yet their stories were unremembered.

Our sense of self and of where we come from is not confined to history books. On reading about Solnit's project it struck me that if women don't see themselves represented in the world around them, the unspoken message is that their stories, and indeed achievements, don't matter. This raised an interesting question. All the men around me, I realised, were living in just that world – a place where men were raised on plinths and streets were named in their honour. Like Solnit, I immediately imagined the entitlement I might feel if my gender was included and the impact that would have on my confidence. The sense of what I might achieve – and of that achievement being normal. It was a window into the world of our culturally dominant gender.

I discussed Solnit's article with James Crawford, the publisher at Historic Environment Scotland. I had contacted him about my bugbear – the lack of memorialisation of women – and asked if he would be interested in commissioning something about women's history in Scotland. I didn't want to write a researched opinion piece – I wanted to take a more creative approach. I honestly wasn't sure if he would be up for that kind of project. But he was. Over coffee we talked about creating an *imaginary* guide that reflected what Solnit had done – a map not only of an underground system, but of a country. A different world …

It came as no surprise when I discovered that, in a 2016 survey by English Heritage, 40 per cent of respondents thought women did not impact history as much as men. It struck me that this is a vicious circle – if women's achievements are constantly downplayed and men's are publicly more valued, equality will remain an uphill struggle and we will continue to remember the men and forget the women. For all members of society to contribute, it is important to show all contributions are valued, be they from mainstream, majority communities or from minorities. While women make up over 50 per cent of the population, they are still a marginalised group. If proof were needed of how controversial this subject remains, the outcry in 2017 in the run up to Jane Austen's appearance on the Bank of England ten pound note is a good example. The argument against this ran that Austen wrote about 'domestic' subjects and therefore was not worthy of commemoration. This chimed a particular bell with me as a novelist. It reminded me of writer and critic Lesley McDowell's view that 'There's a tendency to elevate novels about war above novels about the domestic sphere, and women tend still to write more about the latter. It doesn't make their novels any less serious or important, but they are perceived to be less so.' The truth is, it isn't only books. This idea crosses all media and with it the dominant view that women's issues and indeed lives aren't worthwhile.

In my writing life I have commemorated the stories of lost and unremembered women for years. In archive after archive I have found myself asking 'where are the women?' as I research material for my historical novels. The lack of female documents and artifacts is acute. Historian Bettany Hughes estimated in 2016 that female material makes up a mere 0.5 per cent of recorded history. Over time I became more and more aware that this issue extends into our day to day existence, and when I found out that in the UK only 15 per cent of statues are raised to women and most of those to Queen Victoria, I was incensed. In another medium, as an activist, I co-founded an equality-led perfume company, REEK, which memorialises landmark women including Jacobites and witches. The collection of scents makes the wearer themselves a monument and allows individual women to take a stand by remembering forgotten heroines from the past. On the day I met Jamie, in fact, I had decided to mix a new perfume in memory of the lives of pirate queens – just as fearsome as Bluebeard, Captain Kidd or Henry Morgan – Jeanne de Clisson, Gráinne Mhao (Grace O'Malley) and Ching Shih. Now I had an opportunity to extend that vision to imagine the recognition of hundreds of women.

The way we memorialise our history is key. As George

Orwell noted in *1984* 'He who controls the past, controls the future. He who controls the present, controls the past.' *He.*

In Naomi Alderman's science fiction novel *The Power*, which won the Baileys Prize in 2017, Alderman imagines a world 5,000 years in the future, where women's power is normalised. In this world, evolutionary biology allows society to misread history and show that men are weak. One character – a man – tries to push against this, arguing that history was written by women who chose stories that were more favourable to them. 'They picked works to copy that supported their viewpoint ... I mean, why would they recopy works that said that men used to be stronger and women weaker? That would be heresy, and they'd be damned for it.' Exactly.

Just as I read Alderman's book, in my home city of Edinburgh (where, incidentally there are more statues of animals than there are of women), crime writer Val McDermid created 'Message from the Skies' as part of the programme of events to celebrate Edinburgh's Hogmanay. This was an interactive trail highlighting Edinburgh's female literary history including the novelist Susan Ferrier, whose talent Sir Walter Scott claimed surpassed his own; author D E Stevenson, cousin of the repeatedly commemorated Robert Louis Stevenson (whom she outsold in her day); and internationally renowned writer Muriel Spark, whose collected works had just been republished to mark her centenary. The project provoked a similar response from some of the people who followed the trail – they were shocked that they had not heard of so many of the landmark female writers featured. The answer to that is how could they have done so if these women aren't commemorated? Existing female monuments number a mere five statues in the whole of Glasgow. Day to day, cultural and historical memory is contained around us, in our built environment, and the women are not there.

This landscape, however, is changing. The centenary celebrations for women over 30 getting the vote prompted a flurry of memorials to suffragettes – a movement more radical than anything in mainstream politics today, which achieved extraordinary change. These specific monuments are important. A frustration for many feminists is the proliferation of general monuments. Solnit herself points out that New York's most prominent statue is a nameless woman – a nobody – the Statue of Liberty. This symbol in female form is like so many around the world representing, say, Justice or Peace. These statues are distinct from the commemoration of groups of women and distinct again from individual commemoration. In the UK, recently memorialisation of non-specific female achievement has risen – the statue to wartime female steel workers in Sheffield is a good example. Not that these women shouldn't be honoured, but not one of them has been named.

For me there is a certain dignity and egalitarianism in memorialising groups of women – victims of oppression or activists who banded together. Sisterhood is key to the feminist movement, and general monuments honour that as a way of instigating progress. But there is no doubt that this should not happen at the expense of our high achievers: women who, if they were men, would certainly have streets named after them. In the field of public art there is a drive against the statue – that (typically) bronze and patriarchal rendering of a famous individual – in favour of something more interpretive and meaningful, which truly expresses that person's achievement. In this guide I have imagined many different kinds of monument – traditional statues, yes, but also places of pilgrimage for public engagement, festivals, light installations, murals, parks, altars, benches, cairns, fountains and bells. I have tried to achieve what we talked about when Jamie threw down the gauntlet that day over coffee. Can you imagine a different Scotland, he said, a Scotland where women are commemorated in statues and streets and buildings – even in the hills and valleys?

The result of that conversation is this book – a guide to an alternative country, a Scotland where the cave on Staffa is named after Malvina rather than Fingal, and Arthur's Seat isn't Arthur's, it belongs to St Triduana. Where you arrive into Dundee at Slessor Station and the Victorian monument on Stirling's Abbey Hill interprets national identity not as a male warrior but through the women who ran hospitals during the First World War. The West Highland Way ends at Fort Mary. The Old Lady of Hoy is a prominent Orkney landmark. And the plinths in central Glasgow proudly display statues of suffragettes. Each fictional street, building, statue and monument is dedicated to a *real* woman and tells their (often uncelebrated) stories.

If we cannot imagine it, how can we build it? It has been a huge task and also an honour. I have tried to create something worthy of our astounding female heritage. I hope the time is right and that we are ready to look unflinchingly at the stories we tell and search for the pieces of our history that have been lost. Conversations about women in history and society have never been more relevant, and this guide-book seeks to contribute to those discussions by exploring the connections between gender and place – looking beyond the traditional male-dominated histories that have been repeated for generations.

'Do you think there are enough women worthy of memorialisation?' many people I have spoken to over the course of my research have asked (always nervously). The answer is that we have thousands of pioneering women who have been forgotten, their stories set aside. Often after asking this question people add (continuing worriedly) 'but you don't *only* want to memorialise women, do you? I mean, that wouldn't be fair.' The answer to that is, for myself, I look forward to the day when feminism is no longer relevant and we can simply use the word 'equality' but I fear we are nowhere near it. For this reason, I have not mentioned in this book the many monuments to amazing men but you will notice that I have placed monuments to their sisters, mothers, wives and friends in some places where statues already exist. Where else was I to put them? If this shocks you then I am glad – welcome to the world of the 'other gender' – this is how women feel all the time and they, mostly, internalise it. If a proliferation of imagined monuments to women sets you on edge, why doesn't the real-life proliferation of monuments to men? That is not to forget men's contributions – it is simply to provide a provocation, an opportunity to see this issue from the other side and hopefully return to the existing state of affairs with questions. This is, in fact, what memorials are supposed to do. Ultimately, this book seeks to paint a companion picture of Scotland's history. It is a challenge laid down to all people – men and women together. This issue is one we need to address and is particularly relevant today: the lack of memorials to women was recently discussed in the Scottish Parliament. If this is to be remedied we need to act as allies, together.

While nothing I outline here can alone change the world, my hope is that it chips away at the dominant cultural narrative and confronts how we remember where we have come from. As a novelist, every book I've written in the last decade has been a hymn to the women whose stories I have found in the archives, be it only one short letter. I feel compelled to engage with that material (and

Bettany Hughes is right – it's gold dust). If we want things to change, we need to ask difficult questions about the way our history has been represented and whether some of the things that history currently tells us are valid. We must celebrate our female stories alongside our male ones and make them just as visible. If I can provide a few ideas and take a very small stand, then I'll be proud to have been part of something that I consider hugely important.

Edinburgh, 2019

How to Use this Guide

In *Where are the Women?* we have worked with the existing landscape, adapting it to memorialise Scotland's women. Some real monuments have been included, and in those instances no symbol is required in the text. Those that have been created are marked on the first mention as follows:

Suffragette Square⚷

This symbol ⚷ indicates a feature or monument that exists and has been renamed, rededicated or adapted so that it commemorates a woman or women. Check Renamed Places (see page 406) for the real names of certain monuments.

Museum of Misogyny⚸

This symbol ⚸ indicates that a building, feature or monument is fictional. Sometimes the material for it exists elsewhere (such as in an archive) and has simply been put on display.

The monument may be in memory of more than one woman. Some women are mentioned without raising a monument and are simply associated with a particular place. The illustrated maps provide the locations for a selection of the monuments in each chapter.

Edinburgh

*Do not think that I blaspheme when I tell
you that your great London, as compared
to Dun-Edin, 'mine own romantic town',
is as prose compared to poetry, or as a
great rumbling, rambling, heavy Epic
compared to a Lyric, brief, bright, clear,
and vital as a flash of lightning.*

Charlotte Brontë on Edinburgh, 1850

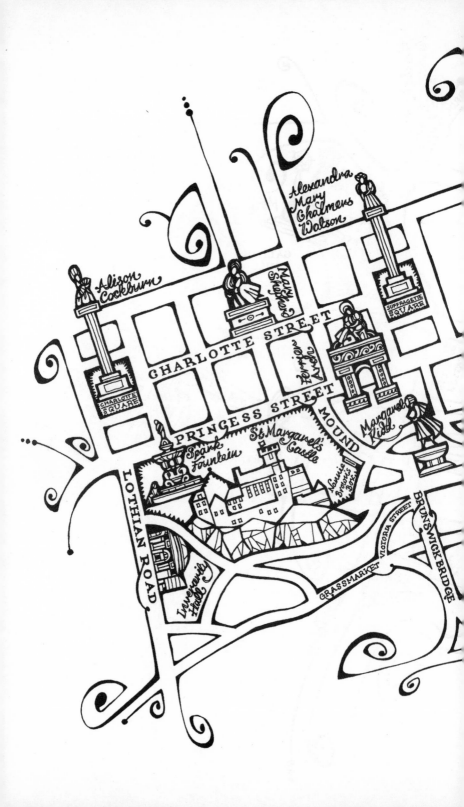

Welcome to Edinburgh: a city of great women! Scotland's capital would still be easily recognisable to Charlotte Brontë – especially the city centre, which is split between the medieval Old Town and the New Town (now over 200 years old), into which the city expanded at the end of the 18th century. The city is surrounded by hills, and one of the best views over the historic skyline is from Triduana's Seat⛰, the extinct volcano about a mile to the east of St Margaret's Castle (see page 21). This hill towers over Holyrood Park and is named after **St Triduana**, who lived between the 4th and 8th centuries. Said to have been so distressed by the amorous attentions of the King of the Picts – who professed to love her beautiful eyes – Triduana tore them out with a thorn and sent them to him, allowing her to continue her life of piety, free from harassment. The ancient centre of worship of Triduana was in the Restalrig area, now part of Edinburgh, where her church is a fine example of 15th century architecture. You can pick out the site of the church with binoculars from the summit of her hill. Triduana's name is also associated to this day with retreats near Forfar and Pitlochry. Beside Triduana's Seat you will see the Livesey Crags⛰, named after **Doris Livesey Reynolds** (1899–1985), a geologist known for her work on metasomatism in rocks and her commentary on the divisive 'Granite Controversy' which split the geological community into two groups – the Neptunists and the Plutonists – who argued whether granite was formed from the universal ocean or from matter made fluid by heat. In 1949 she was the first woman to be elected Fellow of the Royal Society of Edinburgh, and she received the Lyell Medal from the Geological Society of London in 1960. She was not paid for her work at the University of Edinburgh as her husband was based there and it was deemed 'inappropriate' but following her death the crags were named after her in recognition of the impact of her studies. On the west side of the rock face there is a carved⚲ explanation of the geology of the city, which features her research.

The Old Town

The original city of Edinburgh, mostly built during the medieval period, was a mile long and 400 yards wide. This part of town is a magical interlacing of early buildings built around 'closes' or vennels in a herringbone pattern off the main drag – the Royal Mile. These were, in their time, the highest buildings in Europe and, as today, bustling with commerce. At its peak, just before the New Town was built, the city's population (not including the Port of Leith, outside the city's walls) was around 45,000 people – half of them women, many of whom made their mark on the city.

St Margaret's Castle 🏰

It's easy to see why this site was chosen to build the historic castle, on top of sheer crags with approach only possible across the Esplanade to the east. Born in Hungary, **St Margaret** (1045–1093) came to Scotland after the Norman Conquest in 1066, when her ship ran aground in Fife. She was married to the Scottish King Malcolm III, and her Roman Catholic faith had a significant impact on religious life in Scotland. Among her many charitable works she established a ferry for pilgrims across the Firth of Forth at Queensferry. Margaret was known as 'The Pearl of Scotland', and each day served orphans and the poor before she sat down to eat. Hugely influential, she died in this castle, which shortly afterwards was named in her memory. St Margaret's Chapel, the oldest building in the castle complex, is also named for her. The chapel houses the only remaining part of a six piece tapestry✶ called the 'City of Ladies', commissioned in the 1530s by **Mary of Guise** (1515–1560) to hang in her chamber – an appropriate choice as the embroidery shows women very much in charge in the medieval world. Mary was Queen of Scotland and Regent on behalf of her daughter (also Mary) from 1554 to her death. When she died, Mary's body was kept in the chapel for several months before she was laid to rest at a convent in Rheims. Today, a group of local women, all called Margaret, look after the chapel, where you can sometimes spot a wedding taking place.

On the Esplanade, where over 300 women were burned for witchcraft, you will find the Witches' Fountain. Witches were prosecuted in Edinburgh for around a century, with the last burning taking place on this site in 1722. Convicted witches were drowned in the Nor' Loch and their bodies then burned so they could not rise from the dead. There is an Edinburgh urban myth that the ashes of witches were used to help build the Flodden Wall, completed in 1560 to protect the city against a threatened English invasion that did not materialise. It's a great story but inside the castle there is a museum✶ that tells the real tales of Edinburgh's witches – many of whom were vulnerable older women. Among the records on display are those of 50-year-old **Margaret Burges** (c1579–1629), who was accused (and cleared) of lesbian behaviour only to be found guilty of witchcraft, and **Beatrix Leslie** (c1580–1661), in her 80s, accused of having caused a collapse in a coal pit by magic. Not all women went quietly! Moneylender **Agnes Finnie** (died 1645) cursed her tormentors, wishing that 'the devill blaw yow blind' and **Isobel Young** (died 1629) stood up for her right not to see eye to eye with the neighbours who had accused her. She was cleared of nine of the ten charges brought against her, but not of witchcraft. The heartrending story of sisters **Janet Spaldarge** (died 1597) and **Margaret Bane** (died 1597), who were tried separately (Margaret was arraigned in Aberdeen), also merits attention. Margaret was a midwife and, in desperation, claimed Janet had taught her 'the craft' – both sisters were killed within weeks of each other. Another unfortunate, **Jean Weir** (c1604–1670), was notorious in Edinburgh. She was tried not only for witchcraft but for incest with her brother. Jean said that she chiefly turned to magic to increase her capacity to spin wool. At Hallowe'en there is a light show✦ on the castle rock which highlights the sisterhood of these women and their tragic stories.

Inside the castle is a beautiful war memorial with sculptures by **Phyllis Bone** (1894–1972), who became the first female member of the Royal Scottish Academy in 1940. The memorial is dedicated to the many brave souls who died in military action and includes the names not only of soldiers but also of nurses, doctors and auxiliary workers who put their lives on the line. It runs to over a hundred thousand names. The animals who took part are also represented, particularly the many First World War horses. As part of the National War Memorial, there is a specific Women's Hospital Memorial✦ to the pioneering women who set up hospitals during the First World War. This is a 5-metre-long cast bronze plaque showing their stories. The memorial includes images of **Dr Elsie Inglis** (1864–1917), who when she volunteered for the task of setting up field hospitals in 1914 was told by the Colonel in charge at St Margaret's Castle, 'Go home dear lady and sit still.' She did not take his advice. There is a glade in Holyrood Park named after her, a plaque in the High Kirk and another plaque on the first floor of Edinburgh's Central Library. There is a great deal of campaigning for a new memorial to Inglis, who along with her comrades favoured practical monuments to help poor women and their children. Edinburgh's main maternity hospital, founded in 1925, was named after her but closed in 1988 to be replaced by the Simpson Unit at the Royal Infirmary. In 2018 she was featured on the Clydesdale Bank £50 note. Alongside Inglis on the castle plaque is **Dame Sarah Siddons Mair** (1865–1935), who helped create the Scottish Women's Hospitals (see page 63) and was, like Inglis, a suffragette. This monument also honours **Flora White** (1894–1971), who became a lifelong campaigner for peace when her brother was killed after action in the Dardanelles. In 1940, Flora became the assistant editor of the *New Statesman*. Though depicted as a young woman here, she still lives in the memory of many who knew her in her later years in the city, a small and determined lady who favoured tweeds and lacy jumpers. There are often flowers laid at the feet of the plaque featuring these amazing women.

Lady Stair's Close

Edinburgh is a UNESCO City of Literature and, unsurprisingly, a strong literary culture is in evidence throughout the city. On leaving the castle, on the north side of High Street is Lady Stair's Close – named after **Lady Elizabeth Dundas (Lady Stair)** (died 1731), an heiress who lived there in the early 18th century. Her house is now the Scottish Writers' Museum, dedicated to the memory of four Scottish writers ▲ – Muriel Spark (see the Spark Fountain page 56), Susan Ferrier (see the Ferrier Arch (pictured) page 62), D E Stevenson and Dorothy Dunnett. Dorothy (1923–2001) was an Edinburgh institution married to the editor of the *Scotsman* newspaper. She wrote six cult historical novels about Francis Crawford of Lymond, a 16th century Scottish soldier of fortune. Another series, set

The Ferrier Arch

in the 15th century, features Niccolo, an apprentice from Bruges, who becomes a successful Renaissance entrepreneur. She also published a series of thrillers under the name Dorothy Halliday. Her commitment to the arts included a stint as director of the Edinburgh International Book Festival. **Dorothy Emily Stevenson** (1892–1973) was another Edinburgh-based bestselling author who published more than 40 light romantic novels over four decades. She sold 7 million copies in her lifetime – higher sales than her second cousin, the lesser-known Robert Louis Stevenson, achieved in his. Her family did not support her writing and she used to write in the attic of her home at 14 Eglinton Crescent on which there is now a plaque to her memory.

When leaving the museum, look down to see many quotes by Scottish writers etched into the paving stones⚑, such as the following by **Elizabeth Hamilton** (1756–1816), poet, novelist and essayist, who wrote ten books and lived locally in Edinburgh:

> *For me, I boast nor critic lore nor skill,*
> *Nor classic laws for measur'd numbers know;*
> *Enough, to feel the bosom's raptur'd thrill,*
> *The tear that starts – the heart's spontaneous glow!*

Outside the Scottish Writers' Museum on the east side of the close, there is a tree planted in 1973 to honour the Edinburgh Women Citizens Association, which was founded in 1918 to promote women's representation in the post-suffragette era.

If you wander from Lady Stair's Close into James Court, you will find a monument to **Susannah Alice Stephen** (1960–1997) who helped to found the Scottish Society of Garden Designers. Known as Zannah, she died in a diving accident in the Galapagos Islands in 1997. The memorial, erected by her friends, is the work of Edinburgh-born sculptor Frances Polly and takes the form of a seat, with a sculpture of a parakeet and garden trug. In a nice touch across the generations, the monument is overlooked by a portrait of one of Susannah's forebears, Alexander Moncrieff of Culfargie, whose likeness hangs in a window adjacent to James Court in the Free Church of Scotland building.

The Grassmarket

Walk down Victoria Street (named after Queen Victoria, see National Gallery page 61) and you will come to the Grassmarket – Edinburgh's cattle market from the late 15th century until 1911. This is an open, cobbled area skirted with shops, restaurants and bars. Look out for Maggie Dickson's pub, named after a Musselburgh fishwife **Maggie Dickson** (c1701–c1746) convicted of concealing her pregnancy (which was a capital offence) but who survived being hanged in 1724 and was thereafter known as Half-Hangit Maggie. Previously estranged from her husband, they reconciled after Maggie was resurrected and went on to have several more children.

Take the Patrick Geddes Steps along West Port and you'll see the work of **Norah Mears** (1887–1967), who established the Mears Garden ⚑ in 1910 to provide a much-needed green space for residents, particularly children, living in what was at the time a crowded slum. The garden is one of several created in the city's Old Town during the Edwardian era, more than a century later only a few survive.

At the other side of the market, before you turn up Candlemaker Row, peer down the Cowgate at the Magdalen Chapel, where **Janet Rhynd** (c1504–1553), a successful Edinburgh merchant who founded both the chapel and the Magdalen Hospital nearby, is buried. The chapel and hospital provided accommodation and living expenses for a chaplain and seven paupers as well as healthcare on what we would today call an outpatient basis. The terms of Janet's will enjoined the residents to include both her and her husband in their prayers as well as Mary Queen of Scots. This practice was common in the medieval period as it was believed prayers on earth smoothed a spirit's path. The prayers Janet commissioned for Mary were probably a form of sucking up to royalty in the afterlife. The terms of this will were fulfilled at the Magdalen Hospital for around 300 years until the 19th century.

Greyfriars Kirk

On Candlemaker Row you will find the entrance to Greyfriars Kirkyard. Another of the city's wealthy woman, **Margaret, Lady Yester** (1647–1675), is commemorated inside the kirk. Lady Yester contributed 1,000 merks (a substantial sum) to the building of the Tron Kirk on the High Street (the Royal Mile) as well as funding Lady Yester's Chapel on nearby Infirmary Street. When the congregation of the chapel merged with Greyfriars in the 1930s, the commemorative plaque in Lady Yester's memory was moved inside Greyfriars Kirk. In the graveyard there are commemorative stones to many Edinburgh worthies including **Mary Erskine** (1629–1707), a widow who became a successful businesswoman and thereafter lent money to other widows to encourage them into business. In 1694 she funded a foundation in the Cowgate for the schooling of the daughters of Edinburgh burgesses. The aim was to educate orphaned, impoverished girls. In 1706, she bought premises for the Merchant Maiden Hospital, as it was known, and, on her death in 1707, bequeathed money to run it. In 1944 it was renamed the Mary Erskine School – one of the oldest girls' schools in the world and still thriving just outside the city centre. As well as her gravestone there is also a plaque at a house on Queen Street, which was the site of her home.

Also in the churchyard is the grave of **Harriet Siddons** (1783–1844), an actor, singer and the theatre manager of the Theatre Royal Edinburgh. Siddons moved to Scotland after a successful career in Covent Garden and Drury Lane. In Edinburgh, she appeared in around a hundred roles during her six-year tenure and was the first to adapt Sir Walter Scott's novels for the stage. Her production of *Rob Roy* was played by royal command in front of George IV when he visited Scotland in 1822. At her farewell benefit performance in 1830 Scott wrote an address for her, which she delivered to a standing ovation. The speech enjoined the audience to continue to support the Theatre Royal once Siddons had retired. She was mindful of her legacy at the theatre, writing in 1831 'To steer our course with safety is all that can be hoped ... It is so complete a lottery ... that (it) must ever be speculative.'

Outside the churchyard, turn right to have a drink at local pub Paddie Bell's🍺, named after the singer **Paddie Bell** (1931–2005) with the popular folk trio the Corries who went on to host the BBC's Hoot'nanny programme.

National Museum of Scotland
At the top of Candlemaker Row is the National Museum of Scotland on Cupples Street🍺. The street is named after **Anne Jane Cupples** (1839–1896) – a populariser of science who wrote around fifty books, mostly for children. Her titles include *Bill Marlin's Tales of the Sea* and *The Magic of Kindness*. She also corresponded with Charles Darwin, who in her later life, enjoined the Royal Literature Fund

to support her financially. Darwin said he was particularly impressed by Cupples' accurate observations of the emotions of dogs in her stories.

At the bottom of the impressive museum steps there is a fascinating water monument✦ dedicated to the work of inventor **Isabell Lovi** (before 1805–1827). 'Mrs Lovi's beads' were made of glass and used to determine the gravity of liquids. They were employed in the bleaching, distilling and dairy industries – you can see a set inside the museum. The fountain outside, with its glass balls dancing in the water, is a beautiful, artistic interpretation of her work.

Also outside the museum there is a statue✦ of **Charlotte Auerbach** (1899–1994), a Jewish-German zoologist and geneticist who contributed to founding the science of mutagenesis – the study of genetic change and mutation in living organisms. She wrote over 90 scientific papers and was a Fellow of the Royal Society of Edinburgh. She also wrote a book of fairy tales, *Adventures with Rosalind*. In 1976, she was awarded the Royal Society's Darwin Medal.

The museum itself is always worth a visit – a particular highlight is the dressing table set of **Frances Teresa Stuart** (1642–1709), It Girl of Charles II's Restoration court, who modelled for the figure of Britannia on the reverse of the 50 pence piece.

National Library of Scotland
Continue along Brunswick Bridge🏛, which is named after **Caroline of Brunswick** (1768–1821). This 'injured queen' was rejected by her husband George IV, the Prince of Wales (who had already secretly married Maria Fitzherbert, although the marriage was not considered legal). She defied convention by taking lovers and horrified the House of Hanover by insisting that she would be queen when the prince took the throne. The door of Westminster

Abbey was slammed in her face to prevent her attending her husband's coronation. A popular rhyme of the period captures the sentiments of the establishment, if not the public, towards this woman who refused to be pushed out of the way:

O gracious queen
We thee implore
To go away and sin no more
And if that effort be too great
To go away
At any rate.

On the east side of the bridge is the National Library of Scotland, the country's legal deposit library which was established in 1925 and houses some 7 million books, 14 million printed items and 2 million maps. Outside you will see the Flag to the Unknown Woman✤, a copy of the only map of Scotland known to be by a woman in the whole collection – a sampler embroidered at the start of the 19th century by **Margaret Montgomery**. Nothing more is known about Margaret, hence the enigmatic moniker.

Inside, on permanent display, are some of the 57 calligraphic manuscripts✤ of **Esther Inglis** (c1571–1624), a woman of Huguenot descent who lived in the Leith area. Inglis composed miniature books of Protestant texts. Her work is especially noted for beautiful paintings of flowers and the intricate, jewel-studded covers she made by hand. She is thought to have received patronage at Prince Henry's court from 1607 to 1614 and dedicated most of her books to the monarchs Elizabeth I and James VI and I. Unusually for a woman in this period, she signed her work. Also on display are the notebooks✤ of pioneering mathematicians **Jane Sang** (1834–1878) and **Flora Sang** (1838–1925), who, despite their initial objections, were credited with a good portion of the work their father had done on logarithmic tables. The women were presented to the Royal Society Edinburgh in 1874 and honoured for their contribution.

The statue✻ in the library's main hallway is inscribed with the words of **Isabella Bird** (1831–1904), 'Everything suggests a beyond.' Bird, a traveller, writer, photographer and naturalist, wrote eighteen books, including *Among the Tibetans* and *A Lady's Life in the Rocky Mountains*. She visited America, Japan, Australia, Hawaii, China, Korea, Vietnam, Singapore, Malaysia, India, Persia, Kurdistan and Turkey, where she climbed mountains and lived with local people. In the 1890s, Bird was the first female fellow of the Scottish Royal Geographical Society and the Royal Geographical Society. Ever a lady, she took issue with a review of her book in *The London Times* that suggested she wore trousers while mountain climbing in America. *The Times* backed down and apologized. When she died in her bed in Edinburgh her bags were ready and packed to go on another great adventure. Bird funded the building of the clock tower on Tobermory harbour wall in memory of her sister Henrietta and also contributed to several medical facilities in India. Her papers are held in the collection at the National Library.

The ceiling in the main hallway is decorated with a poem✻ that spells out the discrimination faced by Scotland's female typographers in the late Victorian era as the industry changed in response to rapid technological development. In 1886, a correspondent to the *Scottish Typographical Circular* wrote 'if [women] were more largely gifted' with the skills of typesetting 'they would, indeed, be very dangerous rivals'. The truth was that in Scotland women had been rivalling men in typesetting jobs for decades. In the same issue of the magazine, a type-lifter called 'Ella' wrote a poem asking that she and her colleagues be given the recognition they deserved. However, as pay structures changed, many men chose to blame women rather than the changes in technology responsible for their reduction in circumstances. Ella's poem is reproduced in a waterfall of letters that slips over the edge of the ceiling and down the wall.

> *Do not prate arrant nonsense about a woman's sphere,*
> *For that humbug's exploded this many a year—*
> *To be wife and mother might perfectly suit a*
> *Compositrix's desires, but not out of Utah*
> *Is such a thing possible;*

Central Library

On the other side of Brunswick Bridge, the Central Library is the city's main lending library. Inside you will find two small bronze statues ✿, each depicting a figure engrossed in a book. One is the hugely popular Scottish-Russian writer **Eugenie Fraser** (1905–2002), whose memoir *The House by the Dvina* intrigued readers with the story of her childhood before she came to Scotland. The other is **Lucy Walford** (1845–1915), who wrote 47 light-hearted books and was invited to meet Queen Victoria after her majesty found she could not put down Walford's debut novel, *Mr Smith: A Part of His Life*, published in 1874.

On display up the main staircase are 60 watercolours ✿ donated to the library by the friends of **Janet Stewart Smith** (1839–1925). Smith was an illustrator who recorded the early morning life of Edinburgh's Old Town, where she lived, in the mid 19th century. These charming paintings were so often requested that the library had them mounted to allow members of the public to enjoy them without troubling library staff.

The High Court
The city's High Court is on the Royal Mile. You will frequently see reporters outside and, on occasion, protesters. To the left of the main door is a bronze statue✤ of **Margaret Kidd** (1900–1989), who was the first woman QC in Scotland, taking the silk in 1948 and later becoming Keeper of the Advocates Library. She is known affectionately as the 'Father [sic] of the Scottish Bar'. Behind her is a plaque✤ dedicated to the work of Jewish feminist human rights and child welfare campaigner **Ruth Adler** (1944–1994). Adler helped establish the Scottish Child Law Centre and was the first Scottish Development Officer for Amnesty International. It has become a tradition to leave a stone beneath Adler's plaque, which is the Jewish custom in memory of the dead.

St Catherine's Cathedral 🜨
Edinburgh's High Kirk was the parish church of medieval Edinburgh and the home of the Scottish Reformation. It is named after **Catherine of Siena** (1347–1380), who established a convent in 1377 outside Siena. Catherine composed over 400 letters about her faith, several prayers and also wrote her *Dialogue*, which led to her being declared a Doctor of the Church in 1970. When a convent on the south side of Edinburgh was dedicated to her, the area around it became known as 'Sciennes' – a derivation of 'Siena' in French, which was the court language of Scotland in the 16th century. It is in St Catherine's that the legendary rioter and stallkeeper **Jenny Geddes** (c1600–c1660) threw her stool at the pulpit in 1637 in protest against an English prayer book introduced by order of King Charles I, who hoped to standardise church services across the kingdom. She is said to have shouted 'Daur you say Mass in my lug?' as she threw the stool. There is a tablet

in the north aisle that marks where her actions sparked the riot that ultimately led to the Wars of the Three Kingdoms (1638–1651) which included the English Civil War (1642–1651). After she (and other rioters) were ejected from the church, they hammered at the doors and threw stones at the windows. Religious matters in 17th century Scotland were as hot a topic, it seems, as women's rights today. Keep an eye out for the monumental statues of religious subjects by **Mary Grant** (1831–1908), one of the city's talented sculptors, whose work is seen not only in the High Kirk but also in St Mary's Cathedral (see page 53). The interior of the kirk is awash with reminders of Edinburgh's notable women, many of whom worshipped there. **Isabel Williamson** (1430–1493) was a hugely successful cloth merchant who supplied the royal household during the 1470s and, unusually, became a burgess of the city, which meant she had voting rights – uncommon for a woman in the period. She endowed the Altar of St Lawrence in 1489 under her maiden name, Isabel Bras. Another contributor to the church was **Lady Roseburn** (1637–1716), an early printer and publisher who inherited the business when her husband died. She was said to have left it ten times more in profit than her husband left it in loss. Don't forget to take in the private chapel of the sixteen Knights of the Thistle, the highest chivalric order in Scotland, built in 1911. The knights include Her Majesty the Queen, who attends the chapel when she is in Edinburgh.

Signet Library

Outside St Catherine's is the Signet Library, which leads a double life. By day it is the home of Scotland's 'writers to the signet' and a centre for legal research – but by evening it is a renowned concert venue. Mindful of history, the musical programme contains a liberal number of Scottish composers, including the award-winning **Margaret Dare** (1902–1976), whose career as a cellist began at the First World War victory concert in the Albert Hall. Dare also wrote music for children. Another local composer and cellist featured regularly is **Joan Dickson** (1921–1994), founder of the New Edinburgh Quartet. She taught the international cellist superstar Jacqueline du Pré.

Mary King's Close

When the building of the Royal Exchange (now the City Chambers) started in 1753, several tenements on the site were simply bricked up. In modern times these have been opened as a subterranean museum called Mary King's Close. **Mary King** (c1600–c1645) was a successful Edinburgh tailor and cloth merchant who lived and worked on the site. Like Isabel Williamson (above), Mary was a burgess. Tours take place several times a day led by actors wearing historical dress. As well as an insight into Mary King's life, expect to hear about **Alison Rough** (c1480–1535). Another successful merchant, Alison was executed for murdering Alexander Cant, her son in law, with a pair of fire tongs in a heated dispute over her daughter's dowry, which she had not paid. Alison was a difficult woman. After her husband was killed at the Battle of Flodden she took over his business and over several years managed to get into hundreds of petty disputes before this murder case. Her fascinating life story and ultimate execution by drowning in the Nor' Loch can be reconstructed from court records. She managed to escape from prison after she was sentenced but was recaptured. Alison's daughter, Katherine, was also implicated in her husband's murder and sentenced to death, but, as she was pregnant, this was deferred until after the birth. Katherine was luckier than her mother – no sooner had the child arrived than she managed to evade the noose by escaping to Germany.

Back on the street, Mary King and Alison Rough are not the only women whose stories add flavour to the grandeur of the buildings – local businesswomen have always contributed to the life of the city. If you want a real taste of history, ask for a 'Marjorie Cowan' in a local bar, a drink� named after **Marjorie Cowan** (1734–1819), who was the doyenne of her family's papermill at nearby Moray House after inheriting it when her husband died. Her favourite drink was a cup of rum mixed with marmalade, the signature ingredients in her eponymous cocktail. Fired by the Enlightenment, high literacy rates and the growth of Edinburgh as a centre for publishing, Cowan's papermill was a hugely successful business that stayed in the family for generations – a testament to Marjorie's handling of the family's affairs.

Off to the north, at Cockburn Street look out for a collection of padlocks✺ attached to a grille at the top of the close to the memory of **Janet Fockart** (c1525–1596), a moneylender to smart Edinburgh, who advanced huge sums to, among others, the Earl of Orkney. When she died her estate totalled an eye-watering 22,000 Scots pounds, but after her death she was disowned by her family who were embarrassed by her fiscal activities. She lived nearby in what is now Anchor Close. These padlocks are reminiscent of the 'locked boxes' of the period, commonly used for keeping cash safe in the days before modern banking.

Back on the High Street look out for the monument to **Jessie McGregor** (1863–1906), who established a nursing home and maternity centre called the Hospice here. By 1910, this had amalgamated with the Bruntsfield Hospital for Women and Children. The statue✺ of a mother and child, which is carved into the wall of the Tron Kirk, is in her memory. Sometimes you will see flowers and votive candles there, a sign of good wishes for women and children undergoing labour. The scorch marks on the stone attest to the fact that this tradition has been ongoing for over a century.

University of Edinburgh

Head along the Bridges to the University of Edinburgh, founded in 1583, which has been a major institution of learning for over 400 years. The university adopted women's education relatively early, though not without some battles, including a riot near Old College in 1870 against women sitting anatomy exams. It is worth taking time to walk around Old College Quad where the walls are covered in plaques to the university's many groundbreaking female alumni including Sophia Jex-Blake (see page 70).

Old College Quad: South Wall

Starting at the south, the first of a number of plaques★ you will see is to someone who was key in women obtaining access to higher education. **Mary Crudelius** (1839–1877) founded the movement that opened university education to women in Scotland and signed one of the first petitions to parliament supporting votes for women. An early residential hall for female students at the university was named after her. Here you will also find **Susan Manning** (1953–2013), Grierson Professor of English Literature and director of the Institute for Advanced Studies in the Humanities, who was known internationally for her work on transatlantic literature (Manning specialised in finding the Scottish voice in American writing). The university hosts an annual lecture in her memory which most recently was given by Scottish writer Janice Galloway about the legacy of Muriel Spark (see page 56). Featured further along is **Christina (Chrissie) Miller** (1899–2001), who overcame disability and sexism to become a highly respected analytical chemist. In 1928 she produced the first sample of pure phosphorus trioxide, for which she received the Keith Prize, and in 1949 she was one of the first five women – and the only chemist – to be elected to the Royal Society of Edinburgh. With impaired hearing from childhood, Miller lost her sight in one eye in a lab explosion in the 1930s. In her early days as a research assistant she left a window open in the lab so she could climb in at night to keep working.

You will also find a plaque here to **Marion Gray** (1902–1979), a mathematician who discovered a graph with 54 vertices and 81 edges, which proved key to network theory and is still used in network calculations today. While working at telecommunications company AT&T in the USA she became well known for supporting junior colleagues and for her critiques of mathematical journals. She retired to Edinburgh where she took up hillwalking.

Old College Quad: East Wall
Plaques✢ continue with lesbian feminist **Ellen Higgins** (1871–1951), who was Principal of Royal Holloway College from 1907 to 1935 and senator of London University from 1911 to 1935. She was a talented string musician who played violin, viola, cello and bass and later in life took up the clarinet. She also decided to learn Russian at the age of 70 and celebrated her retirement by climbing the Matterhorn with the Ladies Alpine Club. In his memorial address Professor E S Waterhouse said 'She fought a battle for women's education. She believed in it as a right and not as a concession or favour.' There is also a plaque to **Sheila Macintyre** (1910–1960), who

compiled the German–English mathematical dictionary and sadly died a year after she emigrated to the USA to take up a post at the University of Cincinnati. Also here you will find **Marion Ross** (1903–1994), a physicist who, with her research partner, discovered the location of the Beevers-Ross and anti-Beevers-Ross ions. During the Second World War she headed research into underwater acoustics (ie radar) at Rosyth. She loved music and sang in the choir at Holy Rude Church in Stirling, where her father had designed the organ. In 1965 she established the Fluid Dynamics Unit at Edinburgh University where there is still a physics prize given annually in her name. A street at King's Buildings is named after her.

The final plaque on this wall is to **Elizabeth Wiskemann** (1901–1971) who was the first woman to hold a chair at the University as the Montague Burton Professor of International Relations. Before her academic career, in 1930, she worked in Berlin for the *New Statesman*, and was among the first to warn of the dangers of Fascism. Wiskemann was expelled from Germany by the Gestapo in 1936. She spent most of the war ostensibly working as a press attaché in Switzerland, but this was only a cover to allow her to secretly gather intelligence from Germany and occupied Europe. In May 1944, British Intelligence learned that Hungarian Jews were being deported to Auschwitz. When the allies turned down her request to bomb the railway lines to stop the deportations, Wiskemann sent an unencrypted telegram to the Foreign Office, suggesting bombing the addresses of the Hungarian government officials with the power to stop the exodus. When, coincidentally, several of the buildings she listed were hit in a US raid, the Hungarian government thought that Wiskemann's telegram was being acted upon and stopped the deportations.

Old College Quad: North Wall

There are also plaques✣ on the north wall. Students still leave flowers at the plaque dedicated to **Rosalind Mary Mitchison** (1919–2002), a 20th century social historian known as 'Rowy', who broke new ground researching the history of 18th century Scotland including studies of sexuality. She was particularly supportive of other female academics and was renowned for throwing legendary parties on Guy Fawkes night. Also commemorated is Quaker **Elizabeth Nichol** (1807–1897), an abolitionist, anti-segregationist, suffragist, chartist and anti-vivisectionist. Nichol attended the World Anti-Slavery Convention in London in 1840 as one of only six British female delegates. On arriving the women were told, despite their objections, they could not participate and were made to sit in a segregated area. She was the first woman to sit on a school board in Scotland. In 1872 around 1,000 school boards were set up. It was important that women like Nichol took an active part in creating an educational environment where girls could succeed, just as institutes of higher learning were beginning to open to female students.

To the rear of the courtyard look out for **Ailie Edmunds Munro** (1918–2002), who was born in China and moved to Edinburgh at the age of seven. She became a music teacher, author and folk music scholar who furthered the recognition of Scottish folk music through her work at the School for Scottish Studies and the publication of her opus *The Democratic Muse* about the Scottish folk music scene. Lastly there is a plaque to **Kesaveloo Naidoo** (1906–1999), one of the founders of the Passive Resistance Campaign in South Africa in 1946 in which women became a leading political force. Of Tamil ancestry, she served seventeen jail terms for her cause after which she moved to England to live in exile. She returned to vote in the first democratic elections in South Africa in 1994. Her memoir, *Coolie Doctor*, is an intimate history of the anti-apartheid movement.

Behind Old College with its array of extraordinary female achievement, there is a statue✴ at the top of West College Street of **Agnes McLehose** (1758–1841), for whom Robert Burns wrote his famous poem 'Ae Fond Kiss' after they parted for the last time. 'Clarinda', as she was nicknamed, had a passionate on/off love affair with Burns (whom she called 'Sylvander') which was memorialised in their correspondence, valued on Agnes's death at £25 – a large sum at the time. Agnes lived close to this statue, in the now demolished tenements on Potterrow, which today is the site of the Student Union. From a medical family, she was well educated and wrote poetry, which Burns declared was 'worthy of Sappho'. Agnes fled to Jamaica to recon-cile with her husband but found he had taken a mistress on the island. When she returned to Scotland, she and Burns continued to write to each other but did not rekindle their affair. On Valentine's Day you may see what looks like litter peppered around the statue, but is in fact love wishes slipped into the crevices – a local tradition.

St Cecilia's Hall

Back on the High Street, turn left at Niddry Street for St Cecilia's Hall, Scotland's oldest purpose-built music hall built in 1762 and named after the patron saint of music. The hall was so popular during the Georgian era that attendees were asked to leave their swords and the hoops of their skirts at home, so that more people could cram inside. It is named for **Cecilia**, an early Christian, martyred in Rome around AD 230, although some accounts put her death around 50 years earlier. Cecilia was forced to marry a pagan nobleman, and during the wedding sang to God for help. Later she revealed an angel to her new husband.

After her martyrdom, she became patron saint of musicians. She was so highly venerated by the early Roman Catholic Church that her name was placed in the Mass – one of only seven women included.

Museum of Childhood

Walk east on the High Street towards this museum, housed in a former theatre. It was the first museum in the world to specialise in the history of childhood. Inside, as well as five galleries exhibiting historic toys, there is also a library dedicated to Scotland's children's writers, where storytime✷ takes place every day at 11am. In addition to Scotland's many living children's authors the museum celebrates the country's heritage in children's books from the past including the stories of **Mona Noel Paton** (1860–1928), a writer who modelled for her father, the celebrated painter Joseph Noel Paton, and can still be seen in his paintings of fairy scenes in the Royal Scottish Academy. Mona's own works were fresh retellings of *Jack the Giantkiller* and *Beauty and the Beast*, following the French tradition of 17th century feminist storytelling. As a child in 1871 she met Lewis Carroll, author of *Alice in Wonderland*, when he joined the family on holiday on Arran. Later she wrote of Carroll: 'He used to annoy me very much by setting me puzzles, and I retaliated by making some paper stars, and refusing to show him how they were done ... I have also two photographs which he took of me in his rooms at Oxford, and of which I do not approve, as I thought they made me uglier than I was.' As an adult, Mona also became acquainted with Oscar Wilde.

The museum also houses the work of Catherine Sinclair (see Charlotte Square page 52) and **Ann Fraser Tytler** (1781–1857), whose work was enjoyed across the world but is now largely forgotten. Her series of Leila stories about a girl who is shipwrecked with her nurse, father and pet spaniel were bestsellers in their day. The *Gentleman's Quarterly* called her an 'accomplished writer' and said she 'gratified the love of the marvellous which is so beautiful an instinct in children'. Ann's popular books outsold those of her brother, the eminent historian and advocate Alexander Fraser Tytler.

Controversially, the museum library also contains the books✤ of local author **Helen Bannerman** (1862–1946), who wrote *Little Black Sambo*. These are displayed alongside the museum's collection of gollywogs and an explanation of why the institution has taken the decision to show and comment upon the racism of the past. Despite this there are often objections to the validity of this display.

In the museum you can also learn the story✤ of **Lady Jane Dundas** (1811–1897) who in 1895 donated £6,500 to build, furnish and fund the running of a wing at the Edinburgh Sick Children's Hospital in memory of her sister who died aged three. The display telling the story of the hospital includes photographs and historic equipment used on the wards.

The Storytelling Centre

This contemporary centre contains the Netherbow Theatre and is built around one of the oldest buildings in the High Street – the house of misogynist preacher John Knox (see Museum of Misogyny page 240). The Edinburgh City of Literature Trust recently installed an exhibition here called The Marvellous Regimen of Women✤ (a play on Knox's book against female monarchs *The First Blast of the Trumpet Against The Monstrous Regimen of Women*). The exhibition projects holograms of female Scottish writers declaiming their own words as you follow the trail of female voices from medieval times to the mid 20th century from Elizabeth Melville, Scotland's first female poet in print (see page 224) to Muriel Spark (see page 56). There is also a small permanent exhibition✦ about Scottish folk tales and songs. This part of the High Street was home to the Howff, a legendary folk cafe – one of two main venues in the city during the 1970s and 1980s to host Scotland's burgeoning folk music scene. The other was a monthly club called The Heretics at the New Town Hotel. Video of some of these meetings is included in the exhibition – look out for the performances of **Maggie Cruickshank** (1939–2012) and her younger sister **Liz** (died 1990), folk singers and collectors known as The Crookies, who had a huge repertoire of songs, which they generously shared with other folk bands. After carol-singing for charity during the 1960s, the sisters started regularly organising fund-raising concerts in aid of cancer research and local homeless charities.

St Patrick's Church

Take a quick detour down St Mary's Street to the Cowgate, where you will reach St Patrick's Roman Catholic Church. Here you can visit the shrine to **Margaret Sinclair** (1900–1925), a nun declared venerable by Pope Paul VI in 1978. Born and brought up in Edinburgh, Sinclair worked multiple jobs to support her family during the First World War while her father and elder brother were away fighting. Latterly, she worked in a French polishers and a biscuit factory before entering the Order of Saint Clare (or the Poor Clares) in 1923. She died of tuberculosis shortly afterwards and quickly became known as Edinburgh's 'factory girl' venerated for her bravery facing the harshness of ordinary life.

Scottish Poetry Library

Head down the High Street once more and, housed in a modern custom-built building that incorporates part of the ancient city wall, you will come to this library founded by **Tessa Ransford** (1938–2015). Ransford was a Fellow of the Royal Literary Fund and President of the Scottish Centre of PEN International from 2003 to 2006. Her friend **Kathleen Raine** (1908–2003) was also involved in the foundation of the library and received the Queen's Medal for Poetry in 1992. Raine paid tribute to the place her Scottish heritage played in her relationship to poetry when she said, 'On my mother's side I inherited Scotland's songs and ballads … sung or recited by my mother, aunts and grandmothers, who had learnt it from their mothers and grandmothers … Poetry was the very essence of life.'

Inside the library, you can browse books and periodicals and listen to recordings of poetry in English, Scots and Gaelic. Among the Scottish poets in the collection are **Anne Bannerman** (1765–1829), who died in poverty in the city and whose work was supported by Sir Walter Scott, and **Sandie Craigie** (1964–2005), a Cowgate performance poet influenced by the punk era, who refused to allow her work to be published. She co-edited early editions of the counter-culture journal *Rebel Inc* in the 1980s and wryly said of her own work 'it's a bit sweary'. Another local poet in the collection is **Christian Lindsay**, thought to be a cook at the court of James VI in the late 1500s as well as a pioneering female writer. Also on the shelves is the work of **Isa Knox** (1831–1903) who contributed verses to the *Scotsman* as 'Isa' and was regularly employed on the paper in the 1850s before moving to London, where she won £50 at the Crystal Palace for her centenary poem on Burns.

As you stroll back onto the cobbled street, look out for a memorial to **May Drummond** (c1712–1772), who was a Quaker preacher, in what is now Bull's Close. If you look up as you pass you will see hands clasped in prayer in memory of her fundraising for the founding of Edinburgh's Royal Infirmary. This close was formerly named May Drummond Close in her honour but was changed in the 19th century.

The Scottish Parliament
In the shadow of Triduana's Seat, this building houses Scotland's directly elected assembly. Inside, look out for the work of Shauna McMullan, which commemorates the women of Scotland – an impressive ceramic piece that covers all of one wall with raised white handwriting, the words of women talking about their heroines. There are often temporary exhibitions✿ here, most recently about the life of **Teresa Billington-Greig** (1877–1964), who was a suffragette, teacher and trade unionist. In June 1906, she was arrested outside the Prime Minister's house, where it was alleged she was part of a disturbance, and sentenced to either a fine or two months in prison. She chose the prison term and became the first suffragette to be sent to Holloway Prison. She was released quickly, however, because an anonymous reader of the *Daily Mirror* paid her fine. She was then sent to organise the Women's Suffrage and Political Union in Scotland, later resigning over differences with the Pankhursts. However, she remained in the group as a member. For the rest of her life she documented the suffrage movement, staying politically active into the 1950s.

On the exterior of the building and etched into the paving stones there are a huge number of quotations and memorial stones🌢, and one otherwise blank wall acts as a screen✿ for projections about political campaigns, action taken in the chamber and, of course, the many figures that make up Scotland's history – more than half of them women. One biography recently screened there was that of

Annie Altschul (1919–2001), the most significant psychiatric nurse of her generation. Born Jewish in Vienna she fled fascism and trained as a registered mental health nurse. Altschul became a major influence in the post-war development of UK mental health nursing education and practice. She was professor of nursing studies at the University of Edinburgh from 1976 to 1983. Her MSc research and books are classics in the field and she wrote bravely and openly about her own experience of depression in her book *Wounded Healers* in which she says 'The beauty of spring in the Scottish landscape is … a landmark in my recovery which it is difficult to convey to others.' Annie's achievements were recognised in her appointment as one of the first cohort of fellows of the Royal College of Nursing in 1978.

Scotland's parliament takes the commemoration of Scottish culture and politics seriously and particularly encourages women's involvement in political life. After the death of **Margo MacDonald** (1943–2014), an independent politician who campaigned for assisted dying, the Margo Awards were instituted. These trophies take the form of a bell✻ (or clarion call), accompanied by a political book published that year selected by the First Minister,✻ and are awarded annually to six Scottish women who have contributed to politics.

On days when the parliament is in session, at 1pm a biodegradable balloon✻ is launched from the grassy area in front of the main door. This is in memory of a different person each day (with suggestions submitted by the public) and preference is given to those who fostered political change. Women commemorated recently include **Angela Booth Dobbie** (1937–2012), a disability and access campaigner who founded and led the Artlink organisation, and **Janet Chance** (1886–1953), co-founder of the Abortion

Law Reform Association. The balloon is always printed with one of several quotations by **Mary Ann Radcliffe** (1746–1810), a leading figure in the early feminist movement. Often featured is a quote from Radcliffe's book *The Female Advocate*: 'When we look around us, nothing is more conspicuous in the eyes of the world, than the distresses of women.' Accompanying the release of the balloon, there is a short ceremony led by a different member of the Scottish Parliament each day – this is not announced in advance and you may find that you are being treated to the thoughts of a rookie backbencher or those of the First Minister.

Outside the parliament there are three statues. The first✤ is to **Mary Burton** (1819–1909), who convinced the Watt Institution and School of Arts (forerunner of Heriot-Watt University) to open its classes to female students in 1869, and became its first woman director in 1874. In her will she left prizes for evening-class students of both genders, and for the Edinburgh National Society for Women's Suffrage to campaign for women to be admitted as members of parliament. The second statue✤ is to **Chrystal Macmillan** (1872–1937), who in 1896 became the first female science graduate of the University of Edinburgh and was the first female honours graduate in mathematics. She campaigned for women's right to vote and became the first woman to plead a case before the House of Lords in 1908 when she took the male establishment of the University of Edinburgh to court because they refused to let women graduates vote as members of the University's General Council. After this, she became known in the press as the 'Scottish Portia' after Shakespeare's feisty character in *The Merchant of Venice*. Both these women also have university buildings named after them. The third statue✤ is of **Jackie Crookstone** (1768–1797). Little is known of Crookestone's life apart from the heroic stance she took against the Scottish Militia Act 1797. The act aimed to supply the armed forces of Britain's expanding empire with men, but local miners opposed enforced conscription and Crookstone organised a protest march. A female ringleader, she used her drum to orchestrate chants of 'No Militia'. When the act went ahead, a riot broke out and soldiers killed eleven people in what became known as the Tranent Massacre. Dragoons 'mopping up' afterwards were probably responsible for killing her. Her death was never officially recorded and her body lay in a cornfield for weeks until being discovered by harvesters. There is also a bronze statue to her memory further along the coast in the Civic Square in Tranent.

Palace of Holyroodhouse
On the other side of the road is a 17th century royal palace and the ruins of a 13th century abbey. Tours of the palace include the room where the rumoured lover of Mary Queen of Scots (see page 205), David Rizzio, was stabbed 56 times by men led by the queen's jealous husband, Lord Darnley, who felt slighted at not becoming king on his marriage to Mary, only a consort. Later, when Darnley died following an explosion, Mary came under suspicion for his death, and ultimately succumbed to pressure to marry the Earl of Bothwell. The palace is also home to the Queen's Gallery where exhibitions are staged from the Royal Collection. Outside there is a statue✣ depicting 'The Blak Lady' (c1485–c1520), one of a troupe of black entertainers who moved with the court of James IV between Edinburgh and Dunfermline.

As you leave the palace look to your right and you will see a small thicket of trees✣ dedicated to the memory of **Lucky Wood** (died 1717), a famous innkeeper on the Canongate to whom Allan Ramsay wrote an elegy.

Ramsay's words about Lucky's kindness to local writers are etched into the tree trunks:

The writer lads fow well may mind her,
Furthy was she, her luck design'd her
Their common mither, sure nane kinder
Ever brake bread;

The New Town

Though both locations are World Heritage sites, in contrast to the craggy, atmospheric Old Town, the New Town is a bright neoclassical development. Today it is the heart of Edinburgh's business and retail community with shops, offices, banks and restaurants as well as a residential population. Some of the streets and squares are named after Hanoverian royals.

Charlotte Square

Start at the West End at Charlotte Square, named for **Queen Charlotte** (1744–1818). Born in Germany, Charlotte married George III in 1761 and went on to have fifteen children. The queen took an interest in botany and music and was a patron of the arts at the Hanoverian court. She particularly chose to patronise women artists when she commissioned paintings and sculptures. There are eight streets and squares named after her across Scotland.

At the centre of the square there is a statue of **Alison Cockburn** (1712–1794), renowned wit and society hostess in Enlightenment Edinburgh. She described the six-year-old Walter Scott as 'the most extraordinary genius of a boy I ever saw'. Cockburn also wrote lyrics, which were set to the traditional music of *Flowers of the*

Forest. There are public benches and seats surrounding the statue as a reflection of her salon.

Fittingly for the site of the Edinburgh International Book Festival, the square also houses a statue✦ of writer **Dame Rebecca West** (1892–1983) with pen and paper in hand. West's major works include *Black Lamb and Grey Falcon* about her travels in Yugoslavia; *A Train of Powder*, which contains her coverage of the Nuremberg Trials; and *The New Meaning of Treason*, a study of the trial of William Joyce, British fascist. She also wrote the Aubrey trilogy of autobiographical novels, for which *Time* magazine gave her the backhanded compliment of 'indisputably the world's number one woman writer'. When he heard of her death, the editor-in-chief of the *New Yorker* called her 'one of the giants'.

Just off the square, at the bottom of North Charlotte Street, there is a gothic stone spire in memory of children's writer **Catherine Sinclair** (1800–1864), whose most famous novel, *Holiday House*, remained in print for a century. Besides huge success in her writing, she was a popular philanthropist who started a volunteer brigade for the boys of Leith, set up cooking depots for working men, paid for the first drinking fountain in Edinburgh and a hall for lectures, and donated funds in aid of the city's cabmen. This monument was raised by subscription after her death.

West End Village

Behind Charlotte Square, to the west, lies the West End Village. Among a nest of shops, offices, restaurants and bars, search out the De La Barca Mexican bar⚑ named after **Fanny Calderón de la Barca** (1804–1882), whose 19th century journal is considered one of the most important documents about Mexico from the period. She also wrote *The Attaché in Madrid* under a male pseudonym. In later life she was responsible for the education of the Infanta Isabella of Spain for which she was made a Marchesa in 1873.

You will also pass a bronze statue✤ on Coates Crescent – the figure of a man, Walter Sholto Douglas, born as **Mary Dods** (c1790–c1830), who was raised at Dalmahoy House just outside the city. Douglas wrote under the name David Lyndsay and is often featured on flags✤ and banners during Edinburgh's Gay Pride March.

Further along the crescent there are plaques at number 12 to **Jean Milligan** (1886–1978) and **Ysobel Stewart** (1882–1968), co-founders of the Scottish Country Dance Society in 1923. Around the corner, look up to see the magnificent triple spires of St Mary's Cathedral. The building was funded by sisters **Barbara** and **Mary Walker** in their estate – the money being released after Mary's death in 1870 (Barbara pre-deceased her.) The twin spires at the west end of the church are named in their honour – one is called Barbara and the other Mary. Nearby another pair of sisters, **Flora** (1839–1905) and **Louisa Stevenson** (1835–1908) eschewed the family business of building lighthouses in favour of good works. They are commemorated in the name Stevenson Street🏛, which will lead you back to Charlotte Square. Flora was one of the first women to serve on a school board in Scotland and organised ragged schools for the poor, while Louisa campaigned for women's university education, women's suffrage and effective nursing. Their distant cousin Dorothy Stevenson is commemorated at the Scottish Writers' Museum (see page 24).

Lothian Road
Running south from the West End, is Lothian Road, which will take you to a stretch containing two of Edinburgh's theatres and a concert hall. In front of Inverarity Hall🏛

(endowed by the Usher brewing family in memory of **Eliza Inverarity** (1813–1846), an Edinburgh-born opera singer who toured the UK and USA), there is a beautiful wrought iron installation of an open door✷ dedicated to **Jeni Ayris** (1964–2012), who owned popular local cafe Ndebele in Tollcross. She was tragically killed by a suicide bomber in Afghanistan. The programme at Inverarity Hall often includes work✷ by **Helen Hopekirk** (1856–1945), an Edinburgh pianist and composer whose music was influenced by the Scottish folk tradition. The great piano teacher Theodor Leschetizky deigned to describe her as the finest woman musician he had ever known – a tempered compliment.

Next to Inverarity Hall is the Lyceum Theatre, where on the facade you will see a stucco statue✷ of two women – both actresses. **Elizabeth Baker** (died 1778) and her nemesis **Sarah Ward** (1726–1771) wrangled over billing to a legendary degree throughout the 1760s. The women are now side by side in perpetuity above the Lyceum's entrance, though Ward would probably take great pleasure in pointing out her statue is slightly taller than that of Baker.

On the other side of Inverarity Hall, outside the Traverse Theatre, is a podium✷ used by street performers during the Fringe. On the base are the words of **Cordelia Oliver** (1923–2009), who was the *Guardian*'s arts correspondent in Scotland for 30 years from 1963. It reads 'A Scottish national theatre is an activity. It has to start with a company, not a building.' In the hallway of the Traverse there is a video presentation✷ about the life and work of sisters **Anna Maria** (1778–1832) and **Jane Porter** (1776–1850), historical novelists and playwrights whose work predates Sir Walter Scott's, with whom they were acquainted, and who covered much of the same subject matter. Many wonder if Scott 'borrowed' some of their original ideas.

On the other side of the main road there is a statue of a woman and child titled *Victory is Certain* by Ann Davidson, which was unveiled in 1986 by Suganya Chetty, a member of the African National Congress then living in exile in Edinburgh. The statue is in honour of all those killed or imprisoned for their stand against apartheid in South Africa and was the first publicly funded statue in the UK to depict a black woman.

Princess Street and Princess Street Gardens 🏛

Named after Queen Charlotte's six daughters, the **Princesses Charlotte**, **Augusta**, **Elizabeth**, **Mary**, **Sophia** and **Amelia**, this is Edinburgh's main thoroughfare with open views across Princess Street Gardens and St Margaret's Castle. The street itself is extremely busy but a stroll through the gardens is always pleasant.

At the west entrance you will see the Alcock Glasshouse✿. **Lilian Alcock** (1874–1972) was an early specialist in seed pathology. Made a Fellow of the Linnean Society in 1922, she was the first woman appointed to a high-level job at the Royal Botanic Gardens Edinburgh. The glasshouse planting tells the story of her work. In addition, the spectacular collection of exotic Indian lilies✿ in the glasshouse commemorates the lives of two Edinburgh women. The first, **Dr (Margaret) Winifred Rushforth** (1885–1983), was a medical practitioner and Christian missionary who became the founder of a family clinic in Scotland, a therapist and writer. She corresponded with Carl Jung, Laurens van der Post and Prince Charles, who is said to have exclaimed on hearing of her death 'If only I had got to know her sooner!' The second, **Margaret Balfour** (1866–1945), was Chief Medical Officer for

Women's Medical Services in India from 1920 to 1924 and dedicated herself to improving the health of Indian women and babies. She called throughout her career for the employment of more female doctors in India. One bed in the glasshouse is dedicated to the memory of **Christian Ramsay, Countess of Dalhousie** (1786–1839), who was a botanist and natural historian. A genus of tropical plant, *Dalhouseia* is named after her and it is these plants which grow in her honour in the Alcock Glasshouse. The countess travelled in Canada and India where she collected and catalogued many species of plants. She was the only female honorary member of the Botanical Society of Edinburgh.

Next to the glasshouse is the ornate Spark Fountain▲ named for **Dame Muriel Spark** (1918–2004), a novelist, short story writer, poet and essayist born into Edinburgh's Jewish community (she converted to Catholicism in 1954). In 2008, *The Times* rated Spark eighth in its list of 'the 50 greatest British writers since 1945'. Miss Jean Brodie, her most famous character, was inspired by **Christina Kay** (1878–1951), a local teacher whose statue✦ dips her hand into the water on the east side of the fountain. Elsewhere in Edinburgh, a path across Bruntsfield Links is called Muriel Spark Walk, and the steps that connect the Grassmarket to Keir Street are known as the Miss Jean Brodie Steps. There is also a Spark Tent at the Edinburgh International Book Festival.

On the other side of the Spark Fountain, the children's playground✦ is one of nineteen founded by councillor and health campaigner **Euphemia Somerville** (1860–1935) to offer 'exercise, fresh air and happy occupation' to the children of the city.

The church▲ you can see looking westwards from here is that of **St Oda** (born AD c680). It is one of the oldest religious sites in the city, first mentioned around AD 850.

Although born in Scotland, St Oda is principally known in the Netherlands. Miraculously cured of blindness, she became a hermitess. St Oda's graveyard contains many interesting monuments including the grave ⚓ of Glasgow-born poet and writer **Anne McVicar Grant** (1775–1835), who followed her father's regiment to America as a child where she lived among Dutch settlers, French Huguenots, English soldiers, African-American slaves and the Mohawk people. From these experiences she wrote *Memoirs of an American Lady*. Back in Scotland she turned her eye to Scottish life and culture – she especially loved the Highlands. Her book *Letters from the Mountains* is said to have inspired the folk song 'Blue Bells of Scotland'. Also at St Oda's there is a memorial ⚓ to **Agnes Thomson Borrowman** (1881–1955), a pioneering pharmacist who fought for the rights of women in her profession. She was the first woman on the national board of medical examiners and founder member of the National Association of Women Pharmacists. Another notable grave is to the memory of **Phoebe Blyth** (1816–1898), a philanthropist and educationist, and one of the pioneering members of the Edinburgh Society for Promoting the Employment of Women, founded in 1860. She was one of the first three women to be elected to public office in 1873 when school boards were opened to female candidates.

In the graveyard of the neighbouring St John's church you will find the gravestone of **Malvina Wells** (c1804–1887) who was born in Carriacou, Grenada. This is an extremely rare example of the grave of a freed slave. Malvina was owned by George MacLean from Ross-shire. George and his brother John owned over 2,000 people in Grenada, where Malvina's name can be found on the 1817 slave register. She came to Scotland on being freed and became a servant to Joanna Macrae (the sister of her former

Princess Street

owner) for 70 years. Kind messages and flowers are often left on her grave, which has become a place of pilgrimage for supporters of human rights. Malvina was one of very few black ex-slaves in Scotland. Another, **Frances McLeod** (1823–1908) came to Scotland as a child upon being freed by her master who, it is believed, may also have been her father. Frances married in the city but there is no monument to her life (see also Henrietta Fraser, page 288).

Turning back to walk through Princess Street Gardens, you will come to the Tweedie Bandstand⧫ named after **Mary Tweedie** (1889–1963), who was one of the earliest women to gain recognition as an examiner of musical work for Trinity Laban Conservatoire, London. In the 1960s, due to her success in the field, the proportion of women examiners rose in a single decade from 8 per cent to 25 per cent. Beyond the bandstand, at the east entrance, is a colourful kinetic installation⚹ of rotating spirals in memory of **Violante Larini** (1682–1741), a rope dancer, tumbler and celebrated figure in 18th century Edinburgh who was refused permission to perform by local magistrates. Hugely popular, Signora Larini toured the world but chose to retire to Edinburgh, where she died.

Statues⚹ in the gardens include **Marjorie Shaw** (1904–1984), who was *The Times* correspondent in Russia during the Second World War, **Edith Simon** (1917–2003), a Jewish artist and writer, and **Mary Cameron** (1865–1921), an artist whose work was used by the French Government to promote their opposition to bullfighting and who is shown here with a (tame-looking) bull.

Several women's suffrage campaigners are commemorated in this part of the gardens with a series of benches⚹ engraved with a timeline of significant dates in the women's suffrage movement intertwined with the names of key Scottish suffragettes. One of these is **Arabella Scott**

(1886–1980), a speaker who was imprisoned and released under the notorious Cat and Mouse Act and forcibly fed in Perth Prison for five weeks. The novel *A Petrol Scented Spring* by Ajay Close was inspired by her story. Another, **Grace Ross Cadell** (1855–1918), was, with Elsie Inglis (see page 23), one of the first entrants to the Edinburgh School of Medicine for Women set up by Sophia Jex-Blake (see page 70) and therefore one of the earliest women to qualify in medicine in Scotland. Cadell was primarily dedicated to the care of women and children, and as a suffragette she was known for public acts of defiance. She once paid a large fine in small change simply to annoy the bailiffs. She also provided medical aid for other suffragettes, some of whom were released straight into her care after being force fed in prison. Cadell remained unmarried but adopted several children and left her fortune to them, equally between the boys and the girls, when she died.

Remaining in the gardens, at the foot of the Mound, is the city's floral clock♣. It was recently rededicated to the memory of cancer sufferer **Maggie Keswick Jencks** (1941–1995), co-founder of the Maggie's Centres – a network of drop-in centres that help people affected by the disease. The first was opened in 1996 in Edinburgh, just after her death. There is a bust of Maggie at the Hall of Scottish Heroines (see page 204) at the National Monument in Stirling.

Outside the garden gates on the Mound you will come to Nannie Brown's Box✠, a speaker's corner named after **Nannie Brown** (1866–1943), who was born nearby at 125 Princess Street. She was one of only six suffragettes who organised and participated in the historic Women's Freedom League march of the 'Brown Women' from Edinburgh to London over five weeks in 1912. This is often a starting point for political protest marches to the Scottish Parliament today.

The National Gallery of Scotland and the Royal Scottish Academy

Look up at the neoclassical gallery building at the bottom of the Mound and you will see a statue of **Queen Victoria** (1819–1901). Until 2015 she was Britain's longest serving monarch (now overtaken by her great-great granddaughter Elizabeth II) and remains the most commonly memorialised woman in the UK. There are 27 monuments to her across Scotland.

In the plaza beside the galleries you will find digital reproductions❦ of the works of Edinburgh artists. Look out for paintings by **Anna Dixon** (1873–1959), a watercolourist who painted birds, flowers and figures in landscapes and exhibited continuously for 64 years including 94 works at the Royal Scottish Academy, 98 works at Royal Society of Scottish Painters, 107 at the Glasgow Institute for Fine Arts and 2 at the Royal Academy in London. Her pictures of horses and donkeys with children remain sought after.

Inside the galleries it is worth searching out the work❦ of the **Nasmyth sisters**, painters who were renowned in Enlightenment Edinburgh. Their parents ran an art school from their house on Princess Street and later also in London. **Barbara** (1790–1870) painted Scottish subjects, **Elizabeth** (1793–1862) designs for Walter Scott's armoury, **Anne** (1798–1874) Highland scenery, **Jane** (1788–1867) landscapes and **Charlotte** (1804–1884) wildlife. Another popular exhibit is the Flora Macdonald Reid Collection❦. **Flora Macdonald Reid** (1861–1938) exhibited her work for the first time at the Royal Scottish Academy in Edinburgh when she was only 16. She went on to travel widely and lived in Norway, France and Belgium. In 1900 her painting was awarded a gold medal at the Exposition Universelle (a world's fair) in Paris. Her paintings *The Miller's Frau, A Wonderful Tale* and *A Man Convinced Against His Will, is of the Same Opinion Still* all appear on the catalogue in the Royal Academy in the same year. She is best known for her street scenes.

The Ferrier Arch ⚜

At the other end of this block is the world's largest monument to a writer, quite an achievement for a woman who declared 'I could not bear the fuss of authorism.' Designed as a triumphal arch festooned with wrought iron figures, it is dedicated to **Susan Ferrier** (1782–1854). In 1809, Ferrier began planning a novel with a friend. However, apart from one chapter, she wrote *Marriage* alone and it was published anonymously in 1818. Ferrier received £150. The novel was hugely successful and *Marriage* was attributed by many to Sir Walter Scott, who publicly praised his 'sister shadow' and called the book a 'very lively work'. Ferrier's other novels, *The Inheritance* – which owing to the success of *Marriage* she sold for £1,000 (more than Jane Austen received for any of her novels) – and *Destiny* were both critical and commercial successes, and Ferrier became friends with many literary worthies of the day including William Wordsworth and James Hogg. As well as a large effigy of Ferrier herself, the regal arch is festooned with statues of her much-loved characters (some of whom spoke in Scots and in Gaelic). If you look closely, you will spot a representation of the great woman's supporter Sir Walter Scott with his deerhound, Maida, at Susan Ferrier's feet. Edinburgh's main railway station nearby is somewhat dramatically known as Destiny Station ⚜, after Ferrier's last novel, prompting a thousand jokes about 'getting off the train at your destiny'. She is buried at the other end of Princess Street in the graveyard of St Oda's.

Suffragette Square 🏛

Walking northwards from the Ferrier Arch you come to Suffragette Square. The planting❦ in the square is green, white and violet – the suffragette colours. These colours were chosen because the initials stand for Give Women the Vote. On the south side, start at the site of what was Scotland's Suffragette Headquarters and the office of the Scottish Women's Hospitals, which was donated by the Prudential Insurance Company (now Tiles bar). During the First World War 24,000 women served in these hospitals. Outside, there is a statue❦ of **Bessie Watson** (1900–1992) who as a child piped for Edinburgh's suffragette march in 1909 and played to the women incarcerated in Calton Jail. She wore ribbons in the suffragette colours in her hair. Watson famously also piped the train carrying suffragettes returning to Holloway Prison as a result of the Cat and Mouse Act.

The suffragette statues❦ continue around this square, one on each corner. Clockwise from Bessie Watson is **Anna Gillies Macdonald Munro** (1881–1962) who became organising secretary of the Scottish Council of the Women's Freedom League in 1908. In 1912 she walked from Edinburgh to London on Nannie Brown's march (see page 60) and was key in organising summer campaigns down the Clyde coast. When she was imprisoned for this in 1908, her husband sent her a message sewed into a banana as communication was restricted. In 1956 she gave a radio talk about her experiences called *A Honeymoon in Prison* where she talked about how thrilling it was to fox the authorities during the course of the suffrage campaign.

On the northwest corner of the square are **Flora** (1856–1937) and **Rosaline Masson** (1867–1949), sisters who contributed pro-suffrage articles to *Cornhill Magazine*, *Chambers's Journal*, *Blackwood's Magazine* and the *Scotsman*

Bessie Watson Statue

newspaper. Trained as a nurse, Flora was awarded the Royal Red Cross First Class in 1919 and was matron at Rosewell Hospital. She also wrote extensively – in particular, biographies of the Brontë sisters, Wordsworth and Robert Louis Stevenson. Rosaline wrote too. Her best known book, *Poets, Patriots and Lovers*, contains anecdotes about famous writers she met through her circle in Edinburgh, including Robert Browning (whom she claims to have flirted with over a family breakfast – albeit Browning was 71 at the time), J M Barrie and Herbert Spencer (when she visited Spencer in Brighton he refused to meet a starstruck American reader who it seems was thrilled simply to hear Spencer shouting that he was not at home from the safety of a back room).

Lastly, on the southwest corner of the square is a statue of **Margaret Sackville** (1881–1963), founder of Scottish PEN and a pacifist during the First World War. In addition to these statues there is a plaque ✣ to **Priscilla McLaren** (1815–1906), a Quaker anti-slavery campaigner and radical suffragette, who did not live to see women get the vote.

In the heart of the square itself there has recently been a concerted campaign to remove the statue of Henry Dundas, originally on the towering central column, who it was felt was afforded an inappropriately high-profile place in the city's landscape. Dundas's vice-like control of Scottish politics in the Hanoverian era led to him being known as 'The Great Tyrant' and in 1806 he was impeached for misuse of public money. To mark the significant impact women in Edinburgh have had on the field of medicine, campaigning Edinburgh University students recently succeeded in having Dundas's statue replaced by one ✣ of **Alexandra Mary Chalmers Watson** (1872–1936), Edinburgh's first woman to receive an MD (doctor of medicine). Watson was prominent in many women's organisations and contributed to the Cathcart Report, which laid the foundation for a distinctive Scottish health system. A plaque on the statue is inscribed with her words: 'It has been honour enough to have lived through such great times for women and to know that the generation after us will not have the same fight for liberty.' There is an urban myth that Dr Watson in the Sherlock Holmes stories is named after her, but the first Holmes story appeared when she was only in her teens.

The Scottish National Portrait Gallery

North from Suffragette Square, on Queen Street, this fantastic gothic gallery houses the national collection of over 30,000 portraits, which it proclaims are 'of but not necessarily by Scots', although many notable Scottish painters are represented. Look out for the work✤ of one of the earliest Scottish women to make a career from painting, **Anne Forbes** (1745–1834), who was Portrait Painter to the Society of Antiquaries of Scotland. Critic Colin Russell noted 'her importance remains in her struggle against gender prejudice'. In her day it seems she juggled business with political allegiances – being popular with Jacobites seeking portraits of the Stuarts.

As well as the expected portraits of Mary Queen of Scots, Mary of Guise and St Margaret, notable works to search out in the gallery are the paintings✤ of **Leah Leneman** (1944–1999), a Jewish-American historian and cookery writer who wrote about women's history in Scotland and campaigned as a vegan, and **Dora Noyce** (1900–1977), madam of the notorious brothel at 17 Danube Street who quipped cheekily with a wink to policemen sent to raid her premises, 'Go on. Do your duty, officer.'

Broughton Street

At the east end of Queen Street, Broughton Street runs to the north. At the top of the lively street is the James Barry pub🍺, named for **Margaret Ann Bulkley** (c1795–1865), or James Miranda Barry, who studied medicine at the University of Edinburgh from 1809 to 1812. A distinguished army surgeon, Margaret's birth gender was a secret until after her death in 1865, making her the first woman to graduate in medicine from Edinburgh. Out of the pub windows you can see the large '0'🍺 hoisted over Broughton Street which commemorates **Franki Raffles** (1955–1994), a photographer who shot the hugely influential Zero Tolerance campaign. Her photos were originally posted for six months in Edinburgh in 1992 to raise awareness of the reality of child sexual abuse, rape, sexual assault and domestic violence. They are considered a benchmark within the advertising industry.

Further down the street, the statue🍺 at the round-about of two women sitting on theatre seats depicts **Lennox Milne** (1909–1980), who co-founded the Gateway Theatre in a local church, and **Sadie Aitken** (1905–1985) a director and producer who ran the Gateway. The theatre was a venue at the first Edinburgh Festival Fringe in 1947 and between 1953 and 1965 staged 150 productions, giving a generation of Scottish actors their first break in show business. When the church prohibited alcohol on its premises, Sadie hid her gin in the safe. In 1968, when the Gateway became STV's Edinburgh studio, STV paid to fund a seat in Screen 1 at the Filmhouse Cinema in Sadie's honour.

As you pass look into the Mansfield Traquair Centre, named after **Phoebe Anna Traquair** (1852–1936), widely recognised as the first significant professional female artist in modern Scotland and an icon of the Arts and

Crafts movement. Her work includes embroidery, enamel jewellery, book illuminations and huge murals – she painted the interiors of six public buildings. In 1920 she became the first woman elected to the Royal Scottish Academy. Traquair was tiny – the stained glass artist Louis Davis referred to her as 'a woman the size of a fly' and the poet W B Yeats commented she was 'a little singing bird'. Her work however packs a mighty punch and has seen a resurgence over the last twenty years.

Calton Hill

Edinburgh is known as the 'Athena of the North' because of the unfinished monument on this hill, which overlooks Princess Street. You can walk to the top and visit the observatory, built in 1818 to replace an earlier building of 1776 on the same site. Today, this observatory is used by students, and Edinburgh's main observatory has been re-sited on another of the city's seven hills – Blackford Hill. The paving stones set into the ground beside the building depict a 3D constellation of stars and are dedicated to the memory of **Maria Short** (c1787–1869), who sued the city council when they seized her father's telescope after his death. Successful in her lawsuit, she went on to open the first paying observatory on this site and later another on Castle Hill at what is now the Camera Obscura. Looking beyond 'Edinburgh's Disgrace', the unfinished neoclassical building more formally known as the National Monument, you can also see the football stadium on Easter Road, site of the first international women's football match (between Scotland and England) in 1881 – Scotland won 3–0.

Further down the hill you will pass Rock House, home and workplace of inventive Edinburgh photographers David Octavius Hill and Robert Adamson. Visitors can now rent this historic property to experience life on the hill. Note the plaque🌿 raised to **Jessie Mann** (1805–1867) known only as Hill and Adamson's assistant during the 1850s, but who is said to have taken some of the photographs originally credited to them. She always wore long gloves because the chemicals she used to develop their prints had badly marked her skin. The small digital screen🌿 here displays Jessie's photographs. The winning images from an annual Scottish photography competition are displayed here. These are then held in perpetuity by the National Library of Scotland and known as the Jessie Mann Digital Archive🌿.

Next to Rock House there is an unusual installation🌿 depicting an 18th century chemist's workbench with bottles, scales and distilling apparatus – carved in wood and left as if the chemist has only just walked away. This is to the memory of **Elizabeth Fulhame** (c1760–c1810), an experimental chemist whose discovery of photoreduction led to the invention of modern photography. She said she hoped her work would serve as a 'beacon for future mariners' – by which she meant other pioneering women.

Charlotte Street🏛

Running parallel to Princess Street, Charlotte Street is considered the most exclusive of the New Town's shopping streets, the centrepiece of the original New Town design. At each junction you will find a large bronze statue🏛 raised to local dignitaries from the Victorian and Edwardian era. Look out for **Mary Shepherd** (1777–1847), an Enlightenment thinker who exposed errors in the reasoning of her contemporaries Hume and Priestly when she was only in her 20s. She went on to write two books on the subject of philosophy. At the next two junctions stand **Gertrude Herzfeld** (1890–1981), the first woman surgeon in Scotland, and **Marie Stopes** (1880–1958), a pioneer of birth control whose bestsellers *Married Love* and *Wise Parenthood* informed a generation. Then there is **Sophia Jex-Blake** (1840–1912) who, having been refused entry to Harvard because of her gender, enlisted four other women, who together gained admittance to the medical school in Edinburgh. At the end of their studies, the university refused to award them a degree – it wasn't until 1894 that women were allowed to graduate in medicine. Understandably furious, Sophia Jex-Blake became instrumental in setting up the London School of Medicine for Women in 1874 and went on to found the Edinburgh Hospital and Dispensary for Women and Children (later the Bruntsfield Hospital) in a property she donated to the city. A controversial figure, she was described by her contemporary Elizabeth Blackwell as 'a dangerous woman' because of her steely determination to break down closed doors.

And last is the statue of **Eliza Wigham** (1820–1899), a Quaker, anti-slavery campaigner and secretary of Edinburgh National Society for Women's Suffrage from 1867, who wrote *The Anti-Slavery Cause in America and its Martyrs*. She has been described as one of the six key women in the British transatlantic anti-slavery sisterhood, which sought to bring women together to fight slavery. In 1861, author of *Uncle Tom's Cabin*, Harriet Beech Stowe, wrote a rallying cry to women on both sides of the Atlantic that chimed with the sisterhood's message and encouraged Britain to support the cause of American's northern states. 'We appeal to you, as sisters, as wives, and as mothers, to raise your voices to your fellow-citizens, and your prayers to God for the removal of this affliction and disgrace from the Christian world.'

Half way along Charlotte Street you will come to the Assembly Rooms, the heart of Enlightenment Edinburgh, which opened in 1789. Today the building is still used for balls, dances and performances and becomes a major venue during the Edinburgh Festival Fringe. On the lane running down the side of the Assembly Rooms there is a mural✦ which depicts local creatives, some of whom appeared in productions at the venue and went on to become famous internationally. **Mary Ann Paton** (1802–1864) was an opera singer who toured the UK and USA, introducing Bellini's operas to Americans. She is said to have had an astonishing vocal range from low D to an E above the stave. Also there is **Jane Stirling** (1804–1859), who was the unrequited lover of the composer Chopin. She studied under him and after the death of his lover, George Sand, organised his 1848 tour of London, Glasgow, Edinburgh and Manchester. Finally there is writer **Margaret Oliphant** (1828–1897), whose fictional works span 'domestic realism, the historical novel and tales of the supernatural'. She wrote 90 novels, 300 articles, 25 works of non-fiction and 50 short stories. At night, the luminous faces of these women glow eerily as you pass.

Rose Street

Running parallel to Charlotte Street, you can explore the bars and restaurants of Rose Street. It has always been considered a shady thoroughfare and it was here that the 18th century prostitute **Margaret Burns** (c1769–c1792) had rooms. When she was banished from Edinburgh by the Lord Ordinary at the Court of Session, she fought her case. It is said Robert Burns (who was no relation) followed her story closely and she was referred to in the press as the poet's 'poor namesake'. After her death, Burns wrote of her:

Cease, ye prudes, your envious railings,
Lovely Burns has charms: confess!

True it is that she had one failing:
Had a woman ever less?

This quotation is inscribed on a plaque✤ on the corner of Rose Street and Frederick Street in her memory.

Behind the Assembly Rooms, on Rose Street, a local pub, the Fletcher Lounge🍺, is named after **Eliza Fletcher** (1770–1858), an Edinburgh Enlightenment figure known for her sympathy for revolutionary politics and her connections with other women. She founded the Edinburgh New Town Female Friendly Society (the first female friendly society in Scotland) and was instrumental in setting up the influential *Edinburgh Review*.

Glasgow

It's very important for cities all around the world to reinvent themselves, and Glasgow is a good example of that. The Scots are very nice. I don't think they are burdened by their history.

Zaha Hadid

Glasgow is Scotland's largest city and as the inspirational architect Zaha Hadid pointed out, it has successfully reinvented itself time and again – from a small ecclesiastical village to an industrial hub to today's vibrant cultural metropolis. However, Glasgow women would probably take issue with Zaha's comments on history – it is very much the history of this city, in particular its huge growth in the Victorian era and its industrial explosion, that has defined its built environment and the great stories that environment contains. The city's history has made Glasgow a hub for equality-driven politics for over a century as well as home to leading performers and artists – feisty women who have both inspired the world and sought to change it.

City Centre

All over Glasgow you will see the city's slogan emblazoned on buildings and billboards: Jobs for the Girls✷. Typical of Glasgow's history of direct action, the Jobs for the Girls movement started when the post of Keeper of Social History at the People's Palace was advertised in 1989, and Elspeth King (see page 93) was told that there were 'no jobs for the girls'. This prompted the printing of 'Jobs for the Girls' t-shirts worn by many women in the city as a protest. Later the slogan was adopted by the whole city, and is celebrated as a counterpoint to Glasgow's traditional 'hard man' persona.

Victoria Square ▲

The imposing architecture of Victoria Square skirts a plaza peopled by statues✷ dedicated to the city's leading political women as well as one to the square's namesake, Queen Victoria (see page 61). This statue is famously capped by a traffic cone and has become a bizarre landmark

Jobs for the Girls Mural

with souvenirs widely available. The queen is depicted riding sidesaddle. The statue was raised to commemorate Her Majesty's visit to Glasgow in 1849, but Victoria was a regular visitor, opening the City Chambers at the east end of the square in 1888. Inside this grand building you can visit the Roberts Chamber ⚑ where council meetings take place. It is named in memory of **Jean Roberts** (1895–1988), Glasgow's first woman provost, in office from 1960 to 1963. A pioneer, she was instrumental in the planning of Scotland's six 'New Towns', five of which were built from 1955 to 1973.

Outside the City Chambers there is a digital memorial to **Marion Henery** (1910–2001), a communist who helped organise the Scottish contingent of the Hunger March to London in 1932 to deliver a petition of a million signatures protesting against means-testing as a way of determining eligibility for unemployment payments. In retirement she became secretary of the Scottish Old Age Pensioners Campaign and devoted her time to the Campaign for Nuclear Disarmament. The Henery Board ⚑ is updated every quarter and displays the city's minimum wage, living wage, average wage and gender wage gap keeping Glasgow well informed about its wage equality and inequality.

Victoria Square is dedicated to Glasgow's culture of activism which has not only always included women but frequently been led by them – from suffragists to rent strikers and temperance campaigners. The large plinth in the centre is topped by a statue ⚑ of **Eunice Murray** (1878–1960), writer, campaigner and Scottish President of the Women's Freedom League (which operated offices and a tearoom within walking distance, on Sauchiehall Street, see page 103). In 1913 a letter printed in the *Glasgow Herald* declared that if more people could hear Eunice speak, the 'vote would be won without delay'. During the

First World War she worked in a munitions factory and was involved in what she mysteriously termed 'confidential business'. After women got the vote in 1918, Murray was the first Scottish woman to stand for Parliament that year (in Bridgeton), though she did not win the seat. Passionate about women's history, she wrote *Scottish Women of Bygone Days* and headed a campaign for the creation of a Scottish folk museum, which came into being in the 1930s (see Isabel Frances Grant, page 319). The plaque on the plinth quotes her words from 1923: 'It is prejudice, not reason that has delayed the emancipation of women. Every step forward has been won in spite of prejudice … But it is reason, not might, which should govern the world.'

On the northwest corner of the square, opposite Queen Street Station, there are statues✣ to the memory of two more suffragettes. **Jane Allan** (1869–1968) was a major supporter of the militant suffrage campaign and in one year alone donated £650 – a huge sum at the turn of the 20th century. Jane was arrested for window-smashing in 1912, refused to pay her taxes in 1913 and fired a blank at a policeman who was arresting Mrs Pankhurst when she was talking at an event in 1914 (see page 92). While on hunger strike in prison, Jane said that she dreamed of sipping green chartreuse liqueur.

The other statue is of **Agnes Dollan** (1887–1966), who became Lady Dollan in 1946. She was an activist and speaker for the Women's Social and Political Union, the Women's Labour League and the Independent Labour Party and was jailed for a short time in 1917 for protesting the council's rent rises. Lady Dollan also helped to organise the infamous Glasgow rent strike alongside Mary Barbour and Helen Crawfurd (see pages 125 and 103). The first female Labour candidate to stand for election to Glasgow City Council, she remained in office for a decade.

Directly opposite these women on the southwest corner there is a statue✷ to **Madge Easton Anderson** (1896–1982), the first woman admitted to practise law professionally in the UK (under both Scottish and English jurisdictions). She qualified as a solicitor in Scotland in 1920 after she took her case to court following the passing of the Sex Disqualification (Removal) Act of 1919 and won. Latterly she ran a practice in rural Perthshire.

Opposite the statue of Anderson, on the southeast corner, is a bronze✷ of political firebrand **Janey Buchan** (1926–2012). This Labour Member of the European Parliament was a cultural and political activist in Glasgow's fiercest tradition, and an active anti-apartheid campaigner. Mandela embraced her when she welcomed him to Strasbourg, where he was addressing the European Parliament in 1990. Buchan backed the Campaign for Nuclear Disarmament and opposed social injustice of all kinds. She was an early supporter of gay rights. In another cause important to many in Glasgow, she was a champion of the revival of traditional Scottish music. On 27 April (known as Freedom Day in South Africa) flowers are often left at this statue to commemorate her anti-apartheid stance and the campaign's ultimate success. This statue also became a focus for the pro-Remain EU campaign and you will sometimes spot EU flags flying from it.

On the final corner of the square is a statue✷ to **Agnes Hardie** (1874–1951). A stalwart of Scottish Labour, Hardie was a talented platform speaker. She was the first female member of the Glasgow Trades Council and sat on the Glasgow School Board as well as being Women's Organiser of the Labour Party for five years at the end of the First World War. In 1937 she became an MP. A pacifist, she opposed conscription during the Second World War and was nicknamed the 'housewife's MP' because she frequently spoke out at Westminster about food shortages and rationing.

Gallery of Modern Art

A stroll to the south of Victoria Square will take you to Royal Exchange Square where you will find the Gallery of Modern Art. Outside is a sculpture✦ called *Reclining Woman* by Jewish artist **Hannah Frank** (1908–2008). This sculpture is more commonly and irreverently known as the *Mare on the Square*. Hannah signed her early work Al Aaraaf – a star placed between heaven and hell – after the poem of the same name by Edgar Allan Poe. There is a reproduction of her 1928 work 'Girl in a Wood' under the Clelland Road railway arches in the Gorbals. She continued to work into her 90s and was widely recognised as the last living Glasgow Girl (see page 115).

The Lighthouse

After the Gallery of Modern Art, cross Buchanan Street and turn down Carswell Lane⚓, named after writer **Catherine Carswell** (1847–1946), who was fired from the *Glasgow Herald* (which had offices on this site) for an unsanctioned review of the novel *The Rainbow* by D H Lawrence, which was later banned under the Obscene Publications Act. Beneath the street name there is a commemorative plaque containing her words: 'One can and should think with all one's being', which is taken from her correspondence with Lawrence. Carswell went on to write theatre reviews for the *Observer*. Lawrence then mentored her when she was writing her autobiographical novel *Open the Door!* for which she won the Melrose Prize. Ever controversial, her biography of Robert Burns outraged traditionalists by refusing to gloss over Burns's sexual misdemeanours and his drinking. After its publication, she received a bullet in the post with a suggestion that she kill herself. Her personal life was also stormy and in her own words she embarked on a 'rash and foolish marriage to a man I scarcely knew'. He tried to kill her when she became pregnant and the marriage was annulled on the grounds of his insanity in a groundbreaking legal case.

On Carswell Lane, Scotland's Centre for Design and Architecture, the Lighthouse takes its name from its distinctive tower (originally designed by Charles Rennie Mackintosh as a water tank to protect the *Herald*'s warehouse from fire). In the hallway there is a permanent exhibition✣ about **Edith Burnet Hughes** (1888–1971) who is considered Britain's first practising female architect. Hughes won first prize for a war memorial design submitted to the Civic Arts Association early in her career, undertook her first commission in 1916 and established her own architecture firm in 1920, specialising in kitchen design. In 1927, she became the first woman nominated for membership of the Royal Institute of British Architects (RIBA) but RIBA's legal advisers disqualified the vote. Up to the end of the Second World War Hughes was Head of the Glasgow School of Architecture, one of the five schools which make up the Glasgow School of Art. She was finally admitted to RIBA as an Honorary Fellow in 1968, more than 40 years after her nomination.

Outside the Lighthouse you will see a notebook and pen✣ illustrated on the tiles on the building opposite with a quote from the seminal novel by **Dot Allan** (1886–1964), *Hunger March*: 'It was one of those days when you felt God had forgotten the city.' Dot, born Eliza MacNaughton Allan, was a successful Glasgow writer in the 1920s and 1930s whose work was misidentified by the *Times Literary Supplement* in 1934 as that of a man because she did not write about domestic issues – focusing on politics, class and gender issues instead. She wrote ten novels all set across Glasgow – from city centre political rallies to slum tenements and suburban middle-class villas. She also worked as a freelance journalist and interviewed the internationally famous actress Sarah Bernhardt when she appeared at the Pavilion Theatre, a ten minute stroll from here. Dot lived all her life in Glasgow, spending much of her time as a carer for her sick mother, and it seems appropriate that she is commemorated here, in the centre of the city she loved so much.

The Merchant City

To the west of Buchanan Street lies the Merchant City, which over recent decades has become gentrified and is home to bars, shops and galleries. Outside Glasgow City Halls, now a concert hall, you will find a statue✲ of two women peeking through stage curtains as they wait in the wings. This is dedicated to two of Glasgow's well-loved music hall stars – **Marie Loftus** (1857–1940) and her daughter **Cissie** (1876–1943). Marie had Cissie when she was only 18 and went on to become one of Britain's best-paid music hall performers, earning £100 a week in the 1890s. She toured the USA and South Africa. Cissie was a mimic, actress and music hall performer. It was said that 'Glasgow never had a greater favourite.'

Around the corner, in front of the Fellow Glasgow Residents mural is the Magdalene Institute Monument✲. In the shape of a giant mangle, it honours the **girls who were locked up for their sexuality** (often just for having had sex) and made to work for what was seen as moral rehabilitation. There were 20 Magdalene Institutes across the country, including the one in nearby Townhead. These girls, generally aged between 15 and 19, were called 'prostitutes'. However, most weren't sex workers, but homeless and poor, often living on the streets when they were picked up and sent to 'wash their sins clean' by learning laundry and other domestic skills. Some were incarcerated by their parents. The institute in Glasgow was run by the local council and housed about 100 girls at any time. Opened in 1812, it wasn't closed until 1958 after the women had broken out on two occasions and were 'hunted down' by police. None of the women had been convicted of a criminal charge. Despite the fact that these women weren't sex workers, the mangle has become a focal point for calls for further rights for sex workers. As a result red umbrellas✿ are at times fixed to the monument by protesters.

The Gorbals

Continue south across the Clyde over the Marjory Bridge🏛 to the Gorbals, originally known as the Gorballes, once a small town in its own right. The bridge is named after **Lady Marjory Stewart of Lochow**, a 14th century resident who is thought to have founded St Ninian's Leper Colony – the area's first centre of healing. A bust of Lady Marjory appeared on the original bridge she funded in 1345, though that structure is no longer standing. There is a donation box for a homeless charity✿ on the site where **Mollie Gillespie** (1766–1826) ran a lodging house where she was known to charge 3d a bed and always keep two free for the destitute. Over 30 years it is estimated she provided accommodation for 50,000 people. An itinerant broadsheet seller of the period called her 'the most charitable person I have ever met'. There is a huge amount of philanthropy, generosity and militant action in this area's history.

First though, visit its cultural centre – the Citizen's

Theatre, the principal producing theatre in the west of Scotland, founded in 1943. It is said that the building, erected in 1878, is haunted. One of the most commonly seen ghosts is that of a young female strawberry seller who often visits the upper circle. Staff also report sightings of a 'white lady' dressed in Victorian costume who moves between the dress circle bar and the dressing rooms. Inside, the 'Citz' has many interesting features throughout the hallway, the cafe bar and the auditorium. As well as the famous decorative pink elephants, look out for the video installation❦ showing clips of performances by **Madeleine Christie** (1904–1996), a regular cast member at the theatre as well as a TV actor – she appeared in *Take the High Road*, in STV's adaptation of *The Prime of Miss Jean Brodie* and in films including *An Old Lady Shows her Medals*, *Electric Dreams*, *Conspiracy of Hearts* and *Florence Nightingale*.

Commemorated by a plaque❦ beside the box office is **Tessa Fortune Fraser** (1934–2013), a successful businesswoman who was the first female chair of the Variety Club of Great Britain in Scotland. She invested in a production company to make Scottish animated feature films. At the top of the stairs to the grand circle there is a bronze sculpture❦ of a quill and scroll, which is dedicated to three of the city's female playwrights – their signatures are clearly visible etched into the paper. They are **Ena Lamont Stewart** (1912–2006), who wrote *Men Should Weep*, **Joan Ure** (1918–1978), who wrote the revue *Nothing May Come of It* and **Ada F Kay** (born 1929), who as well as penning drama also wrote *Falcon*, an 'autobiography' of James IV of Scotland which first brought the king's homosexuality to mainstream attention. Together these women formed the Scottish Society of Playwrights in 1973 to create a coordinated voice for playwrights in Scottish theatre.

Leaving the Citz, walk to South Cumberland Street to see the original site of the Glasgow Samaritan Hospital for Women, established in 1886 to provide gynecological care for poor women. The hospital had an all-female staff including, during the mid 20th century, **Celia 'Goldie' Goldfein**, reputedly a small and frail-looking lady who worked with the local Bible medical mission and was 'warrior-like' in her determination to rally volunteers. She is commemorated today by the bronze nurse's cap❀ set into the wall on the corner of the street. Today on the site of the hospital there is an ornate stone Celtic cross❀ to **Alice Cullen** (1891–1969). The first Catholic woman to hold a parliamentary seat, she was MP for the area. Cullen was a pacifist, strongly opposed to conscription and was known as 'Mrs Gorbals'. When the queen visited Glasgow, Cullen insisted Her Majesty view an old 'single end' – Queen Elizabeth is reported to have asked 'Is this all?' when she saw the accommodation. Later, the Samaritan Hospital moved as money was raised to add a dispensary, a nurses' home and additional wards, ending up in nearby Coplaw Street.

On Old Rutherglen Road you will pass the Twomax Clothing Factory (now social work offices). **Rita McGurn** (1940–2015) designed the artwork that billows from the chimney. It rotates like a weathervane and is called *Smokestack* 1994. McGurn's design captures the spirit of the Gorbals during its industrial heyday. Since its installation, the foot of the chimney has been clad with a bronze relief❀ dedicated to the trials of the area's women in the 1820s. When female labour was enlisted at local factories, men tried to intimidate the women workers (who were paid less and therefore preferred by factory owners). There were cases of beatings, shootings, sulphuric acid thrown at women to disfigure them, and one worker's mother was murdered.

As a result of this menacing behaviour, one factory owner simply dismissed all his female staff. But opposition to women's labour was not the only danger working women had to face. Around the corner on Ballater Street look out for the installation✤ of empty coffins at the old Adelphi Hair Factory which was nicknamed the 'coffin works' after an outbreak of anthrax in 1878 resulted in three women's deaths. Here you will also find a plaque✤ inscribed with the names of 29 female workers killed in 1889 during the construction of the nearby Templeton Carpet Works when high winds brought the brick facade under construction crashing down into the weaving sheds below. It is common for wreaths of flowers to be left at this monument.

Nearby, the Gorbals Swimming Pool, officially called the Graham Baths⛴, is dedicated to **Lilias Violet Graham** (1917–2008), a woman of aristocratic background who moved to the area as a lay worker with the Episcopal church. She preached that the poor here needed 'not only bread but roses' and established a holiday scheme for children from disadvantaged backgrounds that still runs today. When she inherited her family's manor house near Stirling in 1972, she opened it as a holiday and respite centre.

Turning back towards Marjory Bridge there is an 'eternal flame' monument✤ to **Catherine Taylor** (1868–1930), a Gorbals cinema cashier who is said to have firebombed Ayr Racecourse in 1913 in support of the campaign for women's suffrage. Her involvement was kept secret by her family until after her death. As a result this monument was only recently raised to her memory, on the centenary of suffrage being granted. Along Geneen Street⛴, named for **Sophie Geneen** (1888–1963), known as the 'Mother of Glasgow', who ran a kosher hotel and restaurant, you will find a mural✦ designed in the style of Hannah Frank (see page 83) depicting the Jewish women of the area during the late 19th and early 20th centuries – including **Dr Sara Jacobs**, the first Jewish woman to graduate in medicine from the University of Glasgow in 1923, who had a practice nearby.

Glasgow Green

Across the river enter the park, which is brimming with monuments to Glasgow's sheroes. Near the gate is the Jane Arthur Temperance Fountain🔔. Five of the founders of the Radical Temperance Society of 1836 were women, four from nearby Bridgeton. Worldwide, women were key to the temperance movement because alcoholism so adversely affected the quality of life of married women, who did not have any legal status, could not control of their own finances and were therefore easily subjected to domestic violence and extreme poverty. The temperance movement in Glasgow was supported by **Jane Arthur** (1827–1907), a social reformer and proponent of women's emancipation. From her own pocket, she provided bursaries for a Renfrewshire student and for a female medical student, and from the late 1880s she donated money to support poor patients who were convalescing from illness. As well as this fountain, a street is named after her in Paisley.

Inside the green follow the Droy Walkway✦, which is named in memory of local legend **Doris Droy** (1905–2005), who was given the nickname Suicide Sal and is remembered in song by her rock singer niece Maggie Bell. Droy's risqué material escaped the censor's wrath thanks to her broad Glaswegian dialect. In 1952, the journalist Colm Brogan called her 'The most completely liberated Glasgow comic, Queen of the Queens … her voice would make a pneumatic road drill or an electric riveting machine sound like the soft purring of a contented cat ...'. Look down as you pass along the walkway to see paving stones✹ in memory of several entertainers with links to the city. These commemorate **Lena Zavaroni** (1963–1999) who was a child singer and star of *Opportunity Knocks* born in nearby Greenock. She suffered from anorexia nervosa and died at age 35 of an infection after surgery. Another paving stone is to actress **Morag Hood** (1942–2002) most famous for her roles in the BBC production of *War and Peace*, *Bergerac*, *Z-Cars* and *Heartbeat*. Also commemorated is **Ella Logan** (1910–1969), an international nightclub singer who recorded two solo albums and appeared at both the Copacabana and the Waldorf-Astoria in New York. She sang on television in May 1956 with Louis Armstrong. And lastly, **Maggie Moffat** (1873–1943), an actress and one of the earliest Scottish women to be arrested and incarcerated for protesting the suffrage. Maggie's husband formed a male group to support the suffragettes.

On a plinth at the side of the walkway you will see a huge pair of glamorous legs✹ commemorating actress **Bebe Brun** (1901–1982), who was born Martha Law in Glasgow. She started as a stunt woman. On location in Tilbury Docks director Alfred Hitchcock needed someone to leap between two ships. He offered £50 – an enormous sum in those days – but no-one was brave enough to take the offer. Brun said she would do it for £100. She got the cash (and she caught pneumonia), but her career took off, leading to work with screen legends like Randolph Scott, Lupino Lane and Will Hay. Marlene Dietrich was reportedly furious with Brun because while filming *The Blue Angel* the director decided to use Brun's legs for close up shots (rather than Dietrich's) and had them insured for two million dollars. She retired young after a fun fair accident.

On top of the tall column⚓ visible across the green, you will find a statue of **Margaret Herbison** (1907–1996), the Labour MP for North Lanarkshire who rose to become Under Secretary of State in the Scottish Office and Minister for Pensions and Social Security in Harold Wilson's government. This column has been in place for some time and was originally dedicated to Lord Nelson, though it was decided to rededicate it to Herbison's memory after her death. It was at this column in 1914 that Emmeline Pankhurst was arrested following a rowdy meeting. In 1917, 14,000 suffragettes rallied here to listen to Mrs Pankhurst make a speech on her return to Glasgow. Today, beside the column, there is a bench⚘ cast in the form of books, piled newspapers, medical equipment and protest banners. This unusual monument is to one of the women who attended both rallies: **Dorothea Chalmers Smith** (1872–1944). She was a doctor and militant suffragette so committed to the cause that her marriage failed due to her campaigning, which was not supported by her husband. Dorothea was not put off and went on hunger strike while in Duke Street prison. She was also known to have skipped bail in order to avoid incarceration. There is a matching bench⚘ on the other side of the column – this one cast in the shape of piles of money, pillows, get well cards and architectural plans – dedicated to the work of **Beatrice Clugston** (1827–1888), a volunteer who visited inmates in both prisons and hospitals, and who in 1864 founded a Dorcas Society to help discharged patients. She later raised funds to establish the Glasgow Convalescent Home at Bothwell, the first such institution in the west of Scotland. This was followed by a second convalescent home in Dunoon, then the largest in the country. She went on to found Broomhill Homes for Incurables at Kirkintilloch in 1876. In her later years, a fund was raised to provide her with a pension in recognition of her work. There is also red sandstone and bronze memorial to her in Kirkintilloch's Auld Aisle Cemetery.

The People's Palace

For sixteen years the People's Palace museum in Glasgow Green was curated by Elspeth King (see Jobs for the Girls page 78). Jobs for the Girls t-shirts are still sold in the museum shop❦ with the profits going to women's charities around the city. King's book *The Hidden History of Glasgow's Women* is a classic. The museum's collection reflects her interests and includes material about women's contributions to the city's life.

Look out for the many permanent exhibitions❦ about notable Scottish women. These include recordings of **Agnes Duncan**'s (1899–1997) work. Agnes was a leading choral conductor who formed the Scottish Junior Singers, which provided children's choruses for the Scottish National Orchestra and Scottish Opera. She inspired a generation of singers across class and cultures and believed 'We are the music makers, and we are the dreamers of dreams.' A neighbouring display features **Jessie Russell** (1850–1881), a poet and dressmaker whose feminist work 'Woman's Rights vs Woman's Wrongs' was published in the *Glasgow Weekly*. Another exhibit centres on **Renée Houston** (1902–1980), a comedian who appeared on television and in film. She also performed at the 1926 Royal Variety Command Performance. Renée toured with her sister **Billie** (1906–1972) as the Houston Sisters. Reviews of the period said that the women 'speak like Scots and sing like Americans'. In 1926, Renée wrote a short musical film which she shot with Billie. This groundbreaking work was produced by Lee De Forest using his pioneering Phonofilm process, which played the soundtrack as part of the movie. It was released a year before *The Jazz Singer*. In later life Renée specialised in 'battleaxe' roles including the mother in *Carry on at Your Convenience*.

You will also find material by **Evelyn Cowan** (1921–1998), whose landmark memoir of growing up in the Gorbals, *Spring Remembered*, was published in 1974. She later wrote the novel *A Portrait of Alice* and was active in Jewish charities in the city. Her work forms a significant part of the display in the People's Palace about Jewish life in the area.

Glasgow Women's Library

Opened in 1991, and now sited a short walk to the east of the Green, this brilliant institution grew from the grass-roots project Women in Profile during Glasgow's year as European City of Culture. Originally run by volunteers, it now employs 14 paid staff and houses an impressive archive, which contains material on all manner of female activities – from the suffragette movement to knitting. There are also reading rooms and an events programme. During May the library hosts the Open the Door Festival of **women writers**. On display you will find artefacts illuminating the lives of many Glasgow women and the curators involved are often on hand to talk about the material.

The Women's Library holds monthly discussion groups✢, with memorable incidents from the lives of significant women setting the theme. Recent inspiration has come from **Isabella Pearce** (1859–1929), who wrote the 'Matrons and Maidens' column about female emancipation in the *Labour Leader* newspaper, and **Ingrid McClements** (1948–2008), a feminist and activist, and a trailblazer in development in the voluntary sector. She contributed hugely to communities in Glasgow, particularly to anti-racist work, and to women's organisations such as the

Women's Support Project, Rape Crisis Scotland and the Glasgow Women's Voluntary Sector Network. Other women featured include **Roona Simpson** (1964–2017), sociologist, campaigner and co-author of *Living Alone*, which explored population explosion and falling fertility rates in the Western world, and **Helen Macfarlane** (1818–1860) from Barrhead, who wrote the first English translation of the Communist Manifesto. The daughter of a wealthy mill owner, Macfarlane's story is memorialised in the play *Rare Birds* by Penny Cole. It's always worth popping into the Women's Library – you're sure to find something interesting.

East End

Heading north, tip your hat to the legendary Barrowlands Ballroom founded by local entrepreneur **Maggie McIver** (1878–1958), who also set up the Barras market. The Barrowlands is now one of Glasgow's iconic music venues and is a testament to Maggie's drive and vision. One of the entrances to Glasgow Green is dedicated to her memory.

Beside the Barras is the Saracen's Head pub (the 'Sarry Heid') which was built on the site of a 16th century churchyard. Today the pub displays a mysterious skull, allegedly that of **Maggie Wall**, popularly known as the last witch to be burned at the stake (in Perthshire in 1657). However, this is untrue as sadly witch hunting went on in Scotland into the 18th century (see page 22).

A ten minute walk from the Barras will take you to a large wrought-iron sculpture of a chain, embedded into the pavement on Duke Street. This is in remembrance of Glasgow-born **Mary Macarthur** (1880–1921), who was the general secretary of the Women's Trade Union League and was involved in the development of the

National Federation of Women Workers and National Anti-Sweating League (which had nothing to do with perspiration – it worked against sweatshop labour). In 1909 Mary steered the women chainmakers of Cradley Heath in the Midlands to success in their struggle for a minimum wage and led a strike to force employers to put the rise in place. Mary Macarthur's name and picture is on the statue✝ of Millicent Fawcett erected in 2018 in London's Parliament Square.

Women's Sport Museum✝
On the Gallowgate, this newly built attraction is known as the Barras' Other Ballroom. The museum also houses the Helen Holm Centre for Sports Psychology✝. **Helen Holm** (1907–1971) was a golf champion who represented her country during the 1930s, 1940s and 1950s. The museum showcases an eclectic mixture of sporting memorabilia and honours Scotland's long history of sporting women.

Swimmers included are **Nancy Riach** (1927–1947), holder of 28 British and Scottish swimming records – there is an annual medal in her name awarded to the swimmer who has done most to enhance the prestige of Scottish swimming – and **Helen Orr Gordon** (1933–2014), who represented Great Britain as a swimmer in three Olympics, and Scotland in two British Empire Games. In 1950 she received the Nancy Riach Medal for her services to swimming, she won an Olympic bronze medal in the 200-metre breaststroke in 1952, and was inducted into the Scottish Sports Hall of Fame in 2003. Also featured is **Catherine Gibson** (1931–2013), who had a 16-year swimming career peppered with achievement. She won three European Championships medals and a bronze medal at the 1948 Summer Olympics. This was Britain's only swimming trophy of the contest. In 2008, she was inducted into the Scottish Sports Hall of Fame. **Ellen Elizabeth King** (1909–1994), who represented Great Britain twice in the Olympics, and Scotland at the inaugural British Empire Games in 1930, and **Belle Moore** (1884–1975), a swimmer who was the youngest British woman to win an Olympic medal and who won an Olympic gold at the 1912 games, are also among the remarkable sportswomen featured.

In hockey the key players are **Marjorie Langmuir** (1905–1984), who represented Scotland internationally in three sports (hockey, badminton and tennis) and in 1933 captained the only Scottish women's hockey team to beat England between 1909 and 1972, and **Charlotte Beddows** (1887–1976), Scotland's hockey team captain in 1905 who also won the Scottish Golf Championship several times. Beddows organised the maintenance of Gullane Golf Course during the Second World War.

Highlighted in the golf section are **Dorothy Lee Campbell** (1883–1945), the first woman to win the US, UK and Canadian Women's Amateur Golf Championships, and **Ethel Jack** (1939–2012), who played golf for Scotland in 1955 and from 1962 to 1964. She was president of the Scottish Ladies' Golfing Association from 2007 to 2010 and was renowned for her wicked sense of humour.

In tennis we have **Winnie Shaw** (1947–1992), who twice made the semi-finals of the French Open and in 1973 played in the doubles semi-final at Wimbledon.

The museum also unravels some urban myths around Scotland's footballing history, including the tall tale of 'Scotland's first black female goalkeeper' Carrie Boustead (who was in fact, white and from Liverpool) and the many myths around the team she was said to play for, 'Mrs Graham's Eleven', which, sadly, is also apocryphal.

Glasgow Cathedral

The square in front of the cathedral is the site of the medieval Bishops' Palace, where women accused of witchcraft were imprisoned. Beside the cathedral you will find a garden containing plaques✤ to **Caroline Soule** (1824–1903), an American who in 1880 was the first woman to be ordained as a minister in the UK, serving at St Paul's in Pitt Street; and **Stella Reekie** (1922–1982) who worked with the Red Cross after the Second World War, helping to rehabilitate Jewish children who came out of Belsen concentration camp. Later Reekie became a missionary in Pakistan and from 1968 worked with immigrant communities back in Glasgow. Her home at 20 Glasgow Street in the West End became an open house to international visitors. The statue in the garden✤ is of **Princess Marjory Bruce** (1294–c1317), the daughter of Isobel of Mar and Robert I. The crowns at her feet symbolise that she was the daughter of – and mother of – kings. Marjory was captured after her father seized the throne of Scotland. Edward I ordered her to be confined to a cage in the Tower of London but later imprisoned her in a Gilbertine nunnery. She was released in 1314 following the battle at Bannockburn. It was agreed that she would inherit the crown if both her father and his brother Edward died without male heirs, but she predeceased them both, fatally injured after a fall from her horse while pregnant. Her baby was saved – the future Robert II, the first of the Stewart monarchs. Marjory is buried in Paisley Abbey and there is a cairn to her memory near the site where she was dismounted a short drive northwards.

Also in the small garden you will find a stone✤ to the memory of **Susan Newell** (1893–1923), the last woman hanged in Scotland (at Duke Street Prison) for her part in the murder of paperboy John Johnson. The jury at her trial found her guilty but asked for mercy, which was not forthcoming from the judge. Newell was subjected to emotional and physical abuse by her partner and was under huge pressure at the time of the murder. Only a couple of years later, a man convicted of a similar murder was given life imprisonment, rather than the death sentence.

The Necropolis

There are two necropolises in Glasgow – this huge grave-yard, containing an estimated 50,000 graves and 3,500 monuments, and a smaller Southern Necropolis in the Gorbals. For gravehunters it's worth visiting both. In the smaller yard you will find **Agnes Reston** (1771–1856), the 'Heroine of Matagorda' who went to Spain with her husband during the Napoleonic Wars. As the troops with-drew she bravely tried to rescue her son who was under fire – but failed. Back in Glasgow she died in the poorhouse. Also in the Southern Necropolis are **Magdalene Smith** (c1851–1933) and **Mary McNaughton** (c1878–1933) who died when they were run over by a tram, which they did not see coming because of their umbrella. Their monument is called the White Lady and it is said that its gaze will turn you to stone.

The second, larger graveyard holds the moving Mothers' Monument ✿ to the memory of all **women lost in childbirth**. This is said to have been inspired by **Agnes Strang** (c1810–1843) a 'Beloved Mother' whose grave in the Necropolis depicts a relief of four children mourning. She died in childbirth aged 33. The Mothers' Monument is near Agnes's grave and is often alight with candles and bedecked with flowers and notes. Carved from startling white stone, it shows a mother staring into her baby's face. While deaths in childbirth fell dramatically over the course of the 20th century, childbirth was hugely dangerous in the centuries preceding that, and for sexually active women, pregnancy was unavoidable without effective contraception. This monument, raised in the 1970s, commemorates all women who lost their lives while giving birth and is inscribed simply 'our foremothers, our heroines'.

The Necropolis also encompasses a Jewish cemetery dating back to 1832, where you will find the grave of **Deborah Ascherson** (died 1847), who is buried just outside the Jewish area – possibly because she married out of the religion. In the Christian part of the Necropolis look out for the grave of **Corlinda Lee** (1831–1900), who merged two important traveller dynasties when she married horse trainer George Smith. She famously hosted gypsy balls and read Queen Victoria's palm. There was a stall in her name at the Barras until recently. Nearby are the **Misses Buchanan of Bellfield**, three unsung heroines of Victorian Glasgow. None of them married and they bequeathed £10,000 to the Merchants' House and £30,000 to found a hospital. Their total legacy in today's money is worth approximately £4 million. It is inexplicable that the only monument to them is this grave. You can also visit the grave of **Barbara Hopkirk** (died 1833), wife of Necropolis founder, Laurence Hill; she died aged 40, having given birth to 13 children. She was the first 'Christian lady, moving in the upper or respectable ranks; whose remains were deposited in the cemetery'. However, the first female Christian burial in the Necropolis was that of **Elizabeth Miles** earlier the same year.

St Enoch's Museum of Religious Life and Art⛪

This museum on Cathedral Square houses exhibits relating to all the world's major religions. It is named for **St Enoch**, the mother of St Kentigern (St Mungo). St Enoch, also known as St Teneu, was a 6th century Christian princess who survived banishment, rape and two murder attempts and is the patron saint✤ of the city. She has been described as 'Scotland's first recorded rape victim, battered woman and unmarried mother' in the *Innes Review*, a Catholic periodical. The Welsh prince Owain mab Urien disguised himself as a woman and raped Enoch, whereupon she fell pregnant. When her father found out he sentenced her to death and she was thrown from Traprain Law in East Lothian. On surviving the fall, she was set adrift in a small boat on the Firth of Forth and ran aground at Culross where she gave birth to her son. Both Scottish and Welsh myths have sprung up around her life but she is commemorated in Glasgow as nowhere else. St Enoch Square, on Argyle Street, is home to the St Enoch Centre and St Enoch Subway Station. The square was the site of her chapel and well, which was said to have healing properties. The tree (now long gone) beside the chapel had metal offerings inserted into the bark, left by adherents over the centuries and believed to help women in childbirth. Recently two highly detailed photo-realistic murals by Australian artist Smug have been commissioned in the city on the corner of the High Street and George Street. One depicts St Enoch tenderly breastfeeding her son, Mungo, and the other shows St Mungo as an adult.

Inside the museum is the sculpture✤ of **Sister Marie Hilda** (1876–1951), who founded non-denominational, free therapeutic children's clinics in Glasgow. She was deaf and lectured on emotional deprivation, poverty and ill-health. You will also discover material✤ written by **Janet Hamilton** (1795–1873), a poet and author who lived in what is now Coatbridge. She came from a family of Covenanters and by the age of five had learned to read using the Bible. Her work was mainly religious in nature. The museum houses her manuscripts, which are written in her distinctive self-taught handwriting. A memorial fountain was placed opposite her cottage, and the community centre in Coatbridge is named after her.

Provand's Ladyship⚑

This is the oldest house in the city, dating from 1471. It's home to a small museum of memorabilia relating to some of the city's characters. Of particular interest⚑ is **Jean Cameron** (c1698–1772), who in 1745 led 300 men to the raising of the Jacobite standard at Glenfinnan. Said to be the only woman of rank present, 'Bonnie Jean Cameron' made a striking image and she immediately became famous. As a result her name was blackened by Hanoverian commentators and press, with rumours circulating that she was Prince Charles Edward Stuart's mistress, that after the '45 she had fallen into poverty in Edinburgh, had a wooden leg and died in a stairway in the Canongate. In real life, she lived obscurely after the '45, buying the estate of Blacklaw in Lanarkshire in 1751 and running a school. There is a cairn marking her grave in the small park at Blacklaw where a horse chestnut tree marks the site of her house, which was demolished in 1958. Also look for the artefacts⚑ pertaining to **Maude Galt** (1620–c1670) from Kilbarchan, Renfrewshire, who was charged first as a lesbian and then as a witch. Galt was accused of assaulting her maidservant with what sounds in the court records like a sex toy. We don't know what happened to her – she may have been let off or she may, like many convicted witches, have been drowned and then burned. Provand's Ladyship also houses late-Victorian photographs⚑ of **Rachel Johnston**, a 6 foot 4 inch Irish woman known as 'Big Rachel', who worked as a labourer in the shipyards, a forewoman navvy at the brickworks and a farm worker. Indomitable and always smoking her pipe, she was sworn in as a special constable during a two-day riot in Partick in 1875 as opposing factions clashed over Home Rule being granted in Ireland. It is said she dumped one man, who refused to stop struggling against her, into the Clyde.

Sauchiehall Street

Look out for the large-scale mounted photographs✤ by **Audrey Glover Walker** (1910–1966), who took many shots of the painter Joan Eardley (see page 277). These are on display as banners along the street. Eardley is well known for her pictures of Glasgow tenements, which have become world-famous as representations of the city's working-class life. Fittingly there is also a statue of a large bottle of ginger beer here, on the pedestrian precinct. This is in memory of **May Donoghue** (1898–1958), a shop assistant from the Calton area who discovered a dead snail in her drink while visiting a local cafe with a friend. Her case was taken up (pro bono) by Glasgow solicitor Walter Leechman and resulted in a landmark House of Lords ruling establishing a manufacturer's duty of care to customers. During proceedings, Donoghue was forced to declare herself a pauper in order to be able to continue the case. There is a statue in her memory in Paisley by Mandy McIntosh.

Further along Sauchiehall Street, on the site of a turn-of-the-century suffragette office (which also housed a tearoom), you will see a plaque✤ inset into the pavement dedicated to **Helen Crawfurd** (1877–1954), a gifted orator and one of Emmeline Pankhurst's bodyguards. During the First World War, Crawfurd was involved in grass-roots women's movements including the rent strike, the Women's Peace Crusade, and the Independent Labour Party. An internationalist and proponent of Home Rule, she became Dunoon's first female town councillor. The plaque is inscribed 'Courage springs from facing danger, strong in love of life's delight', taken from the suffragette anthem 'Song of the Women', which Crawfurd wrote.

Willow Tea Rooms

Having undergone recent refurbishment, a visit to these tearooms founded by **Kate Cranston** (1849–1934) is a must. It is said that Cranston made Glasgow a 'very tokio for tearooms'. An eccentric dresser – all ruffles and crinolines long after they had gone out of style – she made up for her lack of fashion smarts with her progressive taste in interiors. Cranston's tearoom was designed by her friend Charles Rennie Mackintosh, who was inspired by the word 'Sauchiehall' which means 'avenue of willow' in Scots, resulting in the willow tree design. Cranston appears on the redesigned Royal Bank of Scotland £20 notes.

Glasgow Film Theatre

Just off Sauchiehall Street on Rose Street, the GFT has three screens, each named after a famous actress from Glasgow. The cinema is affectionately known as the Mason after **Elliott Mason** (1888–1949), an actress from Glasgow who appeared in many Ealing comedies. The Kerr Screen is named after **Deborah Kerr** (1921–2007), a Golden Globe winner, three time winner of the New York Film Critics Circle Award and six time Academy Award nominee. Among her many films are *Black Narcissus*, *The King and I*, *The Life and Death of Colonel Blimp* and *Bonjour Tristesse*. The Gordon Screen is named after Hollywood character actor **Mary Gordon** (1882–1963), who appeared in more than 200 films including *The Bride of Frankenstein*, *Bonnie Scotland* and *Fort Apache*. She also played Mrs Hudson in the series of ten Sherlock Holmes films starting in 1939. Mary was a charter member of the Hollywood Canteen, which entertained troops during the Second World War. She was also active in the Daughters of Scotia, the female contingent of the benevolent society the Order of Scottish Clans, which provided a form of health and life insurance to those of Scottish heritage in North America. The Ure Screen is named after **Mary Ure** (1933–1975), another celebrated Hollywood actor who first won critical acclaim for her role in *Look Back in Anger* and was nominated for an Oscar for her role in *Sons and Lovers*. These talented women all feature regularly in the Finnieston Crane screenings (see page 118).

Glasgow School of Art

Subject to two devastating fires in recent years, the Glasgow School of Art was founded in 1845 and moved to the site on Renfrew Street in 1897. On the campus you can still see work✤ by **Agnes Miller Parker** (1895–1980), who studied here from 1911 to 1917, and joined the school's staff for a short period. She was one of the group of futurist artists known as Vorticists, inspired by Cubism, who worked in London in the 1920s. The main body of her work consists of wood engravings for book illustrations. Also on display✤ is work by **Marianne Grant** (1921–2007). Her memoir, *I Knew I Was Painting for My Life*, recounts her life during the Second World War when she was ordered to sketch death camp prisoners by SS doctor Josef Mengele. She said that 'it hurt to survive', so she devoted herself to teaching future generations about the horror of the Holocaust. The Scottish Government produced an education pack based on her experiences, which was distributed to every secondary school in Scotland.

The Tenement House

This museum at 145 Buccleuch Street was the home of shorthand typist **Agnes Reid Toward** (1886–1975), who lived here from 1911 to 1965. Preserved to show Glasgow tenement life in the early 20th century, it also provides a snapshot of the life of an independent Glaswegian woman. On entering you will hear a recording ✿ of the once popular song 'There's Nae Luck Aboot the Hoose', described by Burns as 'one of the most beautiful songs in the Scots or any other language'. It was written by poet **Jean Adam** (1704–1765), who died in Glasgow's workhouse despite her poetic talents and Burns's praise.

Near the Tenement House look out for the cuckoo sculptures ✿ in the gardens that run up to Hill Street. These are in memory of **Allison Greenlees** (1896–1979) who, with five other girls from Laurel Bank School, objected to the fact they could not join the Scouts. The girls formed the Cuckoo Patrol in 1909, a girl guiding troop which became affiliated to the First Glasgow Scout Group. After a life-long commitment to guiding, Greenlees went on to receive the organisation's highest award, the Silver Fish, in 1939, and in 1953 became President of the Guiding Council for Scotland. The community hall at Whittingehame, Haddington, is named after her.

The Mitchell Library

Opened in 1911, this is Glasgow's largest reference library and houses a photographic archive and sundry special collections as well as the city's annual book festival Aye Write! in March. Look out for the main sweep of stairs ✿ leading in to the impressive building, with giant spines of books on its rises, like a huge reading pile. This features Glasgow authors including **Helen MacInnes** (1907–1985), a classics scholar who also published 21 espionage thrillers. Her novel *Assignment in Brittany* is said to have been used to train Allied personnel to work with the French underground during the Second World War. A novel by **Marion Lochhead** (1902–1985), *Cloaked in Scarlet*, is half way up the staircase. She wrote poetry, biography and history across an impressive range of topics and became a fellow of the Royal Society of Literature in 1955. **Reay Tannahill** (1929–2007) was a historian and novelist known for her non-fiction bestsellers *Food in History* and *Sex in History*. She also wrote under the pseudonym Annabel Laine. Her novel *Passing Glory* won the Romantic Novel of the Year Award in 1990, and makes the next step on this staircase. Towards the top of the staircase influential poet **Veronica Forrest-Thomson** (1947–1975) is represented by her collected works, which inspired Edwin Morgan to write a ten poem sequence tribute to her 'raw moving almost ballad strain'. Next is the work of two sisters. **Peggy Morrison** (1897–1973) wrote hugely successful novels under the name March Cost. Her most famous, *The Bespoken Mile*, tells the story of a cabaret dancer who inherits a house in the country. The top two steps show the work of Peggy's sister, **Agnes Brysson Morrison** (1903–1986), a prolific novelist and biographer who secretly wrote 27 romances as Christine Strathern. Her authorship of these romance novels was not discovered until 30 years after her death, so successful was she at keeping her secret. One of her steps is *The Gowk Storm*, which she wrote as Morrison, and the other is *Love in the Mist*, which she wrote as Strathern.

Hanging on the walls in the Mitchell you will find the work ❦ of painter **Margot Sandeman** (1922–2009), a good friend of Joan Eardley (see page 103 and page 277) and collaborator with the poet Ian Hamilton Finlay. In 1942 Sandeman worked for six months as a code-breaker at

Bletchley Park. Her beautiful paintings of west coast land-scapes, rural settings, interiors and still lives brighten the library walls. Look out for the portraits of her friend and neighbour, the dramatist and poet Robert McLellan.

The West End

Now ranging from up-and-coming Finnieston to the University of Glasgow's extensive properties in the area and the established shops and eateries of Hillhead, the West End of Glasgow developed in the late Georgian and early Victorian period as the city outgrew its medieval boundaries. Travelling westwards, notice the townhouse at 6/7 Blythswood Square, which is said to be haunted by the ghost of **Madeleine Smith** (1835–1928), a Glasgow socialite who was released after the charge of poisoning her lover, Pierre Emile L'Angelier, was 'not proven' in 1857. When L'Angelier threatened to release Smith's love letters, she bought arsenic but though Smith signed the pharmacist's poison book, it could not be proven that she administered the fatal dose. There have been several dram-atisations of Madeleine's story including a film by David Lean and several novels featuring her case such as Wilkie Collins's *The Law and the Lady*.

Kelvingrove Art Gallery and Museum

Built for the 1888 International Exhibition and then opened as a permanent museum in 1901 during the International Fair, Kelvingrove houses a wonderful collec-tion of artifacts. It is worth looking out for the work✤ of **Dr Mary Armour** (1902–2000), a landscape and still life painter, art teacher and a Honorary President of the Glasgow School of Art and the Royal Glasgow Institute of the Fine Arts. The Armour Award, named after her, is given annually for a work of distinction by a young artist, which is then displayed❦ in the museum next to Armour's own work. She especially loved Arran and latterly painted many landscapes of the island.

Also of note is the exhibit❦ about the life of **Dorothy 'Doll' Thomas** (c1763–c1848), the 'Queen of Demerara', who was a free black woman, slave owner and successful businesswoman. She arrived in Glasgow in August 1810 with some of her children and grandchildren, looking to educate the boys in Inverness and the girls at Kensington House. Though a slave owner (registers of the period show her owning about 80 people), she stood up for her slaves including one called Sally, a pregnant black woman who was killed in police custody in Demerara (now Guyana). Doll was a fascinating figure whose story runs counter-intuitively to the common expectations of women of colour during the era. When she arrived in London it was said she had a skirt made out of five pound notes and a necklace of golden doubloons. She certainly was wealthy and leant money to her (white) son-in-laws when their businesses ran into trouble. She also had considerable clout in the Demerara business community.

Kelvingrove Park

A favourite with local students, the park runs to 85 acres with the River Kelvin winding through the middle. One of the main paths, Stephen Way🔔, is named for **Jessie Stephen** (1893–1979), who at sixteen joined the suffragette movement and was the youngest member of a working women's delegation to London, organised by the Glasgow Domestic Workers' Union. Later she worked full time with Sylvia Pankhurst. She was a lifelong committed socialist, trade unionist and pacifist – one of the few working-class women who organised within the suffragette movement.

She dropped acid into pillar boxes as a protest. There is a blue plaque to her in Bedminster where she lived at the time of her death. In 1918, on Stephen Way (then Kelvin Way) victorious suffragettes planted a sessile oak, which has now grown to maturity and is known as the Suffrage Oak. Suffragette sashes�࿓ in violet, green and white are often looped round the branches and sitting beneath it is a small bronze statue✝ of a woman reading. This is dedicated to **Marion Reid** (1815–1902), author of *A Plea for Woman*, written in 1843, the first work to give priority to achieving civil and political rights for women. The book in the statue is engraved with Reid's words: 'The ground on which equality is claimed for all men is of equal force for all women.'

Elsewhere in the park you will pass the Todd Fountain⚱, named after **Margaret Todd** (1859–1918), a school teacher from Glasgow who became one of the first students at the Edinburgh School of Medicine for Women. During her studies she wrote a novel based on her experiences, *Mona Maclean, Medical Student*, using the pseudonym Graham Travers. When her friend Frederick Soddy, a lecturer at the University of Glasgow, discovered isotopes, Todd suggested the name to him, which is Greek for 'at the same place' (in the periodic table). Romantically involved with Sophia Jex-Blake (see page 70), Todd wrote a biography of her after Jex-Blake's death.

The park's Whiskey Bandstand⚱ is not named after the national drink, as many people assume, but after **Nancy Whiskey** (1935–2003), a chart-topping skiffle musician born in Glasgow who is best known for her hit 'Freight Train'. Beside the bandstand, the beautiful floral clock✝ planted with exotic flowers is to the memory of **Margaret Wilson** (1795–1835). A pioneer of women's education across caste in India, she died in Bombay (present

Suffrage Oak and Marion Reid Statue

day Mumbai). Over the course of the year the clock is replanted but is always laid out with the bright colours of the sub-continent.

Kelvingrove Park is peppered with statues✼ of Glasgow women including mental health pioneer **Kate Fraser** (1877–1957), the first woman Commissioner on the General Board of Control for Scotland, and historian **Betty Miller Unterberger** (1922–2012), who spent most of her academic career as a professor of American International Relations at a university in Texas. She was the first woman to be employed as a full professor on the faculty of the university in 1968 and stayed in post until she was in her 80s. There is also **Mary Hamilton** (1884–1966), born and educated in Glasgow. She became MP for Blackburn, and was a governor of the BBC in the 1930s. The charming and unusual statue✼ of two women and a bicycle depicts **Hilda Goldwag** (1912–2008) and **Cecile Schwarzschild** (1915–1998) Jewish refugees who fled from the Nazi regime in 1939. The women lived together in Garnetthill, only a few miles to the south, and worked as turners in the local engineering works during the war. Sadly, Hilda's family was prevented from following her to Scotland and was killed in the Holocaust. Hilda had graduated from art school in Vienna, and after the war she designed scarves for Marks and Spencer. Her paintings were exhibited in small galleries around the city and her portrait of Cecile – a tribute to her friend – is now held by the Scottish Jewish Archives Centre.

Glasgow University

Founded in 1451, Glasgow University is the fourth oldest university in the English-speaking world. It moved to its current location in the mid 19th century, although the design of the main building harks back to earlier times. There are buildings, plaques and statues across the campus which pay homage to renowned female students. The university's earliest female alumni was **Marion Gilchrist** (1864–1952). Gilchrist was also the first woman to qualify in medicine at a Scottish university and was a prominent suffragette. She was chair of the Glasgow division of the British Medical Association – another female first. The Marion Gilchrist Prize is awarded to 'the most distinguished woman graduate in Medicine of the year'. There is a memorial garden to her in Bothwell, where she grew up. It is particularly fitting that Gilchrist signed the death certificate of **Isabella Elder** (1828–1905), who campaigned for women's right to education and devoted herself to philanthropic projects, including endowing a chair of naval architecture at Glasgow University and providing property for Queen Margaret College (originally a women's college, later merged with the university). Elder also made a number of contributions in Govan, establishing a School of Domestic Economy, gifting land for Elder Park and financing Elder Cottage Hospital and Elder Free Library. The *Baillie* (a Glasgow news periodical) described her as 'a true woman, wise benefactress of the public and of learning'. There are three monuments to her at the university – a memorial window at Bute Hall, a plaque and the Isabella Elder Building. There is also a rose garden and statue in Elder Park. Without her, the university would not have accepted female students as early as it did and Gilchrist's career would not have been possible. It should be noted that three other women also graduated with Marion Gilchrist but as Gilchrist had won a high commendation it is her name that came first on the roll.

Another university pioneer is honoured by a statue outside the Queen Margaret Union. **Jessie Campbell**

(1827–1907) promoted higher education for women as early as the 1860s. She gained the support of professors at Glasgow University and arranged lectures for women, initially in natural history, moral philosophy, English literature and astronomy. In 1877 she became the Vice-president of the newly formed Glasgow Association for the Higher Education of Women, with **Janet Galloway** (1841–1909) as its Honorary Secretary. Together they campaigned for women's right to higher education and when, in 1892, Queen Margaret College amalgamated with Glasgow University, they achieved their goal. They are commemorated in stained glass windows in Bute Hall. Another early beneficiary of Elder, Galloway and Campbell's campaign was **Frances Melville** (1873–1962), the first Scottish woman to graduate as a Bachelor of Divinity in 1910. She was a suffragist and advocate of higher education for women, later becoming Mistress of Queen Margaret College. Melville House is named after her and there is an annual award of a Melville Medal in her name for a distinguished candidate in mental philosophy.

Other memorials at the university include plaques to **Merbi Ardesir Vakil**, who in 1897 was the first Indian woman to graduate from Glasgow University and **Muriel Clara 'M C' Bradbrook** (1909–1993), a literary scholar and Shakespeare specialist who became Professor of English and Mistress of Girton College, Cambridge.

Hunterian Museum

Located within the university, this is Scotland's oldest public museum, founded in 1807. It contains many collections of scientific and cultural interest including the work of archaeologist **Anne Strachan Robertson** (1910–1997), who became Under-Keeper of the Museum in 1952. She was also one of the first women to be given professorial rank at the University of Glasgow as Professor of Roman Archaeology in 1974. Also look out for the collection⚶ of paleontologist **Ethel Currie** (1899–1963), the first woman to win the Neill Prize for life sciences in 1945 for a paper about Jurassic ammonites, one of the first three women to become a fellow of the Royal Society Edinburgh in 1949 and the first woman president of the Geological Society of Glasgow.

Hunterian Art Gallery

On the other side of University Avenue is the Hunterian Art Gallery, part of which was originally the home of **Margaret Macdonald Mackintosh** (1864–1933), whose husband, Charles (also a painter and designer), said of her, 'Margaret has genius, I only have talent.' The gallery houses an extensive collection of art including the creations⚶ of the Glasgow Girls, who worked in many media from suffragette banners to jewellery, prints, metalwork and paintings. This collection was first brought together by groundbreaking curator **Jude Burkhauser** (1947–1998), who staged an exhibition of the movement at nearby Kelvingrove Museum and Gallery in 1990. She declared 'Women in the arts have been starved for stories of other women, tales of these maverick sisters whom they might learn from. We followed in one another's footsteps knocking on doors, asking the same questions, rediscovering fire, the wheel, electricity because there was no record of our past.'

On display as part of the Glasgow Girls collection is the work⚶ of **Kathleen Whyte** (1909–1996), embroiderer, textiles expert and teacher of textile arts whose work can also be seen in the Victoria & Albert Musuem, London and Royal Scottish Museum; **Helen Paxton Brown** (1876–1956), who specialised in embroidery and bookbinding; **De Courcy Lewthwaite Dewar** (1878–1959), born in

Ceylon (now Sri Lanka), who became a metalworker and enamellist as well as President of the Society of Lady Artists; Art Nouveau icon **Annie French** (1872–1965), a painter, engraver and illustrator; **Georgina Greenlees** (1849–1932), who specialised in landscapes of tourist Scotland; the impressionist **Bessie MacNicol** (1869–1904), who exhibited internationally and tragically died in childbirth aged only 34; **Ann Macbeth** (1875–1948), a particular associate of Charles Rennie Mackintosh and committed suffragette; **Eleanor Allen Moore** (1885–1955), who was born in County Antrim and studied in Glasgow and went on to paint streets scenes of Shanghai and the Yangtse River when she travelled to China; portraitist **Norah Neilson Grey** (1882–1931), whose work is in many national collections and who served as a nurse in the First World War where she painted and sketched the day-to-day life of military hospitals as well as undertaking her medical duties; and **Jessie Newbery** (1864–1948), an artist and embroiderer who frequently used the suffragette colours – green, white and violet. Newbery's applique work included a stylised rose motif that became one of the symbols of the Glasgow style. As a committed suffragette she supported women throughout her life providing exhibition and studio space for female artists.

If you would like to see more work by Margaret Macdonald Mackintosh head for House for an Art Lover on the South Side. This museum is solely dedicated✢ to Margaret and **Frances Macdonald** (1873–1921). Whereas many women studied art for personal pleasure, these pioneering sisters sold their creative work and, upon graduation, set up their own studio. They exhibited across Europe, becoming particularly famous for their metalwork – a process that women were usually discouraged from because of the dirt and heavy lifting involved. They co-signed their early pieces and even forgot which of them had created what. The sisters were two of the famous Glasgow Four (or Spook School), with Charles Rennie Mackintosh and Herbert McNair, and Margaret in particular is believed to have influenced the artist Gustav Klimt's now world-famous work.

(For the work of Glasgow Girl Jessie King and her associates in Kirkcudbright see page 161.)

Glasgow Botanic Gardens

Dating from 1817, these gardens have not always been the oasis of peace you see today. In January 1914, militant suffragettes **Dorothea Chalmers Smith** (1874–1944) and **Margaret McPhun** (1876–1960) bombed the Kibble Palace glasshouse. Margaret and her sister, **Frances McPhun** (1880–1940) had been students at the nearby university and had both previously been arrested and sent to Holloway Prison for smashing windows in London. On this occasion, the ladies left high-heeled footprints that the police used as evidence against them and these are memorialized today by a 10 foot high metal sculpture✜ of a high-heeled shoe inside the glasshouses. Later, Dorothea was caught trying to set fire to 6 Park Gardens nearby. All these women were hunger strikers while in prison and received hunger strike medals after their release.

Elsewhere in the gardens is the Mann Playpark▲ named for **Selma Mann** (1892–1989), who was Convenor of the Care of Children Committee, which brought more than 300 children to Scotland from Nazi-controlled Europe, saving their lives. Beside the playpark the sculpture✜ of an old fashioned wireless is dedicated to **Kathleen Garscadden** (1897–1991), a much-loved children's BBC broadcaster from 1923 to 1960 known to her listeners as Auntie Kathleen.

As you walk along the path from the playpark you will notice the 'psychedelic' spiral hedge maze❀ which was designed and planted in memory of poet and writer **Helen Adam** (1909–1993), who wrote 'dark stories about lethal women'. A child prodigy born in Glasgow, Helen had her first poems published when she was only four years of age. She went on to become part of a literary movement in San Francisco during the 1950s and 1960s – the era of the Beat Generation. Though frequently connected to the Beat poets, she could in fact be thought of as one of the movement's precursors because of her fascination with traditional ballads and myths, which use rhythm to convey narrative drive. In 1981 she won the American Book Award. The poet Robert Duncan once referred to her as 'the extraordinary nurse of enchantment'.

Behind the maze there is a small outdoor stage known as the Biggar Stand❀, named after **Helen Biggar** (1909–1953), a theatre and costumer designer who worked with the Ballet Rambert. She also co-directed many experimental films and was one of the creatives behind *Hell UnLtd*, recognised as one of Britain's most important early pieces of avant-garde political film. In the 1930s, she joined the Communist Party and was involved in the genesis of the Glasgow Unity Theatre. The Biggar Stand is used for public speaking and more recently for performance poetry with a political slant.

Finnieston Crane

If you are in Glasgow during the summer months it is worth checking the programme of films being screened at this proud remnant of the city's engineering past. Standing 53 metres tall, the cantilever crane originally lifted heavy machinery onto ships for export. Now disused, it is one of only eleven still in existence worldwide. The huge screen✦ that is mounted from the jib becomes an outdoor cinema showing vintage films featuring some of Glasgow's most popular actors, singers and performers of the 20th century. The choices are eclectic and give a flavour of talented Glaswegians over the last hundred years.

As well as the films of women memorialised elsewhere in the city, you might catch footage✦ of **Mary O'Rourke** (1913–1964), who appeared as a boy soprano in variety performances. She regularly packed the Metropole in Stockwell Street and later in life appeared in STV's *One O'Clock Gang*. You will also see **May Moxon** (1906–1996), a child performer on Glasgow's cine-variety shows who went on to found a troupe of dancers, and the Waddell Sisters, **Bertha Waddell** (1907–1980) and **Jenny Waddell** (1905–1984), writers, directors and costumers particularly interested in children's theatre. They toured Scotland and played to the royal nurseries in Glamis, Balmoral and Buckingham Palace several times, entertaining the Princesses Elizabeth and Margaret during the early 1930s and the children of Elizabeth II during the mid to late 1950s. Footage of their show is rare but is sometimes shown as part of a medley of vintage material. There are also clips before the main films showing performers such as **Molly Weir** (1910–2004), who acted in radio plays and was most popularly known as Hazel McWitch in the children's series *Rentaghost* from 1976 to 1984. The song 'Molly's Lips', written by Glasgow rock band the Vaselines, and made famous by Nirvana, is about her. **Janet McLuckie Brown** (1923–2011), an actress and comedian from Rutherglen, also features. She became famous in the 1970s and 1980s for her impersonations of the UK's first female Prime Minister, Margaret Thatcher, and at the height of her popularity her impressions were seen by over 14 million viewers. When she met Thatcher in 1986 at a Conservative Party Conference, the PM asked her 'I know you could have delivered my speech better than I did, but was it all right?'

Clydeside

The last great liner to be built on the Clyde was the QE2, launched in 1967. Today, Clydeside is better known for its TV studios, museums and riverside walk. Follow the bronze arrows✦ to see plaques and memorials to women who influenced the area and indeed the world. These include a plaque✦ to **Ethel 'Camelia' McDonald** (1909–1960), who went to Spain during the Civil War and broadcasted in English for Barcelona Anarchist radio – she was known as the Scots Scarlet Pimpernel – and another✦ to **Margot Bennett** (1912–1980), a screenwriter and crime novelist who also went to the Spanish Civil War as a nurse. A lifelong CND supporter, Bennett later wrote for TV including episodes of *Maigret* and *Emergency Ward 10*. The plaques tell of the impact these women had during the conflict, and of their lives when they returned to Scotland. Also look out for the striking sculpture at Custom House Quay on Clyde Street to Basque-born activist **Dolores Ibárruri** (1895–1989), also known as La Pasionaria (the Passionflower). It is inscribed with her words, 'Better to die on your feet than live forever on your knees.' The statue, with both arms raised defiantly in the air, is to the memory of the volunteers who went to Spain to fight fascism from 1936 to 1939. Sixty-five Glaswegians died on Spanish soil during the period.

Continue to follow the bronze arrows as you walk along the Clyde past the SEC and the Hydro, until you come to a beautiful installation made from old sewing machines known as the Seamstress Statue✦. At the turn of the century there were over 1,200 workshops in Glasgow. The majority of the **employees were women, many from immigrant communities**, often working in extremely harsh conditions. A strike in 1911 led to over 400 female workers being sacked, and it is these women who are commemorated by the statue. One local woman who was actively involved in the strike (and was sacked because of her participation) was **Jane Rae** (1872–1959). Rae joined the Independent Labour Party after hearing its founder, Keir Hardie, speak, and became Clydebank Branch Secretary in 1913, going on to campaign against the First World War and becoming a key player in the cooperative and temperance movements. She once chaired Emily Pankhurst at Clydebank Town Hall and was a local councillor from 1922 to 1928. Later, as a justice of the peace, she had a reputation for dealing harshly with men who mistreated their wives. There is a plaque on Dumbarton Road to her memory, and there is a currently a campaign✷ for an individual statue of Jane to be placed in Victoria Square (see page 78).

On this path you'll also find out about **Christian Shaw** (1684–1750), a threadmaking pioneer who started the industry in Paisley by bringing to Scotland a Dutch process that made strong white thread. There is a kinetic installation✷ here of a spinning spool that commemorates her commercial success. The thread industry in the town would go on to employ seven times more women than men, and the word 'spinster' was coined to describe the unmarried women who worked as spinners – they had to leave their job if they married. There is also a darker aspect to Christian's life – at the age of 11, she gave evidence that led to eight people being accused of witchcraft in the Bargarran witch trials. All eight were killed. There is a red thread running through the otherwise white memorial to mark this time in her early life.

Riverside Museum of Transport

This modern titanium-clad building was designed by **Zaha Hadid** (1950–2016) and won European Museum of the Year 2013. Outside, there is a full-size reproduction of a de Havilland Fox Moth bi-plane✲ and, beside it, two women pilots. In real life these women did not fly together but they represent Glasgow's heritage in pioneering female aviation. **Janet Hendry** (1906–2004) was Scotland's first woman pilot. She obtained her licence on 11 January 1929, narrowly beating another female student. The second woman is **Winifred Joyce 'Winnie' Drinkwater** (1913–1996), a pilot and aeroplane engineer who enjoyed a varied career. The first woman in the world to hold a commercial pilot's licence, Drinkwater won two Scottish Flying Club trophies in 1932 – one for racing and one for landing. Among her many commissions, she flew charters to deliver newspapers to the Scottish islands. Winnie also flew press photographers over Loch Ness to search for Nessie and piloted air ambulances to the Western Isles. On one occasion she captained an air search for a boat of kidnappers. There is a bronze bust to her memory at Clyde View Park in Renfrewshire.

Inside the museum look out for the wonderful photographs✲ of glamorous daredevil sisters **Annie** (1924–2004) and **Chrissie Neil** (1927–1991) who entered and finished the Monte Carlo Rally twice in the 1950s. Annie never sat a driving test, though she drove from the age of fifteen. Between them the sisters won a string of Scottish and British rallying awards. They went on to take over their family pig farm and Chrissie set up a fashion house – Smith Innes. The photo archive, donated to the museum, gives a wonderful insight into the world of mid 20th century rally driving.

Janet Hendry and
Winnie Drinkwater Statue

Glasgow Science Centre

South of the river, the science centre houses exhibitions, an Imax screen and the Glasgow Tower, which at 127 metres affords panoramic views of the city. You can also catch the Clyde paddle steamer the *Discipline*, named after the novel by popular Scottish writer Mary Brunton (see page 370).

Inside the museum you will find hands-on displays built around Scotland's contribution to science, incorporating the work of scientists either from or educated in Glasgow. The female scientists include **Nancy Conn** (1919–2013), the bacteriologist who traced the origin of the deadly 1970 outbreak of typhus at the Water of Leith; **Honoria Keer** (1883–1969), who was awarded the French Croix de Guerre, the Médaille d'Honneur des Epidémies and the Serbian Order of St Sava for her medical work as part of the Scottish Women's Hospitals (see page 63); **Ruth Pirret** (1874–1939), Glasgow's first female BSc graduate who became a nuclear and engineering chemist – she collaborated with nuclear chemist Frederick Soddy at the University of Glasgow, researching the ratio of radium to uranium (a project for which Soddy became a Nobel Laureate but Pirret went unrecognised); and **Muriel Robertson** (1883–1973), a protozoologist and bacteriologist at London's Lister Institute for over 40 years. She made major discoveries about the life cycle of parasites and was elected a Fellow of the Royal Society in 1947. She spent part of her career in Uganda, researching the tsetse fly and also piloted breakthrough research on gangrene, a major cause of soldiers' deaths in the First World War.

Govan

Further along the Clyde it's worth taking in the trio of monuments in Govan, constituency of Scotland's first female First Minister, Nicola Sturgeon. This area is famous for its 'gallus' women whose strength had an impact on those around them. Govan was a centre of activity during Red Clydeside, an era of political radicalism along the banks of the river in the early 20th century. At Govan Cross you will find the 2016 statue to **Mary Barbour** (1875–1958), a local councillor, bailie and magistrate honoured for her role as the main organiser of the rent strikes of 1915. She is one of two women painted on the Clutha Bar memorial and there is also a Mary Barbour Cairn in Kilbarchan in Renfrewshire. Plays, songs and novels have been written about this indomitable Glasgow woman. When rent was overcharged, she famously marched to the council's offices to demand a rebate on behalf of the tenants and encouraged tenants to pelt rent collectors with eggs and flour.

Also look for the rose garden✿ dedicated to **Rose Klasko Kerrigan** (1903–1995), a Jewish communist active in the same period – the short film *Red Rose* was made about her in 1996 and is sometimes shown at the Finnieston Crane screenings (see page 118). Sacked from her first job in a factory at age fourteen for speaking out against the First World War, she went on to join the Communist Party, spending time in Moscow during the mid 1930s. She supported Marie Stopes's work (see page 69) and scandalized Glasgow's only birth control clinic by seeking contraceptive advice before she had any children. She also set up a women's branch of the workers' union at Prudential Insurance and was an early supporter of CND. She attended political meetings up to the time of her death – a lifelong radical.

Another local heroine, **Battling Betty McAllister** (1931–2009), is famous for telling Prime Minister Margaret Thatcher she could 'stick the poll tax where the sun don't shine' when McAllister organised a protest during a visit by the then prime minister. She received a British Empire Medal in 1980 and was Scotswoman of the Year in 1984. There is a blue plaque commemorating her at the site of her old shop Betty's Seafood but she is better remembered by the giant megaphone ✦ outside the Barras known as Betty's Funnel, which bears her motto 'if you shout loud enough, they'll listen'.

Southern Scotland

The sun shone, the land looked prosperous,
my days seemed full of happy coincidences.
I crossed the border so many times that I forgot
whether I was in Scotland or England.

Sophie Campbell, *Telegraph*, **1998**

Flora Wilb
Flowers Meadow

Mary's Brig

AYR

Elsie Mackay's Star

DUMFRIES

Margaret
Skinnider's Telescope

Elspeth's Drinking Fountain

WIGTOWN

Ælfflæd's Priory

Castle Agnes

ST ABBS HEAD

EYEMOUTH

Anna Masterton's Book Benches

Margaret Halcro Coffin

Charlotte Waldie Fountain

GALASHIELS •

Africa's Way

Jean Gordon Footprints

Old Jolly Buccleuch Wood

New Brides' Wishing Well

GRETNA

The Borders

The history of the Borders is a history of conflict as both Scottish and English armies repeatedly captured, lost and recaptured towns, castles, religious settlements and even farmsteads in the region over many centuries. This high level of military and private confrontation is commemorated by annual events known as Common Riding – processions which celebrate the bravery of local men in battle. In the main, women were not involved in the fighting, and Common Riding events (dating back to the 13th and 14th centuries) were male-dominated, but this is changing. In 2014, Selkirk appointed the first female standard bearer, Fiona Deacon, in its Common Riding procession. From the Cheviot Hills to the Lammermuirs, the area's turbulent history is evident in idyllic towns, lush landscapes, abandoned abbeys and country houses. This is perhaps encapsulated best in the tale of one woman who did not shy from battle, the indomitable **Agnes Countess of Dunbar** (c1312–1369), who defended the now-ruined Dunbar Castle (better known as Castle Agnes ⚑) against siege in 1338. Known as 'Black Agnes' on account of her dark hair, when the attacking force (said to comprise 20,000 men) bombarded the castle with rocks and lead shot, Agnes sent her ladies to dust down the ramparts in nonchalant defiance. When English troops threatened to hang her brother, she declared that simply meant she would inherit his earldom. The failed siege ended up costing the English army 6,000 pounds of silver and spawned ballads and poems including a song written by the Earl of Salisbury, who was in charge of the besieging force. 'She kept a stir in tower and trench, That brawling, boisterous Scottish wench, Came I early, came I late, I found Agnes at the gate.' Agnes, an exemplary border steward, is buried at Mordington, north of Berwick-upon-Tweed. Look out for cafes, restaurants and pubs named after her in the Dunbar area.

Eyemouth

Eyemouth is the Borders' main coastal settlement. This picturesque town radiates out from its ancient harbour where you will find a 5 metre-high bronze installation by renowned Edinburgh-based sculptor Jill Watson entitled *Widows and Bairns*. Overlooking the sea, the monument was erected in 2016 in memory of the 1881 fishing disaster when, as the result of a freak storm, 189 people were killed, including 129 local men, some of whom were drowned as their families watched helplessly from the shore. This powerful installation features all **78 widows and 182 fatherless children** in the aftermath of what remains Scotland's worst fishing disaster. These women had to be tenacious – local worthies offered to take their children to orphanages, but the community stuck together and regenerated. Watson carefully researched the history of the tragedy, and the sculpture's tiny figures accurately portray the real people who were left behind. The local museum houses a tapestry which also depicts the disaster.

Eyemouth is home to several local galleries which specialise in work from the Mak'Merry Pottery founded by **Catherine Blair** (1872–1946). A stalwart campaigner for women's rights, Blair opened her farm near Tranent (30 miles away) to weakened suffragettes who had been on hunger strike in prison, and cared for them during their recovery. This was absolutely in keeping with her hands-on approach – an example of the suffragette maxim 'Deeds not words.' Outraged that the 1921 census only named the man of the house, she took her children to the barn for the night so that, in a separate property with no man present, she would have to be individually recorded. She founded the pottery in 1917, the same year that she began the Scottish Women's Rural Institute, to provide an income for local women. Pieces made there are now highly collectible.

On Victoria Road, outside Eyemouth Parish Church there is an unusual monument✦ to **Margaret Halcro** (c1647–1725). This takes the form of a mechanical figure, which at noon sits up in her coffin. Margaret 'died' at the age of 27, shortly after her marriage to a local minister. Her body was taken to the churchyard at nearby Chirnside to be buried. That night, a graverobber opened the coffin and attempted to remove a ring from Margaret's finger. Unable to do so, he took his knife and tried to sever the finger. Margaret regained consciousness, sat up in the coffin and screamed, and the man ran off in fright. Halcro went on to have five children, who could claim their mother 'died' before they were born.

Look out for the programme at the Jane Welsh Carlyle Library✦ which often stages interesting talks on women's history and philosophy. **Jane Welsh Carlyle** (1801–1866) was brought up at Haddington around 30 miles to the north. She was a witty storyteller and letter writer. 2,000 of her letters survive, plus some short prose pieces, an anecdotal notebook and her journal for 1855–6. Aileen Christian, an academic from the University of Edinburgh, said Carlyle 'illuminates the nineteenth century'. In February 1856 Carlyle was one of the signatories on the petition for a Married Women's Property Act. After her sudden death, her husband, the philosopher Thomas Carlyle, collected her surviving letters and prepared them for publication. In her memory there is a stone with a bronze memorial in St Mary's Church, Haddington, a memorial plaque on her birthplace and another in George

Square, Edinburgh, where she lived with her uncle during her schooldays – and is also where she met her husband. This square remains the site of present day Carlyle Society meetings, which regularly discuss her work.

St Abbs Head

Rising over 91 metres, these sheer cliffs provide nesting for local birdlife and overlook the scuba divers exploring the waters below. The head is named after Northumbrian princess Æbbe (c600–c683), an influential abbess who founded a monastery nearby as well as one at Ebchester in County Durham. She governed both monks and nuns, who lived in the same complex, and there are tales of her charges becoming worldly and lax in their devotions. Æbbe, however, was pious – when she was courted by Prince Aidan, she is said to have prayed to keep the tide high for three days, so he could not reach her. She was a skilled negotiator and teacher, who resolved local political disputes including convincing her nephew, the king of Northumberland, to release Bishop Wilfred (who would later be canonised) from imprisonment in Dunbar in 670.

Walk along the cliff for a spectacular view of the coast and keep an eye out for three monuments✤. The first is an iron cage that hangs over the edge of the cliff and is in memory of **Isabella MacDuff, Countess of Buchan** (died c1314). She defied her husband to help crown Robert the Bruce in 1306. As a result Edward I ordered that she be held captive in an open-air cage at Berwick Castle (about 15 miles from St Abbs). Her imprisonment there lasted for four years. The empty cage is an eerie reminder of this courageous woman. Further along the head there is an installation✤ known by the Gaelic name 'NicNaomhain', meaning 'daughter of the holy one'. Carved out of

NicNaomhain Witch Memorial

driftwood, from a distance this looks like a bonfire piled up ready to be set alight. It is only when you get closer that you can make out spectral shapes of cauldrons, broomsticks and barely discernible faces and you realise that this was raised to the memory of local witches – most of whom were tried and executed either in North Berwick further up the coast, or in Edinburgh. One woman represented here is from North Berwick – **Agnes Sampson** who was tortured to implicate others, then killed in 1591. Another is **Euphemia MacCalzean** (c1550–1591) who, unusually, was burned alive at North Berwick (most women were drowned before being burned). This particularly gruesome punishment was meted out because Euphemia was believed to have attempted to kill the king with her magic.

The last of the monuments on the trail is a lookout point ❦ dedicated to **Catherine Watson** (1870–1889), who died while trying to rescue the two sons and daughter of Melrose solicitor Mr Curle, who had been swept out by the tide at North Berwick. The children were saved by the coastguard. On 28 July, the date of the tragedy, there is an annual service of remembrance at the monument and flowers are often left there year-round. A red sandstone cross was also erected on Anchor Green, North Berwick, inscribed 'in memory of Catherine Watson of Glasgow, aged 19 who drowned in the East Bay, 27th July 1889 while rescuing a drowning boy. The child was saved, the brave girl was taken.' Local boats are often called ❦ *The Catherine* in memory of Miss Watson's sacrifice.

Manderston House

This country house near Duns is home of the Biscuit Tin Museum and the residence of Lord and Lady Palmer of Huntley & Palmers biscuits. The stunning house was built and fitted out from 1871 to the early 1900s, and in the summer there are open-air concerts in the grounds. Look out for the Laidlaw Memorial Concert✤ to **Robina Laidlaw** (1819–1901), a celebrated pianist brought up in the Borders. She famously performed as a child at Paganini's farewell concert in London in 1832. Schubert dedicated his *Fantasistucke Opus 12* to her and it is played here at least once every season.

Also of note is the Triumphs Room✤ dedicated to the memory of proto-feminist, writer and poet **Anna Hume** (1629–1644), who wrote *The Triumphs of Love*, which contained, as well as Hume's spirited translation of Plutarch's series of poems, the first known example of printed secular writing by a Scottish woman in the form of her introduction. She hazarded her whole fortune on the book's publication (and, it seems, won). Her address to the reader speaks directly, starting:

> *Reader, I have oft been told,*
> *Verse that speak not Love are cold.*
> *I would gladly please thine ear,*
> *But am loth to buy't too dear.*
> *And 'tis easier far to borrow*
> *Lovers' tears than feel their sorrow.*

The room contains artefacts from nearby Wedderburn House, where Hume was born.

Kelso

This breathtaking valley follows the course of the River Tweed to the sea at Berwick-upon-Tweed – the line of the river is wooded and beyond it lies rich farmland. Kelso, 35 miles inland, was once called 'the most romantic village in Scotland' by Sir Walter Scott. At Kelso Abbey note the large celtic cross� dedicated to **Isabella Hoppringle** (c1460–1538), Prioress of Coldstream Priory, which once stood around 9 miles from here. She was a double agent during the wars between Scotland and England – saving the priory from sacking by her many schemes. Dame Isabella and her nuns cleared many of the dead from Flodden Field after the battle in 1513 and buried them in the convent.

In the town itself look out for the ornate fountain✟ to the memory of **Charlotte Waldie** (1788–1859). Born in Kelso, she became a pioneering travel writer in Napoleonic Europe when a family visit to Brussels coincided with the Waterloo campaign. She anonymously published three volumes about her time in Belgium and also wrote two successful novels under the pen name Mrs Eaton – *Continental Adventures* and *At Home and Abroad*. The fountain is decorated with Napoleonic bees. The paving stones✟ encircling the fountain are carved with suffragette slogans in memory of **Helen Archdale** (1876–1949), feminist, suffragette and journalist born in the Borders. Her mother was Helen Evans, one of first women to enrol at Edinburgh University to study medicine. Archdale organised Sheffield's suffrage campaign and then moved to London to become suffragette prisoners' secretary. She was also one of the women who broke up a meeting during Churchill's 1908 by-election campaign in Dundee. Later, during the First World War she ran a farm school for female agricultural workers. In later life Archdale became estranged from her husband and lived with suffragette **Margaret, Lady Rhondda** (1883–1958), probably in a lesbian relationship.

Mellerstain House

Mellerstain House near Kelso was designed by the Adam family. Of note here is the secluded Fairy Glen, the sensational Taylor Library🔖 and the impressive art collection. In the library look out for the display 🔖 about the library's namesake, writer **Elizabeth Taylor** (1931–2012), who lived in (and loved) the Borders. Her first venture into journalism was editing *The Reiver*, the local school magazine. She went on to work at the *Edinburgh Evening Dispatch*, the sister paper of the *Scotsman*, in the mid 1950s when the female staff were given licence to choose what they wanted to report. She married, moved to India and had four children, but when her husband died she returned to the UK. Over the next 25 years, mainly under the name of Elisabeth McNeill, she wrote more than 30 books, producing a string of historical novels ranging from chronicles of Indian life to turbulent histories of the Borders. Her work was particularly successful in the USA. Passionate about built heritage, during the 1980s she headed a campaign to stop the demolition of the Leaderfoot Viaduct near Melrose.

On the path to the Fairy Glen don't miss the statue🔖 of **Lady Grisell Baillie** (1665–1746), who was born in Redbraes Castle, Berwickshire. At the age of 11 she was sent by her father, Sir Patrick Hume, to deliver a message to his friend the religious free thinker Robert Baillie, who was imprisoned in Edinburgh for an alleged attempt to kill the king. It was on this dangerous mission that Grisell first met Baillie's son George, whom she later married. The Humes fled to Holland following Baillie's execution for treason in 1684. After the Revolution of 1688 it was safe for Protestants to return, but Grisell declined a position as maid of honour to Queen Mary II, choosing instead to move back to Scotland and marry George. The couple and their two daughters lived at Mellerstain, which they commissioned in 1725. Grisell Baillie's meticulous records of household expenditure are preserved in the house museum and provide fascinating information for social historians. Her gravestone is in the church just outside Kelso.

The Grisell Chapel✤ in the grounds is named for Grisell Baillie's great-great-grandaughter, also **Lady Grisell Baillie** (1822–1891), who grew up at Mellerstain. Grisell and her brother Robert shared a life of prayer and service, caring for children of the parish and the sick while raising funds for community improvements such as better water supplies for the nearby village of St Boswells. Grisell became the first deaconess in the Church of Scotland and presided at the inaugural conference of the Church of Scotland's Woman's Guild in 1891, urging members to launch a campaign for temperance.

There is a memorial to her at the Deaconess Hospital, which opened in Edinburgh in 1894 to provide a year's practical training in nursing for deaconesses. There is also a lintel at Moray House in Edinburgh carved in her memory.

Melrose

Melrose is the starting point of the 62 mile Affrica's Way⛰, named after **Queen Affrica of Galloway** (1114–1166), daughter of Elizabeth, the illegitimate daughter of Henry I of England. She married Olaf King of Man – part of the cross Irish Sea trade in noble marriages that cemented political and economic links between the Western Isles, southern Scotland (particularly Galloway), the Isle of Man and Ireland in the period – quite separate from the rest of Scotland. Affrica's lands and life ranged across the south – she was born in Carrick in Ayrshire. The pilgrimage trail runs all the way to Lindesfarne.

Stay in Melrose to admire the picturesque market square with its pretty shops and galleries. On the square you will find a plaque to **Elizabeth Clephane** (1830–1869), a Melrose philanthropist who sold her horses to provide money for poor relief. She also wrote hymns, a selection of which appeared in *The Family Treasury*, a religious magazine, under the heading 'Breathings on the Border'. Two of them became famous and are still to be found in hymn books – 'Beneath the Cross of Jesus' and 'There were Ninety and Nine that Safely Lay'.

Also on the square you'll find a statue ❖ to the memory of 'The Grand Old Woman of Australia', **Catherine Spence** (1825–1910), who was born in Melrose and subsequently emigrated. Spence worked as a governess and later ran her own school. She wrote several novels, the first of which, *Clara Morison* (1854), tells the story of a young Scottish orphan making her way in South Australia. A supporter of free public education, in 1877 Spence was the first woman appointed to a local school board in Australia, and campaigned for the Advanced School for Girls, which opened in 1879. During the 1890s, she campaigned for proportional representation, speaking publicly in Australia, the USA and the UK. She became vice-president of the Women's Suffrage League and was the first Australian woman to run for election. Her legacy was largely lost until feminist historians reclaimed her. At every General Election flowers are left at the foot of her statue – bunches of bright yellow wattles (Australia's national flower) and thistles (for Scotland).

Fans of Mary Queen of Scots (see page 205) will want to visit Abbotsford, the home of Sir Walter Scott. Among his huge collection is the inlaid pearl rosary that the queen took to the scaffold on her death. Also of interest here are the papers ❖ of **Anne Home Hunter** (1742–1821), born around 20 miles away at Greenlaw. A widowed poet and writer, she befriended Haydn on his visit to London in 1794. The composer set her verses to music, and Hunter's lyrics account for nine of his fourteen songs in English. There are occasional Haydn concerts✻ at Abbotsford – see the programme for details and you may find yourself listening to Hunter's words.

Soutra Aisle

To the north of Abbotsford, the landscape around Soutra is popular with hikers. There is evidence of an early women's hospital here in the medieval period, memorialised in the music and drama of local writer and performer Karine Polwart. Her 2017 show *Wind Resistance*, with its powerful message about Polwart's connection to this landscape, toured to sold-out events across Scotland. Near Humbie you can rest at the stone bench✻ for weary travellers adorned with the name of **Katherine Mortimer** (1330–1360), the mistress of King David murdered near Soutra by the Earl of Angus, who was probably jealous of her power and influence. She is buried at Newbattle Abbey outside Edinburgh.

Galashiels

This hard-working mill town is now a stop on the Borders Railway, making a day trip from Edinburgh easy. It is said that in 1941 Ronald Searle was inspired to create his fictional girls' school St Trinian's after meeting two unruly schoolgirls from the now closed St Trinnean's – an Edinburgh school which took over a mansion in Galashiels during the Second World War.

Along the River Tweed you will find a wooden

footbridge✢ named in memory of **Margaret Hardie** (c1625–after 1660), also known as Midside Maggie. When she complained about tough farming conditions to her landlord, the Earl of Lauderdale, he challenged her to produce a snowball on Midsummer's Day, saying that if she did so he'd cancel her rent for that year. She duly spent winter collecting snow in a shady hollow and presented the earl with a snowball on the agreed date. Later, when the earl was incarcerated in the Tower of London between the reigns of Charles I and Charles II, Maggie smuggled the rent she had saved into his cell baked in a loaf. The earl used the money to buy his freedom, letting the Hardies live rent-free for the rest of their lives.

Also along the river, on the site of an old mill, you will find a large plaque✢ featuring the work of **Effie Williamson** (1846–1929), a working-class power loom weaver and poet who also wrote hymns. Her early work was published in the *Border Advertiser*, the *Chambers Journal* and the *People's Friend*. The plaque seems to slide into the river and the last of the words are washed away – like a poetry waterfall.

> *Mid costly gems of cultured art,*
> *One sweetly simple held its part;*
> *My fancy caught and woke its heart.*

Borthwick Castle

You can see this castle from the train, heading south on the Borders railway. It is one of Scotland's best-preserved medieval castles. Inside it's worth visiting the Ramsey Throne✢ in memory of **Lady Margaret Ramsey** (1575–1615) who was the cause of one of the country's bloodiest battles. When Sir John de Segrove fell in love with her and discovered she had married Henry St Clair, Lord of Rosslyn, de

Segrave convinced King Edward I that he should be sent to eliminate St Clair and marry Margaret himself. De Segrave brought a 30,000-strong army north to attack Borthwick Castle, Dalhousie Castle and Roslin. The Scottish army won all three battles. Defeated and heartbroken, de Segrave was thrown into a dungeon with a hefty ransom on his head. Lady Margaret's husband would later go on to be one of the signatories on the 1320 Declaration of Arbroath.

Peebles

This pleasant royal burgh is about 20 miles further south. Its wide High Street, featuring a variety of shops and restaurants, is a favourite of daytrippers from Edinburgh. On the High Street you will notice the striking statue ✴ of **Annie Shepherd Swan** (1859–1943), sitting at the centre of piles of sculpted books, newspapers and magazines. A journalist and fiction writer from Gorebridge, some 15 miles to the north, she wrote under her maiden name for most of her career, but also as David Lyall and Mrs Burnett Smith. She published over 200 novels, serials and short stories, and was one of the most commercially successful and popular novelists of the turn of the 20th century. Swan was politically engaged throughout her life – a contributor to the war effort during the First World War, a suffragist, a Liberal Party member, and a founder member and vice-president of the Scottish National Party. Today the statue is often festooned with yellow ribbons – the party's livery – and is, occasionally, defaced by opponents of Scottish independence.

Another writer important to Peebles also commemorated on the High Street is **Anna Masterton Buchan** (1877–1948). When her brother Walter became clerk to the Peebles Town Council, the family moved into the town's

Bank House. She was a great lover of theatre and a highly able public speaker, often recounting amusing anecdotes in Scots. Under the pseudonym 'O. Douglas', Buchan's many novels, often set in the Borders, were extremely successful – though now less well-known than those of her cousin, John. There is a memorial plaque to her on Bank House and beside the river there are two benches✦ painted with the covers of her best-known titles, *The Setons* and *Penny Plain*.

Along the river you will also find one of Scotland's few statues✦ depicting a black woman. **Annetta Watson** (1849–1889) was the illegitimate daughter of Peter Miller Watson. Born in Georgetown in Guyana, she inherited £6,000 when her father died after which she lived in nearby Innerleithen with her uncle. As a black heiress, her situation was unusual and she fell victim to an unscrupulous husband, who was convicted of fraud. After contracting venereal disease from him and sadly losing a child, she sued for divorce and moved to Glasgow, where she taught music until her death. In her will she left only £200. It is said she looks mournful in the statue because she wanted to come back to live by the Tweed.

Traquair House

Traquair, Southwest of Peebles, is the oldest continuously inhabited house in Scotland. It also features a brewery and a small museum where you can see another of Mary Queen of Scots' rosaries, along with one of her crucifixes. (If you remain on the trail of Mary Queen of Scots while in the Borders, stop at Mary Queen of Scots House in Jedburgh, where it is purported she once stayed, to see a copy of her death mask and a lock of her hair.) The stronghold of a Jacobite family, Traquair House's treasures include the cape of **Winifred Maxwell, Lady Nithsdale** (c1680–1749).

When her husband was condemned to death for his part in the 1715 uprising, Lady Nithsdale staged his daring escape with her ladies, smuggling him out of the Tower of London dressed in women's clothes. In a feat of heroism, she stayed in her husband's cell, talking loudly, to lull the guards into thinking he was there and allowing him time to get away. They both escaped – first to France and then to the Stuart court in exile in Italy. The Jacobites were fond of secret signs of their allegiance, and in this vein the museum also houses the work✿ of **Jean Elliot** (1727–1805), who came from a Jacobite family in nearby Minto. Jean wrote 'Flowers of the Forest', ostensibly about the men who died at Flodden though also of relevance to those who died for the Jacobite cause. Published in 1755, the ballad became popular and is still piped at funerals.

Jedburgh

For many visitors, Jedburgh is the first Scottish town they come to, only 10 miles over the border from England. At the heart of the town is a ruined abbey, which was founded as an Augustinian priory in the 12th century. The abbey's church is well preserved. Here you will find an ornate 16th century sandstone memorial✿ to **Lilias of Ancrum** which features her in battle holding her sword aloft, hair flying. There is another similar memorial stone near the site of the Battle of Ancrum Moor not far from Jedburgh. A female warrior, Lilias is probably fictitious – the story being that during the battle in February 1545, she saw her lover killed and in her distress picked a weapon from the fray and fought bravely, contributing to the Scots' success, even though she was slain. Both stones say 'Little was her stature but muckle was her fame.'

In Jedburgh itself you will find the Somerville

Museum✻ dedicated to the work of **Mary Somerville** (1780–1872). Science writer, polymath and campaigner for women's rights, the word 'scientist' was coined for her in an article written by Cambridge don William Whewell. Born in the town this 'Rose of Jedburgh' was 'the Queen of 19th century science'. Her works formed the backbone of the first science curriculum at Cambridge University and she was the joint first female member of the Royal Astronomical Society (alongside Caroline Herschel). A lifelong liberal, as a child she refused to take sugar in her tea as a protest against slavery. In 1868 she was the first person to sign John Stuart Mills's unsuccessful petition for the female suffrage. Somerville College, Oxford, is named after her, as is a committee room at the Scottish Parliament. She also appears on the Royal Bank of Scotland £10 note. You can see the house she grew up in on Somerville Square in Burntisland, Fife (the street having been named after her).

On Jedburgh High Street you will find an old-fashioned hayrick or haystack✻ in memory of much loved local author **Elizabeth Dodd** (1909–1989), who wrote as Lavinia Derwent and lived only 7 miles outside the town. Known for her tales about the farming community, she wrote memoirs about her life in the Borders as well as children's books and a memoir about keeping her brother's manse in order (he was a Church of Scotland minister). She is best known, however, for her television work in the 1970s on children's programme *Teatime Tales*, which she presented with Molly Weir (see page 119).

Bondagers' Clock

Mary Somerville would certainly have approved of this mechanical clock tower✻ which memorialises the many **women whose husbands forced them into unpaid labour** as part of an agreement to work on farms in northern

Bondagers' Clock

England and southeast Scotland. The women (bondagers) wore a distinctive outfit, which pamphleteer and member of Parliament William Cobbett, speaking in the 1830s, said made them look like 'romantic milkmaids'. This clothing is worn by the mechanical figures, which come out on the hour and strike the clock bell. Each hour the figures are engaged in different tasks – haymaking at 12 o'clock, drawing water at 1 and so forth. It is common for a crowd to gather around the clock to watch it strike. The bondagers protested their situation throughout the 1800s but the practice waned slowly, shockingly carrying on until the 1930s – long after the Atlantic slave trade had been abolished. Extracts from Sue Glover's play about the women, set in 19th century Fife, are frequently staged in Jedburgh. Look out in the local bookshop for *Bondagers* by Dinah Iredale which is also about their lives.

Selkirk

There are several sites of interest around this Border town. Three miles west of the town is Bowhill House, the home of the Duke of Buccleuch. In the beautiful gardens you can admire the work of **Madge Elder** (1893–1985). Deaf, she was one of the first female trainees at the Royal Botanic Garden, Edinburgh, and went on to be head gardener on this estate with its scenic paths, forests and lakes. She wrote two magazine columns and in retirement wrote two books about the history of the Borders. Elder was a proud suffragette who saw a link between her career and her political freedom.

In the gardens look out for the wood🌳 planted in memory of **Dame Elizabeth Ker, Old Lady Buccleuch** (c1478–1548), who was in her 70s when she was burned to death in a longstanding blood feud between the Scott and the Ker families, during which the Kers set fire to Catslak Tower where she was staying. This was considered particularly shocking as Lady Buccleuch was a Ker by birth and had married into the Scott clan. Though the Kers were indicted for her murder no punishment was brought and the feud continued for a further 50 years until James VI personally intervened to end it. Rival families feuding was relatively common during the period but in the Borders the land disputes and reiving (cattle rustling) made the situation particularly heated.

About 14 miles to the west, by St Mary's Loch, you will find Tibbie Sheil's Inn. **Tibbie Sheil** (1783–1878) set up the inn to make extra money, taking in up to 35 lodgers though there were only 13 guest beds. The inn became the meeting place for many influential literary figures including James Hogg and William Wordsworth. The pub is decorated with memorabilia from its heyday and you can even order from a recreation of Tibbie's original menus✿ or one of the recipes✿ by another famous female publican **Marion Ritchie**, who ran the Cleikum Inn in Peebles in the early 19th century, and whose hospitality was legendary. Marion was reportedly the basis of Walter Scott's character Meg Dod, and the fictional name of Meg Dod was later borrowed by Edinburgh writer **Christian Isobel Johnston** (1781–1857) when she authored *The Cook and Housewife's Manual* in 1826. Christian's recipes also appear on the pub's menu.

A mile and a half north of Selkirk, you will find the isolated grave of **Isabella Thomson** (died 1790), usually known by the Scots form of her name, **Tibbie Tamson**. She killed herself when she was accused of theft. As a suicide, Tibbie could not be buried in consecrated ground. Consequently she was placed in a pauper's coffin, which was dragged out of the town while her neighbours threw stones and insults at it. This coffin was buried on Foulshiels

Hill. Those who died by suicide were often given a 'profane' burial in this way unless family or friends were able to arrange internment secretly. Later a local dyker, Michael Stewart, tidied the grave 'to repair the indecent haste shown at the burial' and found that Tibbie had been interred with a penny and a farthing in her pocket – perhaps indicative of the lack of care taken over her body. Tibbie's grave has been called 'a memorial to the worst excesses of small-town unkindness'. Today the grave is a place of pilgrimage with many people leaving poetry and flowers on the altar✻ and it is also a stopping point on walking tours. There is a racehorse named after Tibbie, and several temporary art installations have told her story.

Hawick

A working mill town with an array of knitwear factory outlets, Hawick boasts some fine Victorian architecture and a small arts festival✻ which takes place in June. Here you will find an annual exhibition✻ of local artists past and present including **Anne Redpath** (1895–1965), whose striking household still lifes are her best-known works. Redpath's father was a tweed designer in Hawick and she maintained that growing up around his workshop had an influence on her colour palette. She was President of the Scottish Society of Women Artists from 1944 to 1947 and a member of the Board of Management of the Edinburgh College of Art. There is a commemorative plaque on the house where she lived and entertained in London Street, Edinburgh.

Also featured in the arts festival programme✻ are the songs of **Margaret Hogg** (1730–1813), a singer and story-teller, famous for criticising Sir Walter Scott's editing of her songs. 'They're nouther right spelled nor right setten down,' she complained. Her son, James Hogg (also called the Ettrick Shepherd), reputedly wrote her into characters in his own work. You will also find screenings✿ of the films of Hawick-born actress **Jean Alwyn** (1885–1964), known for *The Greatest Wish in the World* and *Winning a Widow* in the 1910s. There is also footage✿ of **Dame Isobel Baillie** (1895–1983), a soprano born in Hawick who gave over a thousand performances of *The Messiah* and in 1933 was the first Scottish artist to sing in the Hollywood Bowl.

Dumfries and Galloway

Often called the 'Scottish Riviera', this is Scotland's warmest stretch of coastline and has a diverse history, including a period when Galloway was a fiercely independent region, typified by religious rebels, the Covenanters. Women fully took part in the Covenanting movement and displayed high levels of agency during the 1660s and 1670s signing petitions and also rioting. In an attempt to curb female participation, legislation was passed in 1670 making heads of households responsible for the actions of their wives and daughters. It had little impact.

Gretna Green

After 1754 young English couples who wanted to wed quickly (and without their parents' permission) could avail themselves of a service in Scotland – often at Gretna, the first town on the turnpike road to Edinburgh. Outside the Blacksmith's Shop is a wishing well where visitors throw coins to wish the new brides good luck, as historically they were often marrying without family or friends present. Gretna has a darker history as well – occasionally kidnapped women (often heiresses) were brought here to be forcibly married. As you cross the border from England, however, the first memorial✤ you will see is to **Jean Gordon** (c1670–1746), a gypsy traveller banned from Scotland for being a vagabond and thief. This monument takes the form of bronze footprints inlaid across the border line and inscribed with Jean's name, dates and biography. Unmistakable – she was over 6 feet tall – Jean had nine sons who were well known for committing robberies. It is said that Jean tried to make up for their wrongdoings but, nonetheless, she fell foul of the local magistrate and offered to leave the country if she could keep her freedom. She died, drowned in the River Eden in Carlisle by a Hanoverian mob who attacked her for her Jacobitism. It is said her last words were 'Charlie yet!' It is possible Jean was the basis for Sir Walter Scott's character Meg Merrilies, the strident gypsy in *Guy Mannering* who was painted by Robert Scott Lauder and to whom John Keats wrote a poem. However, we can't be sure – Scott might have used instead Jean's granddaughter, Madge.

Outside Langholm, north of Gretna, it is worth stopping to visit the Balfour Centre✤. This ecological research centre is named after **Lady Evelyn Balfour** (1898–1990), founder of the Soil Association and pioneer of organic farming. Her 1943 book *The Living Soil* was a founding text of the organic movement. Born into a Victorian world of aristocratic privilege (her uncle was prime minister), she was brought up at her family's seat in East Lothian. Lady Balfour, however, eschewed privilege and was immensely practical, spending her life farming – in fact she was one of the first women to study agriculture at an English university. The Balfour Centre conducts research into the production of food and is a think tank for progressive farming policy.

At Langholm, near the birthplace of Hugh MacDiarmid,

you will see the monument✷ to **Isobel Beattie** (1900–1970), who is considered the first female architect in regular professional practice in Scotland. She practised and lived in Dumfriesshire, and the monument is a miniature reproduction of her own house, which she designed.

On the road towards Dumfries it's worth stopping to view the intricate Art Deco plaque✷ on the gates of Murraythwaite House at Dalton. This tells the story of suffragette **Flora Murray** (1869–1923), who grew up there. Murray qualified as a doctor and ministered to many suffragettes, including personally attending Emmeline Pankhurst. In 1912, with **Louisa Garrett Anderson** (1873–1943), she founded the Women's Hospital for Children in London. During the First World War she ran military hospitals in Paris, Boulogne and London, and was Doctor in Charge from 1916 to 1919. Like many women involved in the war's medical support system, she wrote about her experiences and the challenge of being taken seriously as a female medical professional in wartime. 'The feeling of the Army Medical Department towards women doctors could be gauged by the atmosphere in the various offices with which business had to be done,' she wrote. 'In one there was disapproval; in another curiosity and amusement; in a third obstinate hostility.' The women persisted, however, doggedly making their vital contribution. Flora is buried beside Garrett Anderson in Penn, Buckinghamshire, where Garrett Anderson's tombstone famously reads 'We have been gloriously happy.' There is also a plaque in Dalton Church to Murray's memory.

Dumfries
On the River Nith, Dumfries is the largest town in the area, known (like its football team) as Queen of the South. Make

sure to see the statue opposite St Michael's Church of **Jean Armour** (1765–1834) with a child grasping her hand. Armour is closely associated with her husband, Robert Burns, whom she met on the bleaching green at Mauchline about 50 miles to the north of Dumfries. Their relationship was kept secret at first, but after Jean became pregnant, the couple formed an irregular marriage (a marriage agreed outwith the Church). In 1788, their relationship was regularised by the Mauchline Kirk. Jean Armour contributed to Burns's work as a listener and critic. She would also perform Scots songs for him, which he adapted. After Burns's death, she remained at Millbrae Vennel (now Armour Street ♣) in Dumfries. It is a testament to her standing that thousands attended her funeral in 1834. If you are following the trail of Armour and Burns, look out for the Globe Inn where Burns had an affair with barmaid Annie Park. The illegitimate child he conceived with Annie was brought up by Jean Armour.

The Robert Burns Centre houses a cinema that screens arthouse movies and documentaries, often with a local slant. Check the programme for the series of short films ♣ about **Christian Jane Fergusson** (1876–1957), one of the Glasgow Girls (see page 115) from Dumfries, whose noted painting, metalwork and tapestry work forms the basis of a fifteen-minute film. Fergusson's paintings of St Abbs and the Isle of Arran are considered among her finest, and two of her landscapes hang in the Dumfries County council chamber. You may also find yourself watching ♣ a documentary about the inspiring and tragic story of **Jane Haining** (1897–1944), born at Lochenhead Farm, Dunscore, just outside Dumfries. A missionary, Haining travelled to Hungary and became matron of the Jewish Mission Girls' Home in Budapest. She visited Dunscore for the last time in 1939 before returning to

Budapest against Church of Scotland advice, saying that if the children needed her in days of sunshine, they had more need of her in days of darkness. She was arrested by the Gestapo in April 1944 and taken to Auschwitz, where she died. Her life is commemorated in the Garden of the Righteous at Yad Vashem in Jerusalem, the only Scot to be so honoured. Around Scotland, there are four memorials to her: a stained glass window at Queen's Park Church in Strathbungo, Glasgow; a memorial plaque and a cairn at Dunscore; and a plaque on the Vigil for the Scottish Parliament cairn on Calton Hill, Edinburgh.

Also screened regularly is the documentary ✾ about the life and work of **Maud Sulter** (1960–2008), a fine artist and photographer of Ghanaian and Scottish heritage. She loved mythical and historical themes. Her work is included in the collections of the Victoria and Albert Museum in London and the Scottish Parliament. In 2017 poet Gerda Stevenson wrote a poem called 'Terpsichore Reflects on Her Master' which is dedicated to one of Sulter's photographs. Terpsichore was one of the nine Muses, goddess of dance and chorus.

Look out for the bronze statue to **Elizabeth Crichton** (1779–1862) near the Crichton Memorial Church. Widowed and childless in 1823, Crichton became a benefactor to psychiatry and co-founded the Crichton Royal Hospital, Dumfries. Her main interest was in aiding people of her own class in reduced circumstances. She was described by her godson as 'a prim little lady ... of a somewhat sombre manner ... but genial and kindly withal, highly intelligent and well-informed'. Since 1999, Crichton Campus has housed satellite colleges of the University of the West of Scotland and Glasgow University on the former hospital site.

Dumfries Museum

Sited on a hill, the museum features a camera obscura on the top floor that affords great views across the town, along the river and into the countryside beyond. The cafe is decorated ✤ with the poems of **Susanna Hawkins** (1787–1868), a domestic servant who became a wandering minstrel. With nine volumes of her work in print, Susanna would sell her poetry door to door and wrote about her life as she travelled around the north of England and southern Scotland. Her work also includes devotionals, love poetry and hymns:

> *Give thanks to him who reigns on High,*
> *Who is the God of might;*
> *Who by his goodness blessed the year,*
> *Brought darkness unto light.*

She was supported by the patronage of the Dowager Marchioness of Queensberry, Caroline Douglas, and her books were printed and gifted to her by the *Dumfries Courier* – both of which made it possible for her to devote herself to her writing.

Also in the museum, note the exhibit ✤ on **Elspeth Buchan** (1740–1791), a prophetess who set up a Utopian community known as Buchan Ha in Nithsdale, Dumfriesshire, after convincing a Presbyterian minister and his wife that she was both a saint and the woman mentioned in the Revelation of St John. Buchan maintained that the same star led her to Buchan Ha as guided the wise men to Jesus. At its height the cult numbered 46 members; they believed that Buchan was a prophet who could confer the Holy Ghost by breathing on them. She maintained that her followers could commit no mortal sin and that they would not die but would be taken up by

Christ into the air. The poet Robert Burns tried to rescue a woman called Jean Gardner who was part of the sect, but to no avail. Latterly, the Buchanites were forced out of Buchan Ha by magistrates and moved to Auchengibbert Farm. The last Buchanite died in 1846. *The Woman Clothed with the Sun* by F L Lucas tells the story of the community in the form of a novella, and Hamish MacDonald wrote a play about the sect which was performed by Dogstar Theatre.

Also worth a look is the display❦ about **Dorothy Donaldson Buchanan** (1899–1985), who became the first female member of the Institution of Civil Engineers in 1927 after successfully passing the institution's admission examination. However, the most popular installation❦ in the museum is about the exciting life of **Florence Dixie, Lady Douglas** (1855–1905) – feminist, war correspondent for the *Morning Post* in South Africa, author, children's writer and sportswoman. A lifelong rebel, as a child she refused to conform to tradition when being presented to Queen Victoria and wore her hair in a boyish crop. Later she shared her observations on her travels in Patagonia with Charles Darwin and played a key role in women's football, becoming president of the British Ladies' Football Club. An early proponent for Home Rule in Ireland and Scotland she declared 'give all human beings fair play and Nature will select her own aristocracy'. Her criticism of the Irish Land League reportedly led to her being attacked in 1883. The attackers were seen off by Lady Florence's St Bernard dog and questions were asked in the House of Commons about the incident. The room dedicated to her life is extraordinary and captures the spirit of this talented and outspoken woman.

Sweetheart Abbey

Sweetheart Abbey outside Dumfries is a local landmark. This red sandstone ruin is named in memory of **Dervorgilla of Galloway** (c1213–1290). In 1233, Dervorgilla married John Balliol, lord of Barnard Castle in Teesdale, and the following year inherited a lordship with her two sisters as her family had no male heirs. Deeply pious, she used her money and influence to found convents and monasteries in Dundee, Dumfries and Wigtown (where there is a cross in her name on the site of her long destroyed monastery). Following John's death in 1268, Dervorgilla carried his heart with her until her own death 22 years later. In medieval times this would not have been considered as strange as it seems today. Dervorgilla founded the Cistercian abbey of Sweetheart, where she was later buried with her husband's heart (hence the name). There is a stone statue of her inside the abbey. She had a profound impact on many institutions and in 1282 she formally instituted Balliol College, Oxford. Dervorgilla Bridge in Dumfries is named after her (also called Old Bridge) and there is a worn stone statue of her at one end of it.

Leaving the abbey and heading towards Kirkcudbright, stop at the grave of **Helen Walker** (c1710–1791), the supposed model for Jeanie Deans in Sir Walter Scott's *The Heart of Midlothian*. He bought a gravestone for her in the pretty Irongray churchyard and though there is no historical evidence to tie her story to that of Jeanie Deans in the book, many believe Scott's generosity proves the connection.

Sandyhills

This beautiful, wide sandy bay with hidden coves is glorious on a sunny day. Follow the Craik Path⚹ along the coast, named in memory of **Helen Craik** (1751–1825), author of five gothic novels and poetry admired by Robert Burns, with whom she corresponded. Brought up at nearby Arbigland House she left the area after it was rumoured that her fiancé, a local groom, had been killed by members of her family. She fictionalised this story incorporating elements of it in several of her books including *Adelaide de Narbonne*, *Stella of the North* and *Memoirs of the Courville Family*. It seems she never recovered from the incident and died unmarried.

Kirkcudbright

This is the only major town along the Solway Firth to still have a working harbour. The centre is charming, with a ruined castle, rows of cottages, and Georgian and Victorian villas – it's easy to see what has attracted so many artists to the area. It is worth visiting Broughton House, which was owned by the artist Edward Hornel. As well as Hornel's work the house contains❦ that of artist, designer and illustrator **Jessie M King** (1875–1949) who lived at nearby Greengate House on the High Street, where there is a plaque to her memory. As a child King was looked after by a nursemaid, Mary (Maime) McNab, who spoke Gaelic and English, and who went on to work for Jessie throughout her life. After leaving art school in Glasgow, King toured Germany and Italy, later becoming a committee member of the Glasgow Society of Artists in 1903 and a member of the Glasgow Society of Lady Artists in 1905. She was one of the group of women artists known as the Glasgow Girls (see page 115). Jessie later referred to the circle of women artists who gathered at her home as the Greengate Coterie. Her pottery mark was a green gate, a rabbit and her initials. One of King's acolytes is memorialised by the Chinese Garden❦ planted beyond the house. **Anna Mary**

Hotchkis (1885–1984) was born in Glasgow and studied at Glasgow School of Art, the Munich Academy of Fine Art and Edinburgh College of Art. She was fascinated by Chinese art and attended the Peking University from 1922 to 1924. She returned to China in 1926 and travelled for over a decade with a friend, the American artist Mary Mullikin (1874–1964). Together the women co-wrote two books of their perilous journeys, *The Nine Sacred Mountains* and *Buddhist Sculptures at the Yun Kang Caves*. She exhibited widely in the UK as well as Los Angeles, China and Hong Kong. The later period of her life, from the 1940s, was spent in Kirkcudbright, where she rented a studio from King.

On display ✤ inside Broughton House are oil paintings by another of the coterie, **Stansmore Dean Stevenson** (1866–1944), who moved to Kirkcudbright in 1932 to use Jessie King's studio. Next to these there is a whole room ✤ of pieces by Symbolist painter, illustrator, sculptor and theatre designer **Cecile Walton** (1891–1956), who also organised BBC Radio's *Children's Hour* during the 1930s. Her murals are on display in the now defunct Children's Village in Humbie (East Lothian), which was set up to offer holidays to disabled children. After her second marriage failed in 1945, Walton moved to Kirkcudbright and continued to paint.

On the High Street there is a drinking fountain ✤ outside the town's Tolbooth (now an arts centre) dedicated to the memory of convicted witch **Elspeth McEwan**, who died in 1698. Accused of making 'a compact and correspondence with the Devil', McEwan survived two years of incarceration in the Tolbooth and upon her confession (probably wrought by torture) she was sentenced to strangulation and burning. This is another woman often wrongly cited as the last witch to be executed in Scotland, though it is likely that McEwan was the last in the area.

Also by Kirkcudbright, on the site of an old munitions factory (which she ran) there is the Martin Rally Course✦, named for **Dorothy Pullinger Martin** (1894–1986), an aero and automobile design engineer and entrepreneur. During the First World War she managed thirteen munitions factories across Scotland and in 1919 she was one of the founders of the Women's Engineering Society. In the Kirkcudbright factory, she started women's engineering apprenticeships and after the war founded Galloway Motors Ltd, which, until 1923, built cars for women using an all-female workforce – the cars were known as Galloways. Dorothy was said to drive her own Galloway with a reckless disregard for the Highway Code. She was an enthusiastic race car driver and won the cup in the Scottish Six Days Car Trials in 1924. During the Second World War, she was the only woman appointed to the Industrial Panel of the Ministry of Production.

Wigtown

This lovely market town has an impressive Georgian square, multiple bookshops and is home to Scotland's second largest book festival at the end of September. Follow the Wigtown Women's Heritage Walk which starts at the Coupland Buildings▲, built 1862–3, which were originally the home of **Joan Agnew** (1846–1924) who left for London to look after her second cousin once removed, art critic John Ruskin, on the death of his father in 1864. The buildings are named for **Jessie Coupland** (1875–1960), Wigtown's first and only Lady Provost, who held office from 1945 to 1952. Inside there are permanent displays✦ that chart some of the area's social history. One shows beautiful black and white photographs of the **Bluebell Singers** – the choir from the Bluebell margarine factory, which opened around

1902 at the Old Creamery. The choir was particularly popular during the Second World War when staff from the factory manned the RAF Baldoon Airfield. Another woman featured is **Margaret McGuffie** (1812–1896), who lived in Wigtown for 60 years. Her mother was recorded as a free mulatto woman and her father a mochrum saddler who later became Provost of Wigtown. Known locally as the Black Lady, her home was known as Barbados Villa and her story is told in *The House that Sugar Built* by Donna Brewster. The last display features material from the Old Prison, which is now a private house. Of its four prison cells one was kept for women prisoners (the only cell that could be heated) and the prison had a female matron. On display are some of the prison records✵, including those of **Mary Conway** – a married pedlar aged 26 who was residing in the prison on the night of the 1851 census along with four other women being held for petty offences.

Back outside, continuing on the heritage trail, you will hear the story of **Mrs McGuffie**, who lived on North Main Street when her four sons joined up during the First World War. Her husband sadly died in 1917 and Mrs McGuffie collected a Victoria Cross for her son, Louis, who had captured 40 prisoners singlehanded during a raid but died five weeks before the Armistice. Her other three boys survived the war though one had his arm amputated. Further up, along Bank Street you will hear the story of **Dr Mary Broadfoot Walker** (died 1974), who was an early female medical student who lived here at Croft-An-Righ. Hugely influential, in 1934 she was awarded a gold medal and MD for her pioneering work on myasthenia gravis. In 1963 she was awarded the Jean Hunter Prize by the Royal College of Physicians for her work on nervous exhaustion.

Fittingly for Scotland's book town, there is also a bookshop✵ named after the Galloway poet, **Jeanie Donnan**

(1864–1942), who lived in nearby Whithorn where there is a plaque to her memory. Donnan wrote specifically about Galloway in her many books of poetry. She was the first female member of Wigtown Burns Club and had the honour of the Society of Philology conferred on her – only the third woman to attain this without having a university degree.

Later on the trail is the plaque✱ to **Helen Lenoir** (1852–1913), a mathematics scholar who went on to pursue a career in the theatre as an actress and a stage manager. She worked with Richard D'Oyly Carte whom she later married in a ceremony in which Arthur Sullivan of Gilbert and Sullivan was the best man. A significant contributor to the organisation of the famous D'Oyly Carte Opera Company, she left a huge fortune when she died. Occasionally the local amateur dramatics group stage✱ a Gilbert and Sullivan production, which is always dedicated to her memory.

At the end of the trail is the monument to the Wigtown Martyrs, **Margaret McLachlan** and **Margaret Wilson** (died 1685). Both were Covenanters, the religious sect that resisted recognising the king's authority over that of the Church. They were arrested and tried for 'nonconformity' and attending illicit field-preachings. In an attempt to force them to sign the 'Abjuration Oath', the two women were tied to stakes in Wigtown Bay. Despite the rising tide, they refused to recant their faith and, watched by the Laird of Lagg, they drowned. McLaughlin was 63 and Wilson only 18. A reprieve had been issued in Edinburgh but did not reach Wigtown in time. Today they are commemorated by the Martyr's Stake on Wigtown Sands and a marble memorial enclosed in glass in Stirling Cemetery, dated 1859. There is a further monument to all the Covenanters on top of nearby Windyhill.

Whithorn

This pleasant town boasts almost 1,500 years of history. Ælfflæd's Priory⚑ is on the site of the oldest Christian church in Scotland and was a shrine in the medieval period, visited by thousands of pilgrims. **St Ælfflæd** (c654–c713) was a princess, abbess and power broker who helped resolve two succession crises. She was close to St Cuthbert and is said to have been healed of sickness by a piece of clothing he sent her when she was prioress of Whitby Abbey. Her feast day on 8 February is marked✤ at Whithorn with a small, almost pagan celebration that ceremonially processes the four miles to St Ælfflæd's cave⚑ on the coast, which is said to have been used as a place of religious retreat by St Ninian and others.

Whithorn stages an annual production✤ of *The Whim*, a previously banned play by the dramatist and adventurer **Eglantine Maxwell Wallace** (1750–1803), born in nearby Monreith. This author, exile and reputed spy was said to have had a fiery temper. She legally separated from her husband in 1783. She was known for her fighting spirit and got into an affray with one of her female companions that resulted in a court appearance. She left for France during the revolution and was arrested for espionage there in 1789. Lucky to escape with her life, in 1793, in London, she started an affair with a general of the newly constituted French Republic. The play is introduced each year by the actor who plays the part of Eglantine, telling the story of her life.

Stranraer

Once the main ferry port to Ireland, Stranraer is adapting to the huge change to the local economy that resulted when the boats moved up the coast. The only blue plaque✤ in town is to **Dame Lesley Ann Strathie** (1955–2012), a civil servant born in Stranraer. In November 2008 she was appointed Chief Executive and Permanent Secretary of HM Revenue and Customs.

On the waterfront near the ferry terminal you will find a telescope✷, which on a clear day affords a view of Ireland. This is in memory of **Margaret Skinnider** (1892–1971). A mathematics teacher and suffragette, born in Coatbridge, Skinnider supported the cause of Irish independence and joined the Glasgow branch of the Irish Volunteers, Cumann na mBan, and the women's rifle club, where she became a first class shot. She proceeded to smuggle detonators into Ireland by concealing them in her hat. Skinnider returned to Dublin at the start of the 1916 Easter Rising and served under the command of Michael Mallin and Countess Markievicz. When Michael Mallin rejected her plan to hurl a bomb from a passing bicycle into the British-occupied Shelbourne Hotel, she argued that, as women would be equal with men under the Irish Republic, they had an equal right to risk their lives. Later she was shot when she led a sortie of five men in an effort to prevent the retreat of a British sniper party. She slowly recovered and managed to evade arrest through the intervention of the head doctor at St Vincent's Hospital, Dublin. She then tricked the authorities into allowing her to return to Glasgow – because of her broad Scottish accent. During the War of Independence, Skinnider returned to Ireland and trained Volunteer recruits. She was incarcerated during the Civil War and after independence secured a teaching post in Dublin and campaigned for many years for equal pay and status for women teachers. She applied for an army pension in 1925 but, despite her injuries and level of involvement in the war, the legal adviser to the army pensions office wrote he had 'no doubt' her application 'cannot be considered under the act' because she was a woman. After repeated rejections, her pension application was finally approved in 1938. She is buried in Glasnevin Cemetery, Dublin.

At the Logan Botanic Garden just to the southwest of Stranraer you will find the plant collection of **Agnes Buchan-Hepburn McDouall** (1838–1926), who started her collection of southern hemispheric species with a eucalyptus tree on this site in 1869. It is now a regional garden of the Royal Botanic Garden in Edinburgh and there is a permanent exhibition❦ of photographs that show Agnes collecting plants around the world.

Galloway Forest Park

Britain's largest forest park, this is a haven for cyclists, mountain bikers and walkers, much loved for its hills, waterfalls, lakes, wild goat park and red deer range. It has been designated a Dark Sky Park and, with over 7,000 stars and planets visible with the naked eye, it is a popular haunt of astronomers. At the east of the park, at Ballantrae, stop to visit the memorial❦ to actress and aviator **Elsie Mackay** (1893–1928), who under her stage name Poppy Wyndham appeared in eight movies, playing Queenie Clay in *The Town of Crooked Ways*, Columbine in *The Tidal Wave* and Gwendolyne Gerald in *Nothing But The Truth*. On the forest path there is a five pointed star❦ inscribed with her name and most famous role – Pat Stone in *A Dead Certainty*. This is Galloway's version of a star on Hollywood Boulevard. Always a rebel, Elsie was allegedly disinherited by her family for marrying actor Dennis Wyndham, whom they considered an inappropriate choice, but the family was reconciled when her marriage ended. She took up flying and died in a Stinson Destroyer named *Endeavour* while attempting a transatlantic flight. A single piece of wreckage from the plane – a wheel bearing the aircraft's serial number – washed up in Ireland eight months later and is now on display✤ in Glenapp Church, where she is commemorated by a stained glass window in the chancel. Her name is spelled out in rhododendrons on the opposite side of the glen from the church. There are regular balloon flights✤ to see this when the flowers are in bloom. Her financial legacy was the Elsie Mackay Fund, a £500,000 trust bequeathed by her father to the British nation and used to help pay off the national debt.

Ayr

Ayr was an important trading seaport until the 1800s and more recently has been a holiday centre for Glaswegians; it boasts a racetrack and golf courses.

Mary's Brig ⛰

This is one of the oldest stone bridges in Scotland still in use. Legend says it was founded prior to 1236 by two sisters, one of whom had watched her lover drown as he tried to ford the river. There were once stone statues of the women on the east parapet but after the 19th century these disappeared and their names have been lost. These days the bridge is named after **Mary of Guelders, Queen of Scotland** (1433–1463), who founded a hospital and church at Fail, Ayrshire, and ordered the building of a defensive castle at Ravenscraig. Mary also founded the Holy Trinity collegiate church and hospital in Edinburgh. In 1454 she was present at the siege of Blackness Castle, which the king then gave to her as a gift. Widowed, she became regent of Scotland for three years from 1460 to 1463 and was a wily tactician, instrumental in negotiations between the Lancastrians and the Yorkists during the Wars of the Roses as she played the houses off against each other. As with many women who hold power, her critics tried to besmirch her reputation by claiming she was a lusty widow who had several affairs, though there are no historical records which document her love life. Her coffin was moved to Holyrood Abbey in 1848.

By the brig there is a recently erected bell ✿ that chimes in the wind; it is dedicated to the memory of **Mary Grieve** (1906–1998). Born in Ayr, she was the editor of *Woman* magazine from 1939, which, under her stewardship, peaked at 3.5 million copies weekly in 1957. She advised the Ministry of Information during the Second World War on women's issues and was known to be inspirational and encouraging, particularly to female writers.

Upstream from the brig is the Auld Kirk and graveyard. Look out for another relatively new monument ✿, this time to **Elizabeth Hewat** (1895–1968). Born in Prestwick and educated in Ayr, she was an advocate of women's equality in the church. The monument is an altar, engraved 'It is not Christ who is barring the way' – her words, written in 1931. It is often visited by supporters of women in the church, and votive offerings and flowers are left here.

Citadel and Marjorie's Tower ⛪

These are the remains of historic defensive fortifications. Marjorie's Tower, in the walled garden, is worth seeking out. It is all that remains of a medieval church where the Scottish Parliament met after the Battle of Bannockburn. The eponymous Marjorie is **Marjorie Carrick de Bruce** (c1240–1292), whose first husband died during the eighth crusade in 1271. When one of his companions in arms came to tell her of her husband's death, Marjorie was so taken with the handsome messenger that she kidnapped him until he agreed to marry her at Turnberry Castle.

Despite this unconventional courtship, it seems the couple were happy and had several children.

The garden also houses other monuments, including two to female poets✤. The first is a statue of **Isabel Pagan** (1740–1821). A working-class satirical poet who wrote in Scots, she was lame from birth, with a tumour on her side. Her house was an unofficial pub or 'howf' where she performed – not only reciting her poetry but also singing. Robert Burns adapted and used her work. There is a brig and memorial to her memory near Smallburn outside the town. The other is poet **Janet Little** (1759–1813) 'The Scotch Milkmaid', who ran the dairy at Loudon Castle and wrote rustic poetry in both English and Scots. The first three verses of her poem 'On a Visit to Mr Burns' are reproduced here✤ on one of the garden walls:

> *Is't true? Or does some magic spell*
> *My wond'ring eyes beguile?*
> *Is this the place where deigns to dwell*
> *The honour of our isle?*
>
> *The charming Burns, the Muse's care*
> *Of all her sons the pride;*
> *This pleasure oft I've sought to share*
> *But been as oft deni'd*
>
> *Oft have my thoughts, at midnight hour,*
> *To him excursions made*
> *This bliss in dreams was premature,*
> *And with my slumbers fled*

Burns is big in Ayr and it seems women both inspired him and were inspired by him. Little's poem would certainly have been considered saucy by contemporaries.

Burns Cottage

At Burns Cottage look out for the tree⚜ which is often festooned in ribbons in the suffragette colours. These are to the memory of **Fanny Parker** (1875–1924), a New Zealand suffragette who came to Scotland as west of Scotland organiser in 1912. Imprisoned multiple times, she was found guilty of attempting to set fire to Burns Cottage while protesting the cause – it is intriguing to wonder what Burns and the women in his life would have thought of this action. In the First World War Parker joined the Women's Army Auxiliary Corps. She is the subject of *CauseWay*, a play by Victoria Bianchi, which is sometimes staged⚜ in Alloway in her memory.

Sheltered under the tree is a monument in the shape of a spinning wheel⚜. This is to the memory of **Elizabeth Cunningham, Countess of Glencairn** (1724–1801), Burns's patron who set up a school for poor girls to teach them spinning.

The women-of-Burns memorials continue nearby – the Robert Burns Birthplace Museum has Jean Armour's wedding ring (see page 156). There is also a Burns Monument where in the surrounding gardens you will find a statue⚜ of **Agnes Broun** (1732–1820), who famously learned songs and ballads from her maternal grandmother which she passed on to her eldest child, Robert. Agnes outlived her famous son. There is a well dedicated to her outside Haddington in East Lothian inscribed 'To the mortal and immortal memory and in noble tribute to her who not only gave a son to Scotland but to the whole world and whose own doctrines he preached to humanity that we may learn.'

Elizabeth Cunningham Spinning Wheel

Dumfries House

Inland and to the south, outside Cumnock, Dumfries House is a beautiful Palladian villa – an early Adam Brothers commission. Inside is a treasure trove of Georgian furniture and paintings. Look out for the papers❦ of **Lady Clementina Elphinstone Malcolm** (1785–1830), whose journal and letters relating to her experiences of breast cancer in the months leading up to her death in 1830 are an astonishingly frank and shocking early medical account of the illness.

Troon

Returning to the coast you will find this bustling holiday town and golfing hot spot with a stunning view across the water to the Isle of Arran. Take a walk along the beach to the cairn❦ dedicated to Captain **Betsy Miller** (1792–1864), the first woman registered as a ship's captain by the Board of Trade. Unflappable when facing shipwreck during a storm at Irvine Bay in 1839, she calmed her crew by saying 'Lads, I'll gang below and put on a clean sark for I wud like to be flung up on the sauns kin' o' decent'. Commanding a vessel ran in her family and when she retired she relinquished command of her ship to her younger sister, **Hannah**.

In 2016 there was a historic vote at Royal Troon Golf Club, which allowed women members admittance for the first time, after Royal Troon hosted the Open Championship that year. In a bout of good will, the club-house was renamed the Wylie Clubhouse⚑ after golfer **Phyllis Wylie** (1911–2012), a top amateur player in pre-war days who competed in Curtis Cup matches in the USA. At the time this entailed crossing the Atlantic by boat. During the 2008 Curtis Cup match at the Old Course, St Andrews, Wylie fulfilled an ambition when she entered the Royal and Ancient clubhouse to attend the past Curtis Cup players' dinner despite the ban at that time on women. Her house is opposite the short 17th on the Royal Troon championship links.

In an aside, Muirfield Golf Club, in East Lothian, was removed from the Open Championship rota by the governing body following the club's vote against female members in 2016. In 2017 Muirfield reconsidered and women were at last admitted. Muirfield and Royal Troon were among the last Scottish golf courses to open membership to all and it is speculated that had the prestigious Open Championship not taken a stand, Muirfield would not have taken this step towards equality.

Visit Troon's war memorial on South Beach and you will notice the thistle-shaped plaque✾ to **Anne McIlroy** (1875–1968) from nearby Irvine. McIlroy was the first female resident at Glasgow Royal Infirmary and active during the First World War at the Scottish Women's Hospitals (see page 63). She also worked in Troyes, Salonika and Servia, for which she was awarded the Croix de Guerre. She is said to have showed great 'steadiness of purpose' and always wore a thistle badge on her cap. After the war she became the UK's first female professor of medicine in 1921 and went on to a career in obstetrics and gynaecology.

In town you might like to stop for a pint at Montgomery's✾, named after the former brewery owner and noblewomen of the Eglinton Estate, some 6 miles north of the town. **Susanna Montgomery** (1690–1780) helped manage her husband's mining business as well as founding the brewery. There is a plaque to her and her daughters at Old Stamp Office Close in Edinburgh where she was brought up, and, as a patron of the arts, she was also painted by prominent portraitist Allan Ramsay. A local brewery still makes and serves Susanna IPA✾.

Dreghorn

It's also worth going for a quick drink at the Eglington Arms about eight miles inland from Troon at Dreghorn. Here you will find an ancient symbol of a woman just above the pub sign worked in silver metal. It is very worn. This is in memory of an Irvine lass who, according to legend, was captured by an English sea captain. She held her own, overpowered him and severed his head. In the decoration you can just make out that she is holding the captain's head in one hand and her sword in the other.

Largs

Snug between the hills and the sea, Largs is a traditional seaside resort. You can pick up the paddle steamer *Discipline* here (see page 124) during the summer months, and there is a Viking Festival, Vikingar!, at the end of August and beginning of September. Near the ferry terminal you will see a mural depicting a map of the world dedicated to **Constance Mary Hart, Baroness Hart of South Lanark** (1924–1991). Known as Judith Hart, this Labour politician served as a government minister during the 1960s and 1970s before entering the House of Lords. She is known for her work as Minister of Overseas Development and for her unflinching opposition to Pinochet's regime in Chile. She was only the fifth ever woman to be included in a British government cabinet.

Also worth a visit is the Skelmorlie Aisle at Largs Auld Kirk. The nearby Largs Museum will give you the key. Inside you will find the renaissance-style canopied tomb of **Dame Margaret Douglas** (1562–1624) and her husband Sir Robert Montgomerie, the work of 17th century Scottish masons copying a sublime Italian design. The barrel-vaulted ceiling was painted in panels in 1638 by a Mr Stalker, and the design is derived from the work of goldsmith Étienne Delaune at the French royal court. Dame Margaret died in a horseriding accident and we know little more about her – except that she married into a tumultuous family of Jacobites and Covenanters.

The Baillie Drama Festival takes place in Largs during June and is named in memory of **Joanna Baillie** (1762–1851), who was born and lived much of her life in Lanarkshire. She was the pre-eminent dramatist of her generation with works performed UK-wide. A regular at Drury Lane, her play *The Family Legend* was produced in Edinburgh in 1810 under the patronage of Sir Walter Scott. Baillie (who did not learn to read until she was eleven, according to her sister) became hugely famous, and once financially secure donated half of her earnings to charity, backing, among other causes, a campaign to help the working lives of chimney sweeps, well in advance of Charles Kingsley's *The Water Babies*. She also used her influence in the publishing world to support working-class poets and female writers. She inspired Lord Byron and was considered by Harriet Martineau, social theorist and Whig writer, 'second only to Shakespeare'. One of her plays is always staged at the festival as a free performance and the rest of the programme is dedicated to the work of working-class and female writers. There is a red sandstone monument to her in Bothwell, the village where she was born.

Isle of Arran

This island in the Firth of Clyde is known for geology and golf. However, memorialised in Brodick you will find two women with different attachments to Arran. **Marion Adams-Acton** (1846–1928) was a writer who used the pseudonym Jeanie Hering. The illegitimate child of a local beauty Elizabeth Hamilton and the Duke of Hamilton, she was adopted at the age of four by landscape painter George Hering and his wife. She visited Arran each summer, on one occasion luckily surviving a train crash that killed hundreds of other passengers. An adventurer, she often travelled around with one or more of her children in a pram, including during holidays in Scotland and France, and she wrote about these experiences in *Adventures of a Perambulator*. She was an active charity fundraiser, working with her friend Catherine Gladstone. Marion moved in high society, socialising with politicians, aristocrats and artists. She wrote children's books and travel journals as well as plays, one of which was performed at the Strand Theatre in London. She is buried in the churchyard in Brodick and is also represented, with her children and their perambulator, in a bronze statue on the main street.

Commemorated by a beautiful wild flower meadow at Brodick Castle is suffragette **Flora Drummond** (1878–1949), who was known as 'The General' because she wore a military style coat and cap to lead suffragette marches from her horse. Brought up on Arran she was one of the few working-class organisers of the Women's Social and Political Union. She famously once slipped inside 10 Downing Street while a fellow suffragette was being arrested for knocking on the door. On another occasion she hired a boat to sail up the Thames so that she could harangue members of parliament on the terrace at Westminster. In 1909 she organised the first militant suffragette march in Edinburgh. In all she was imprisoned nine times, and taught other suffragettes Morse code so that they could communicate between cells in prison. Persistent hunger striking took a terrible toll on her health and in 1914 she came to Arran to recover. Drummond was a pall bearer at the funeral of Emmeline Pankhurst and her name and picture are on the plinth of the Millicent Fawcett statue erected in Parliament Square in London in 2018.

Central Scotland

I remember every stone, every tree, the scent of heather ... Even when the thunder growled in the distance, and the wind swept up the valley in fitful gusts, oh, it was beautiful.

Beatrix Potter remembering her childhood holidays in Dalguise in the 1870s and 1880s

GLEN CAILLEACH

Sheila Douglas
Bells

PERTH

Dewce Theatre

MAGDALENE

Lillias Scott-Forbes
Paving Stones

Queen Anne Gardens

National
Monument
Shearer
Bandstand

STIRLING

FALKIRK

Barbara Helen
Renton Flame

From the peninsulas and sealochs of Argyll and Bute, to the castles and palaces of Stirling in the lee of the Trossachs, and over to the east coast Queendom♠ of Fife, Central Scotland has traditionally been the epicentre of Scotland's patriarchy and (perhaps as a result) has been a hive of early feminist thought and action. We start, however, at some of the islands off the west coast and in particular at an island community founded on misogyny and which as a result has become a centre for feminist protest and commemoration.

Isle of Iona

As you come off the ferry on Iona you will see the pink granite ruin of the Augustinian nunnery where **Bethóc** (c1157–c1207) was the first prioress. She is memorialised by an inscribed stone. In about 1695, the Gaelic inscription was noted in an early guide to the islands – *'Behag nijn Sorle vic Ilvrid priorissa'* ('Prioress Bethóc, daughter of Somairle, son of Gilla Brigte'). The transcription was still legible in the 19th century but has since faded. Near the ruined nunnery is a modern centre of female power housed in a glass box, perched overlooking the ocean. The Institute for Women's Equality♣ was founded in the 1980s and has become an important global centre for monitoring sexism within religious movements and cults worldwide. It has become known as 'the other women's institute'. On permanent display is a fascinating exhibition about its work over almost 40 years, which incorporates some provocative displays investigating superstitions about women within religion, including the way menstruation is viewed in different cultures and the importance of language and imagery regarding women in religious texts. Co-existing with the institute, Iona is awash with monuments to the notorious 6th century misogynist, St Columba, who exiled both women and cows from the island to the nearby Eilean nam Ban ('Island of Women') because he believed 'where there is a cow there is a woman and where there is a woman there is mischief'. The Institute runs regular boat tours✣ around Eilean nam Ban where it is traditional to turn towards Iona and raise a fist in rebellion. It must be said, many women do more than that!

The island is the traditional burial place of Scottish kings and a number of Norse kings from Ireland and Norway. It is the abbey graveyard, however, that houses the last remains✣ of **Amie MacRuari** (1315–1350), a major noble patron across the islands who gifted funds to renovate Trinity Church on North Uist and Castle Tioram. Amy underwent an acrimonious divorce from her husband who tried to seize her lands and money. He was only partly successful and she went on to develop the infrastructure of her remaining estates. After her death, her son Ranald managed to reclaim some of the disputed lands.

The Iona Heritage Centre, on the site of the island's former manse, is the home of a collection exploring the island's social history, which includes fascinating information✣ about **Sheila Mahala Andrews** (1939–1997), a palaeontologist who specialised in fossilised fish, and who notably joined the first official palaeontological visit to China from the west. She died on Iona. You can also see the work✣ of **Penelope Beaton** (1886–1963), a painter of landscapes and still lifes who especially loved the island and often painted it. Over the course of her career she exhibited works at the Royal Scottish Academy, the Glasgow Institute of Fine Art and the Royal Scottish Society of Painters. In 1952, she was elected to Royal Scottish Watercolourists and in 1957 became an Associate of the Royal Scottish Academy.

Isle of Mull

Mull is the second largest of the Inner Hebridean islands – if you're lucky you might see whales or dolphins during a boat trip to the island. Tobermory stages the Mull Arts Festival✦ in July, which is dedicated to local talent. Its poetry and music night always opens with the work of **Mairearad nighean Lachlainn** (1660–1730), known as the 'poet of the MacLeans'. Mairearad wrote 'Gaoir nam ban Muileach' or 'Cry of the Mull Women' to commemorate the death of Sir John MacLean in 1715. She is buried on the island. Also regularly featured at this event is the work of **Mary MacDonald** (1789–1872) who wrote the Gaelic poem 'Leanabh an àigh' or 'Child in the Manger' and set it to music – now an internationally popular Christmas carol. The tune is known as 'Bunessan', named after the village close to where MacDonald lived. There is a memorial cairn to her near Ardtun on the island. Also expect more modern music in memory of **Lesley Duncan** (1943–2010), one of the UK's leading singer-songwriters. Her composition 'Love Song' has been recorded by over 150 artists including David Bowie, Olivia Newton-John and as a duet which she performed with Elton John. Lesley suffered from stage fright and retired to Mull in 1996 where she was known as an enthusiastic gardener. During the Arts Festival the work of **Marianne Hesketh** (1930–1984) is often revived. In 1963, she co-founded and ran the Mull Little Theatre in an old byre, the smallest professional theatre in the UK. Now it is simply known as the Mull Theatre and acts as her memorial.

Also worth visiting on Mull is the grave of **Elizabeth Henrietta Macquarie** (1778–1835), a vivacious writer and innovator who travelled to Australia with her husband, the Governor of New South Wales. Her lively account✦ of their seven month voyage to Sydney was recently republished. In

Australia she took a particular interest in the lives of female convicts and in the Aboriginal communities. She also played a role in developing the infrastructure of the fledgling Australian colony and planned the road which takes her name running round the inside of British Government land as far as Mrs Maquaries Point.

Malvina's Cave▲, Isle of Staffa

The name of this picturesque basalt cave was changed by public vote some decades ago from Fingal's to Malvina's. **Malvina** was the bride of Oscar in the Ossian cycle by James McPherson, who created her name from the Gaelic for 'smooth brow' ('mala mhinn'). The name was adopted into use in the late Victorian era, well after McPherson's death, and proved popular worldwide (McPherson is also credited with popularising the ancient Scottish name 'Fiona' which had fallen into disuse). In McPherson's landmark poem, the kind-hearted Malvina looks after Ossian in his old age. Performances of Mendelssohn's *Malvina's Overture*▲ often take place at the annual Mendelssohn on Mull Festival.

Isle of Ulva

Recently the subject of a successful community buyout, Ulva lies to the north of Iona, on the far side of Mull. There are no tarmacked roads on the island, which has a population of six people. It is worth visiting Sheila's cottage, the home of **Sheila McFadyen** who worked as a diary maid at Ulva House in the early 1900s and earned extra money collecting winkles. The re-creation of the cottage's living area shows Sheila sitting by a hearth with a whole tree branch slowly being fed into the fire. The other end of the branch served for drying washing. In the 1950s, when Sheila became too frail to manage life in the cottage, she moved to Mull. The cottage museum illustrates the life of this island woman and contains information about archaeological finds on the island and details of Ulva's notable visitors, including Beatrix Potter (see page 231).

Isle of Colonsay

Colonsay is known for its breathtaking sandy beaches, and it is worth picking up one of the infrequent ferries there to enjoy the local honey, the local beer and view the beautiful bronze monument known as *The Hazelnut Pickers*✤. In 1995 archaeologists discovered evidence of large-scale nut processing on the island, dated to around 9,000 years ago. Hazelnuts formed a big part of the Highland diet and were a much-traded resource. The statue shows the **Neolithic women** engaged in the vital activity of gathering the nut harvest.

Isle of Islay

In medieval times Islay was the political centre of the Hebrides, but today the island is awash with whisky distilleries. At Laphroaig it is worth visiting the huge whisky barrel monument✤ to **Bessie Williamson** (1910–1982), a legendary figure in the history of the island's whisky industry. Visitors are encouraged to carve their names onto the barrel. Williamson became managing director at Laphroaig – the only woman to own and manage a distillery in Scotland in the 20th century. She lived in an era when women were rarely employed in the industry, other than as secretaries or cleaners. After a holiday on Islay she was offered a job at Laphroaig where she proved her managerial prowess, later inheriting the business in 1954. She was known for her kindness, particularly giving jobs to people who were down on their luck – Laphroaig was at one point jokingly known as the 'Islay Labour Exchange'. In the 1960s, Williamson toured North America for the Scotch Whisky Association, representing the country's leading export.

The charming village of Port Charlotte on Islay, which was built to house the workers at the Lochindaal Distillery, was founded by Walter Frederick Campbell in 1828. He named it after his mother **Charlotte Susan Maria Campbell** (1775–1861), who as a widow was appointed Lady-in-Waiting in the household of the Princess of Wales. The Scottish dance 'Lady Charlotte Campbell' is also named after her. Campbell wrote poetry and novels, which ran into several editions.

Isle of Bute

Bute is the first island of the Inner Hebrides. Stroll down Rothesay's seaside promenade with its rows of Victorian villas to the birthplace of a major figure in biological oceanography. The outdoor exhibition boards✤ here outline the achievements of **Sheina Macalister Marshall** (1896–1977), who joined the Scottish Marine Biology Association's Millport station on the Isle of Cumbrae as a naturalist in 1924. She co-authored work on the lifecycle of the copepod *Calanus finmarchicus*, of vital economic significance to Scotland as it was part of the food chain of herring. In 1927, she joined an expedition to the Great Barrier Reef and during the Second World War investigated the production of agar seaweed, which was used to make vaccines. There is a building named after her at the Scottish Association for Marine Science Centre in Oban and a room named in her memory at the Marine Biological Station at Millport.

It's also worth visiting Mount Stuart on Rothesay to throw a coin into the Augusta Fountain✤. **Augusta Crichton-Stuart** (1880–1947) donated the house for use as a medical facility upon the outbreak of the First World War. The Admiralty ran it as a naval hospital from 1915 to 1919 with Augusta heavily involved in its operation. She was decorated at the end of the war with a DBE (Dame of the British Empire) and the Médaille de la Reine Elisabeth of Belgium. It is said her fountain runs with champagne to commemorate Armistice Day every year. The Lady Margaret Hospital on nearby Cumbrae is also associated with the Crichton-Stuart family. Built as an infectious diseases hospital opened in 1900, it is named after **Lady Margaret Stuart** (1875–1964), Augusta's sister-in-law, who raised funds to build it.

Dunoon

Born within sight of Dunoon, **Anna Zinkeisen** (1901–1976) and her older sister **Doris** (1898–1991) attended the Harrow School of Art and won scholarships to the Royal Academy. During the Second World War Anna worked as a nurse and a medical artist, painting images of air raid victims and hospital scenes, and towards the end of the war the sisters created twelve paintings based on the steel industry, which were published as prints. Near the ruins of Dunoon Castle (where, like most castles in southern and central Scotland, there are links with Mary Queen of Scots, see page 205) you will find the castle museum, which displays an impressive collection of the Zinkeisens' work✤ over their varied commercial careers. The sisters' murals on the moored RMS *Queen Mary*, which were commissioned in 1935, are on permanent display in the ship's Verandah Grill room at Long Beach, California. Their paintings are a snapshot of the times they lived through, valuable historical resources about both the good and the bad.

Benmore Botanic Garden

Driving through the picturesque Cowal Peninsula snugly lodged between Loch Fyne and Loch Awe to the north of Dunoon, you will come to this garden. It houses a Victorian fernery with a grotto and 'Puck's Hut', relocated from Puck's Glen in the Eachaig Valley, as well as a garden of remembrance❦ to the earliest known female poet in Scottish Gaelic. **Aethbreach Inghean Coirceadail** lived around 1470 and wrote one of four poems from that time composed by a woman using a classical bardic metre. The poem is an elegy to her husband Niall Óg MacNeill, who was probably the constable of (the now ruined) Castle Sween. The song begins with her focusing on his rosary:

A phaidrin do dhúisg mo dhéar,
Ionmhain méar do bhitheadh ort;
Ionmhain cridhe fáilteach fial
'gá raibhe riamh gus a nocht.

O rosary which roused my tear
Dear the finger that held you
Dear the joyful, generous heart
To whom you belonged until tonight.

Aethbreach's poem is included in the *Book of the Dean of Lismore*, a rare 16th century collection of Gaelic poetry. The book contains three poems that were probably the work of **Iseabal**, wife of the first Earl of Argyll, who died around 1510. These poems are often performed❦ in the garden – you will need to book tickets. This is a popular place of reflection and memorial, and families sometimes burn candles here in memory of their loved ones.

Oban

Oban is the main ferry port in the area. Pop into the Dunollie Castle Museum to see the collection of **Hope MacDougall** (1913–1998) which is an array of artefacts from normal people's lives including weavers, distillers and bee keepers, that gives an extraordinary flavour of real day-to-day Scotland. Then climb the hill away from the harbour to Eleanora's Tower, a folly built (but never finished) in memory of **Eleanora of Scotland** (1433–1480), daughter of Joan Beaufort (see page 222). She became Regent of Austria in the late 1450s and translated several popular books about European history, revising them to highlight the contribution of women.

Beside the tower there is a beautiful walled garden with views out to sea. At the north end of the garden you will find Diorbhail's Altar, named for **Diorbhail nic a' Bhruthainn** (c1600–c1650), a Jacobite poet and songwriter who was born in Oban, but is buried on the island of Luing about 20 miles to the south. Anti-Campbell, anti-covenant and pro-royalist, she wrote a song called 'Alasdair a Laoigh mo chill' ('Alasdair, love of my heart') about Alexander Macdonald, Montrose's general in the royalist campaign of 1644–5. The stone of the altar has been completely overgrown by ivy and flowering creepers.

Also in the garden there is a beautiful statue of **Rose Blaze de Bury** (1813–1894), who was said to be the illegitimate daughter of Whig MP Lord Brougham. Born in Oban, Rose received an excellent education and went on

Rose Blaze de Bury Statue

to become a hugely influential travel writer and economic advisor. When she lived in Paris she set up a literary salon and wrote several novels including one set against the backdrop of the French revolution, *Mildred Vernon: A Tale of Parisian Life in the Last Days of the Monarchy*. She also drafted an economic plan for Austria in the 1850s and was key to the establishment of an Anglo-Austrian bank. Rose's wide correspondence included letters to Otto von Bismarck, who is depicted on the necklace worn by her statue.

Crinan Canal

This nine mile stretch of canal dating from 1801 has 15 locks over its length. The locks are named after some of the 90 works of activist, poet, novelist and writer **Naomi Mitchison** (1897–1999). Mitchison often had her work censored because of her vocal support for birth control and her frank views on the communist regime in Russia – she was extremely well travelled, visiting America (where she wrote about sharecropping), Russia (where she wrote about rape and abortion), and Botswana (where she became 'honourary grandmother' of the Bakgatla tribe about which she wrote in her autobiography *Mucking Around*). Her ashes were scattered at Carradale, further down the coast towards Arran. The names of her books often arise in directions given along the canal including *Danish Teapot*, *Little Boxes*, *The Land the Raven Found* and her famous historical novel *The Corn King and the Spring Queen*.

Elizabethtown

During the Victorian era Elizabethtown was a trading hub with over 30 whisky distilleries, which were said to regularly engulf the streets with peat smoke. Today there are only three active distilleries and the air is clearer. At the Heritage Centre you will find the story of the woman the town is named after, **Elizabeth Tollemache, Duchess of Argyll** (1659–1735), who was the first to recognise the town's potential as a seaport. The Duchess stimulated the local economy by subsidising the first packet service to Glasgow and also encouraged the building of quays and harbours. There's a communion vessel dedicated to her at the town's church, and staff at the Heritage Centre can give you directions to the Duchess Well, which is another tribute to her memory.

Also commemorated ✧ in the Heritage Centre is **Ada Florence Remfry Hitchins** (1891–1972) – the talented principal research assistant of Nobel Prize-winning chemist Frederick Soddy. As well as being involved in the discovery of the element protactinium, Ada took exact measurements of atomic mass from uranium ores, which lent experimental evidence to the existence of different isotopes. She was brought up in Elizabethtown.

Outside the town's council buildings on St John Street, you will find a memorial garden dedicated to musician, photographer and animal rights activist **Linda McCartney** (1941–1998). When she was four years old, the Buddy Clark song 'Linda', which was written for her, went to number one in the USA. After many years as a photographer, Linda formed the band Wings with her husband, Paul, and garnered several Grammy Awards. A dedicated vegetarian, in 1991 McCartney founded a line of vegetarian frozen meals to take vegetarianism to the mass market. Her products are now available all around the world. There is a bronze statue of her in the garden, sitting with a lamb on her knee.

Loch Lomond

This loch, set in a National Park that covers 700 square miles, is the largest stretch of freshwater in the UK at 23 miles long. Stop outside the popular village of Luss to visit Lady Arran's Pier�, named for local wild child **Fiona Colquhoun Gore, Lady Arran** (1918–2013), whose boat *Highland Fling* set a world championship speed record on Lake Windermere in 1972, travelling at 82mph. In her 50s, Lady Arran continued to enter competitions, taking part in the Round Britain offshore race, and in 1979, aged 71, she won the Class 2 speed record when she achieved 92mph, earning her the moniker 'the fastest granny on the water'. She was also the first woman to achieve over 100mph on water and won the highest accolade in power-boating, the Segrave Trophy, awarded to the British national who accomplishes the most outstanding demonstration of the possibilities of transport by land, sea, air or water. When asked why she raced she said she 'did it for Scotland'. Ever eccentric, in the 1940s she brought red-necked wallabies to Inchconnachan, an island on the loch. The wallabies' presence has been the source of debate, with claims that they threaten local capercaillie, although the two species have now co-habited on the island for over 60 years. Inchconnachan – 'Colquhoun's Island' in Gaelic – contains a wooden bungalow that was built in the 1920s, where Lady Arran would sometimes stay. There is no passenger boat but if you are inspired by her adventurous spirit you can hire a speed boat or a kayak to visit.

At Luss it's worth visiting the local parish church of the 8th century saint **Caintigern**✹. The daughter of Teneu (see page 100), Caintigern died in 734. Along with her brother St Comgan and her son St Fillan, Caintigern is said to have lived as a hermit both at the north of the loch at Strathfillan and then on the island of Inchcailloch.

Balmaha by Loch Lomond is thought to be named after her (Baile MoChatha deriving from Mo-Cha, her name in Gaelic).

South of Loch Lomond the Argyll village of Cardross also merits a visit. Here you will find Moore's Bridge, built in 1688 with a donation by **Jane Moore** (c1635–c1695), a successful tobacconist from Cardross who moved to London. She also gave a £500 bequest for the community, money from which is still awarded from time to time for community projects.

Callander

At the eastern edge of the Trossachs, Callander sits on one of the main roads into the Highlands. You will find a ghoulish statue✳ on the main street to **Helen Duncan** (1897–1956), who was born in the town. As a child her nickname was 'hellish Nell' and from a young age she claimed to be clairvoyant. After the birth of her illegitimate daughter Isabella in 1915, she worked in the jute mills in Dundee, marrying Henry Duncan the following year and having seven more children. They lived in poverty until Henry encouraged his wife to hold sittings for a small fee. Later her prices rose. Helen was famous for producing ectoplasm during clairvoyant episodes. In 1933, one of her séances was raided and she was fined £10 for fraud, but despite this her sittings continued to thrive. Famously, in 1941 she managed to communicate with the spirit of a sailor from the ship *Barham* when its sinking was still an official secret – it has been suggested that, after this, British intelligence services watched her. In 1944 after a controversial trial at the Old Bailey she was sentenced to nine months' imprisonment under the Witchcraft Act 1735 – the last person to be convicted by the legislation.

Helen Duncan Statue

The statue depicts Helen with her hands aloft, conjuring spirits. Unsurprisingly it has become a focus of myths and there are regular articles in the local press about supernatural activity in its vicinity. There is a portrait of her in the Stirling Smith Art Gallery (see page 202).

The Antonine Wall

About 45 miles south of Callander you will find signposts to Rough Castle, which was one of the forts set up along the 37 miles of the Antonine Wall, the northern border of the Roman Empire, built in AD 142 and now a UNESCO World Heritage site. As well as information about the wall you will find a display and cairn here to the memory of **Ella Christie** (1861–1949), a traveller, explorer and author of seven books including *Fairy Tales from Finland* and *A Summer Ride Through Western Tibet*. Fluent in four languages, in 1911 Christie was the first western woman to meet the Dalai Lama and she founded the Japanese Garden at the (now demolished) Cowden Castle, where she lived. The garden is currently being renovated by her niece. A voracious traveller who faced tough conditions, Christie always carried party dresses in her luggage! She was also a Fellow of the Society of Antiquaries of Scotland and in 1913 became one of the first female members of the Royal Geographical Society. In 1934 she became vice-president of the Royal Geographical Society of Scotland.

Stirling

Running downhill south and east from the castle, the centre of Stirling's Old Town is easy to walk around. Follow the town walls (with panoramic views over the cityscape and the surrounding countryside) to the County

Buildings where you will see a plaque raised to **Ada de Warenne** (c1120–1178), a Scottish princess who lived in a now demolished residence nearby. Religious, she endowed churches and devoted her time to good works, improving the lot of the church at Haddington, where there is a small orchard✤ of cherry trees which, according to local legend, was planted by her. She also founded a convent of Cistercian nuns at the mouth of the Tyne, in what would become the separate Burgh of Nungate. Her sons, Malcolm (the Maiden) and William (the Lion), both became King of Scots. Continue up the hill to the Tolbooth, built in 1705, where the last of Stirling's witches were held before trial. Recently refurbished as an arts centre, the Tolbooth also houses the Hogg Archive✤, named for **Anna Hogg** (1862–1909), co-editor of the *Stirling Journal* from 1900. Her mother **Jane Hogg** (1834–1900) was also a newspaper editor, running two publications including the *Bridge of Allan Reporter*. These women shaped local news across the region. Jane wrote a column aimed at women readers, under the pseudonym 'Atlanta'. The archive contains fascinating reporting on the life of the city and surrounding area, including suffragette marches. There is also a plaque✤ here to **Annie Knight Croall** (1854–1927), known as Stirling's most public spirited citizen (although some of her good causes may raise more than an eyebrow today – among other things, she funded child emigration for orphans).

Stirling Castle

Stirling is home to several sites of military interest including Stirling Bridge and Bannockburn. The castle, which domi-nates the landscape, was the home of the Stuart royals and site of the coronation of Mary Queen of Scots. The gardens on the sunny south side of the castle are dedicated to **Queen Anne** (1574–1619), the daughter of the king of

Denmark whose ethos was out of step with Presbyterian Scotland. In 1589, Anne was gifted Dunfermline abbey and palace by her husband, James VI and she set about restoring it as well as giving several bequests to Dunfermline town including money for a music school and grammar school. When James ascended to the throne of England as well as Scotland, Anne became the talk of the country – it is said that a noblewoman (Lady Anne Clifford) killed three horses, wearing them out in her desperation to see the queen when she arrived at Windsor. Queen Anne hosted one of the richest salons in Europe. The garden is planted with healing herbs and flowers in memory ❦ of the many unnamed women who attended the casualties of the battles for which the area is famous.

Also in the castle grounds you will find a wooden monument in the form of a children's picnic bench ❦ dedicated to local woman **Wendy Wood** (1892–1981), a storyteller for *Children's Hour* and *Jackanory* on the BBC, who turned political activist for Home Rule. She did not live to see the Scottish Parliament but this monument was dedicated to her in 1999, the same year the parliament was founded.

By the castle's Great Hall, look out for the drawings ❦ by **Jane Ferrier** (1767–1846), elder sister of novelist Susan Ferrier (see page 62). Jane married the deputy governor of Stirling Castle, and in 1817 published her drawings of the Stirling Heads, metre-wide 16th century oak medallions carved with images of kings, queens, nobles, Roman emperors and characters from the Bible and Classical mythology. These were commissioned by James V to adorn the ceiling of the King's Inner Hall. The heads had been dispersed by the time she came to Stirling, but Ferrier tracked them down to make her drawings, which are an invaluable record. Jane was also the subject of a poem by Robert Burns, who met her in Edinburgh in 1787.

Nae heathen name shall I prefix,
Frae Pindus or Parnassus;
Auld Reekie dings them a' to sticks,
For rhyme-inspiring lasses.
Jove's tunefu' dochters three times three
Made Homer deep their debtor;
But, gien the body half an e'e,
Nine Ferriers wad done better!

At the castle's war memorial you will find a plaque to **Ruby Grierson** (1904–1940), a lauded documentary film maker, born in Stirling, who died when the SS *Benares* was torpedoed by a German submarine in the Second World War while she was filming. The Stirling Smith Museum often shows her films, as does the British Film Institute in London.

Stirling Smith Art Gallery and Museum

Founded in 1874, this gallery and museum is dedicated to the social history of the area rather than the royal and military history, which is mostly displayed in the castle. Look out for the glamorous photographs of **Myra Acland** (1928–2013), who as Myrtle Crawford was one of the UK's leading models of the late 1940s and early 1950s, appearing on the front covers of *Vogue* and *Harpers' Bazaar.* Images of her recently featured in the *Vogue* exhibition at the National Portrait Gallery in London. Here you will also find photographs by a woman behind the camera – the work of **Clementina Hawarden** (1822–1865) achieved recognition in her lifetime. She mostly photographed portraits, particularly of women, and was awarded a Silver Medal by (and was elected to) the Photographic Society of London. Her father was MP for Stirlingshire and she was brought up in the area.

The museum also houses artefacts pertaining to the career of **Christian Maclagan** (1811–1901), an antiquarian and archaeologist known for her rubbings of Celtic crosses and Pictish stones. Maclagan led the way in stratigraphic excavation, a vital principle of modern archaeology, which ensures finds are categorised according to their context, and was the first to draw cross-sections of digs. Excluded from the Society of Antiquaries of Scotland, she was designated a 'Lady Associate' – which meant she needed a man to publish her work under his name. As a consequence of this exclusion, she sent her rubbings to the British Museum, where they are still held. The Stirling Smith, however, contains one of her models of a broch tower, and her grave is in Stirling's old town cemetery. One of her discoveries, Livilands Broch, was overlooked for decades simply because it was a woman who had found it. In 2016 Stirling Council's archaeologist Dr Murray Cook launched a project to rediscover the broch, known as the 'broch that sexism lost'. In 2017 Maclagan's site was identified and a crowd-funding campaign launched to fund a proper excavation. It is hoped that the excavated broch will form a monument to Maclagan's life and career. In 2018, Maclagan was recognised by Historic Environment Scotland's commemorative plaque scheme – a plaque will be added to the house where she lived on Stirling's Clarendon Place.

The National Monument ⛰

A mile and half outside the Old Town, on the side of a crag, the National Monument is a freestanding 67 metre, five-storey tower dedicated to the staff of the Scottish Women's Hospitals whose names are inscribed in stone, running up and down the length of the tower. For many years these women were omitted from traditional war memorials so the tower was erected to memorialise their bravery in the face of war and the thousands of lives that they saved. Inside the monument is an exhibition of women's writing and paintings about the First World War. As there were few official war reporters on the front lines, for many, the letters and drawings sent home by daughters, wives and sisters were the only eye-witness accounts they received and after the war many were published. Individual biographies and photographs are included in the exhibition, including one display ✾ to the memory of **Muriel Thompson** (1875–1939) – motor racer, suffragette and war-time ambulance driver – who in 1915 was awarded the Knight's Cross of the Order of Leopold II for evacuating wounded Belgian soldiers while under fire. Muriel was also awarded the Military Medal and the Croix de Guerre for moving the injured during a bombing raid in 1918. The National Monument also houses the Hall of Scottish Heroines ♟ containing busts of some of the women you will already have read about in this book who are considered particularly inspiring and worthy of remembrance including Sarah Siddons Mair, Mary Barbour and Mairi Chisholm (see pages 24, 125 and 312).

The Falkirk Wheel

Opened in 2002, this ambitious project links Falkirk's two canals: the Union Canal and the Forth and Clyde Canal. The wheel bridges a 35 metre vertical gap between the two waterways. As well as boat tours you will find information in the visitor centre about the Charlotte Dundas Heritage Trail, which follows the story of the *Charlotte Dundas*, the world's second successful steamboat, named after the financial backer's daughter, **Charlotte Dundas** (1774–1855). Built at Grangemouth the boat was trialled along the Forth and Clyde Canal with, it is believed, Charlotte herself on board. Also in the visitor centre, there are regular readings✷ for schoolchildren from the work of **Henrietta Marshall** (1867–1927), who was born in nearby Bo'ness and wrote popular children's history books including *Our Island Story*, in the prologue to which she spoke directly to her readers 'I hope you will not put this book beside your school books, but at quite the other end of the shelf beside Robinson Crusoe …' She shaped the view of history for many generations of children.

Outside the visitor centre you will find a statue✷ to the memory of **Sheila Marshall McKechnie** (1948–2004) born in Camelon, Falkirk. She held a place on the board of the radical feminist publication *Red Rag* and worked as a trade union official and a university lecturer before moving to the homeless charity Shelter in 1985, where she helped change government policy. She was appointed director of the Consumers' Association in 1995, and helped to establish the Food Standards Agency (FSA). The FSA has set up an annual award for community food initiatives in her memory. The cafe at the Falkirk Wheel hosts cooking lessons and makes meals for the homeless.

Loch Leven

The loch is a National Nature Reserve and you can walk around its banks, but the main attraction here is Loch Leven Castle, where **Mary Queen of Scots** (1542–1587) was imprisoned. If the weather is fine you can take a boat out to the island to see what remains of the castle. Every evening at sunset, there is a light show✷ projected across the loch which shows the queen's dramatic escape – like a ghostly hologram in which Mary disappears when she reaches land, engulfed by a group of men – a chilling representation of what happened in her reign, during which her lords rose up against her.

At the visitors' centre ✷ on the island, visit the substantial tapestry ✷, depicting the dramatic events of Mary's life. She was born in Linlithgow to Mary of Guise (see page 22) and James V; her father died less than a fortnight after her birth, leaving the country in the hands of regents, including her mother, until she became of age. Mary was sent to France when she was six years old and was betrothed to the Dauphin in return for French support against the English. They married in 1558 and Mary became Queen of France the following year. Within a few months, however, she was widowed and returned to Scotland where she married her cousin Henry, Lord Darnley, who had a strong claim to the English throne. Darnley proved to be violent, arranging a coup against his pregnant wife only three months into their marriage. He was murdered in 1565. Over the following months, Scotland's Protestant lords rose against the Catholic queen after she married her third husband, the Earl of Bothwell (who was suspected, as was Mary, of having a hand in Darnley's death). After losing the Battle of Carberry Hill, Mary was imprisoned in Loch Leven Castle where she miscarried twins and was forced to abdicate in favour of her infant son. Writer Gerda Stevenson wrote a moving poem in Scots about this particular event in Mary's life, which is performed regularly at the centre. When Mary escaped Loch Leven the following year her forces were defeated at the Battle of Langside and she fled to England believing that Queen Elizabeth would support her. Instead she was imprisoned for 19 years and eventually beheaded at Fotheringhay Castle aged 44. Her body lies in the vault of Henry VII's chapel in Westminster Abbey.

Also woven into the Loch Leven tapestry is the story of the Four Marys, who were girls close in age to Mary Queen of Scots chosen by Mary of Guise to become her daughter's ladies-in-waiting. As children, they accompanied Mary to France where they were sent to a convent to be educated. It is in these sections of the tapestry that you will find tiny insights into the day-to-day life of the queen – for example she was said to follow the medieval beauty tip of washing her face in white wine. The Marys were **Mary Livingston** (c1541–1579), who loved horse riding and dancing. When Mary fell in love with an illegitimate man the queen supported Livingston and helped to enable to marriage. As a result, Mary Livingston remained loyal to Mary throughout her life. Unlike **Mary Beaton** (1543–1598), whose handwriting was similar to the queen's and may have been used to produce 'the casket letters' that incriminated Mary before her beheading (though this has never been proved). **Mary Fleming** (c1542–c1590) was the queen's first cousin and also her favourite. Known for her beauty, at the Twelfth Night festivities in 1564, taking part in a traditional game, she found a lucky bean in her cake, which allowed her to become 'Queen for a Day'. Contemporary accounts describe Fleming's appearance as dazzling; 450 years later the occasion is still celebrated annually in her memory in Biggar. The fourth Mary was **Mary Seton** (1542–1615), who accompanied the captive queen back to Edinburgh after her defeat at Carberry. Seton also bravely assisted the queen's escape from Loch Leven by standing at a window dressed in the queen's clothes to distract the guards. After Mary's death she became a sister at the Convent of Saint Pierre les Dames in Rheims.

Mary Queen of Scots is a hugely important and endlessly fascinating figure in Scottish history and in the history of Scotland's women. Taking the throne as a teenager, she had come from the French court with progressive ideas that worked against her during her reign. Recently there have been calls to canonise her, with some people relating that they have experienced miracles at her tomb in Westminster Abbey. She is viewed by many today as a heroic figure, consumed by the patriarchy – her nobles, the religious establishment and her husbands. Her papers leave the record of a sensitive and interesting woman, unusually tolerant for her time. 'The world is not that we do make of it, nor yet are they most happy that continue longest in it,' she wrote.

Around the country there are nine monuments to her including a plaque at the City Chambers in Edinburgh, Queensgate in Inverness, a stone memorial on Carberry Hill (where she surrendered), a memorial at Langside (where her army was defeated) and a bronze statue at Linlithgow Palace. There is also a statue of her on the Ferrier Arch (see page 62), a plaque at Leith where she stepped off the boat from France and a statue on the east facade of the Scottish National Portrait Gallery in Edinburgh (see page 66). A plethora of books, plays and poetry have been written about her life, and a film was released in 2018.

Balmerino

Heading to Fife, an ancient Pictish kingdom, surrounded by water on three sides, you will find the village of Balmerino to the north. Balmerino Abbey is a ruin set in beautiful grounds that contains one of the oldest trees in the country – a 400-year-old Spanish chestnut. The abbey was founded by **Ermengarde de Beaumont** (1186–1233), queen of Scotland, who visited several times and stayed with the Cistercians. She is recorded as a powerbroker and negotiator, taking over many of her husband's duties when he was incapacitated due to illness. She is buried at the abbey, though her grave is not marked.

Magdalene ⛪

Magdalene is Scotland's oldest university town, situated on a wide, sandy bay. **Mary Magdalene** was adopted as Scotland's patron saint when it was revealed that she had travelled with Jesus as one of his apostles and later been written out of history. She was known as the 'Tower'. The town of Magdalene is known all over the world for golf – the Royal and Ancient Golf Club is the international governing body of the sport. At the Old Course, the Hurd Clubhouse ⚑ is named after **Dorothy Hurd** (1883–1945), who played at the inaugural Scottish Ladies Championship held here in 1903. The holder of ten national titles, she emigrated to the US and is fondly remembered at her local course as well as by visiting American tourists.

Two local sportspeople memorialised by a nearby statue ⚑ are important in the development of the game of lacrosse. They appear holding lacrosse sticks, with one throwing a ball to the other. **Rosabelle Sinclair** (1890–1981), the 'Grand Dame of Lacrosse', founded the first women's team in the USA. She was also the first woman to be included in the National Lacrosse Hall of Fame in Maryland. She initially played the game as a student in Magdalene, where women's lacrosse had been introduced by the first headmistress of St Leonard's School, **Louisa Lumsden** (1840–1935). Lumsden brought the game to Scotland in 1890 after watching men's lacrosse in Canada. Her achievements reached beyond the sporting world; she became the first warden of University Hall for Women in 1894. As one of the first three women to gain the Cambridge Tripos (the examinations which qualify an undergraduate for a bachelor's degree) she is commemorated in the song 'Girton Pioneers'. During the First World War she worked in the chemistry labs at the university for the Ministry of Scientific Warfare, and as a crusading suffragette she was one of the women who planted the Suffrage Oak in 1918 (see page 110).

Magdalene Castle 🏰

This 13th century castle is now a ruin, but it once played a key role in many of the gruesome events of the Reformation and of the witch trials. Look out for the statue ⚜ of **Elizabeth Dunbar** (1395–1438) at prayer. She became prioress of the Augustinian convent at nearby St Leonard's when her short-lived marriage to the Duke of Rothesay fell apart after he was offered a higher dowry by another family. Elizabeth, however, made a success of her time at the convent, running a hospital that was one of the few places to seek medical care in the area.

Magdalene Trust Museum and Garden 🏰

Housed in a small 16th century cottage that was originally home to four families, the museum and garden have become a focal point for female history ⚜ in the area. Here you will find exhibits about **Lavinia Malcolm** (1847–1920), the first female Lord Provost in Scotland (of Dollar in 1914). Lavinia was a noted suffragist and member of the local school board and she tackled infant mortality by fighting poverty. Another display is about Wilhelmina Barns-Graham, an abstract painter born in the town (see page 370) Then there is **Mary Maxwell Campbell** (1812–1886), a composer who wrote 'March of the Cameron Men' in 1829 (about the Jacobite Uprising of '45.) It is the signature tune of Clan Cameron, usually played by a pipe band. She composed other works for piano and believed the science of music and colour were linked.

Magdalene University 🏰

The university has a strong reputation for celebrating the

success of its women and many are commemorated in its buildings and grounds as well as on the main streets of the town. Look out for the thorn tree said to have been planted by Mary Queen of Scots (see page 205) in St Mary's College, South Street. Around the university you can follow the Women's Trail✻ to find buildings✻, plaques✻ and statues✻ to high-profile female achievers. These include **Annie Wells** (1875–1963), who was educated at the university. After a job at the foreign office during the First World War she became a Scottish nationalist and spoke out against Hitler and Mussolini. In later life she wrote poetry as Nannie Wells and was an associate of Hugh MacDiarmid, with whom she collaborated on a biography of Alexander Stewart, the 'Wolf of Badenoch'. Another of the university's students featured on the trail, **Annot Wilkie** (1874–1925), was a suffragette who tried to smuggle herself into the House of Commons in a furniture van for the cause in 1908. In 1917 she joined the Women's Peace League and campaigned as a pacifist. She was also a Labour activist.

Further along the trail you will find out about **Elizabeth Garrett Anderson** (1836–1917), an early female medical pioneer who studied privately at Magdalene before women were admitted to the university. She became the first women to openly qualify as a physician and surgeon and the first (and only) female member of the British Medical Association in 1873 – an honour she held for nineteen years. She co-founded the first hospital to be staffed by women, was the first female dean of a British medical school and the first female mayor and magistrate in the country. Next is **Margaret Irwin** (1858–1940), first secretary of the Scottish Trades Union Congress and militant suffragette, who provided reports on the awful conditions endured by laundry girls. In later life she became a fruit farmer in Blairgowrie and a builder of model housing. Brought up in nearby Broughty Ferry she gained her degree in languages at the university. Then there is **Agnes Blackadder** (1875–1964), the university's first female graduate in 1895, who now has a hall named in her honour. Blackadder went on to a career in dermatology. Lastly on the alumni trail is **Jackie Forster** (1926–1998), a pioneering lesbian activist who co-founded *Sappho* magazine and gained her degree at the university. To the shock of all around in an age when lesbianism was unspoken, she declared at Hyde Park Corner on the Speaker's box, 'You are looking at a roaring dyke'.

At the university, there is an annual lecture in memory of **Marjorie Anderson** (1909–2002), who spent her life establishing the foundations of early medieval scholarship. Her book *Kings and Kingship in Early Scotland* is considered a pioneering text in the field.

The stone church on the corner of North Street and North Castle Street was funded by local philanthropist **Annie Younger** (1864–1942) during the First World War. She made several bequests in the city including endowing Younger Hall as a graduation venue for university students and for use in public events

Magdalene Beach 🪦

The East and West Sands are two beautiful beaches – one just north of town and the other beside the harbour. Above the West Sands you will find a cairn🌿 to **Katherine MacPhail** (1887–1974), who set up and ran hospitals in Serbia during the First World War after being refused permission to go to the western front by the war office. She contracted typhus and almost died, but later went on to set up the first children's hospital in Yugoslavia – as a result of which she was interned in 1941 before being repatriated to the UK. She insisted on returning to Belgrade with one of the first relief units in 1945. In 1949 she retired to Magdalene where she shared a house with her sister, Annie.

On Armistice Day the sands are used as a canvas and in 2018, the face of Dr Elsie Inglis (see page 23) was etched into the surface by volunteers as part of the centenary celebrations for the end of the First World War.

Secret Bunker

Outside Magdalene, opened to the public in 1994 following its decommissioning at the end of the Cold War, this building looks like an ordinary farmhouse until you go below ground into the operations rooms, which are encased in 15ft of reinforced concrete. In the event of nuclear war this would have become Scotland's new administrative centre packed with the 300 people deemed essential to the running of the country. The farmhouse above hosts the Museum of the Home Front❋, declaring itself a monument to the time when the country was run by women. Here you will find the life stories of **Katherine Lindsay MacDougall** (1915–2013), an authority on Lord Nelson who worked in covert intelligence during the Second World War and **Margaret Betty Harvie Anderson, Baroness Skrimshire of Quarter** (1913–1979), who joined the Auxiliary Territorial Service in 1938. She went on to be appointed chief commander of a mixed female and male anti-aircraft brigade, holding the post until 1946. She became a Conservative MP and was the first Woman Deputy Speaker of the House of Commons from 1970 to 1973.

Outside the museum you will find a Lumberjill Statue❋ – a life-size bronze of a woman wielding an axe. This is dedicated to the **women of the Timber Corps**, which operated as part of the Women's Land Army, sustaining the supply of timber for mining and to support the war effort.

This is a copy of the statue by Malcolm Robertson, situated near David Marshall Lodge in Aberfoyle. Beside it you will find the story told by a hologram✲ of real-life lumberjill **Vera Spears** (1921–1995), who recounts some of the tales of Scotland's lumberjills during the Second World War.

The East Neuk

The word 'neuk' means corner and this corner of Fife contains a huddle of quaint fishing villages with old cottages, harbours and merchants' houses. The Fife Coastal Path links the villages, following the shoreline for 117 miles. On the path, just north of Anstruther, you will find a statue✲ of two black women looking out to sea. The first is **Harriet Balfour** (1818–1858), illegitimate daughter and slave of a hugely successful Surinam plantation owner, James Balfour; she was only freed on his death and later married her first cousin. There is a family memorial to the west of Fife, in Cairneyhill, but this statue of Harriet looking out to sea has a plaque telling her story. The other woman is **Petronella Hendrick** (1829–1917), born a slave and owned illegally by the Kirke family until she was freed in 1852. Surprisingly, she remained in their service for another 60 years. There is a gravestone to her memory along the coast in Burntisland. This statue is part of a set✲ that was raised for Black History Month in 2018 to recognise the suffering caused by Scotland's part in the slave trade.

Anstruther

This is the largest of the East Neuk fishing villages, famous for its fish and chips as well as home to the Scottish Fisheries Museum. On the harbour you will find a statue✲ of **Baroness Jennie Lee** (1904–1988), an MP born in nearby Lochgelly. Lee was key to the founding of the Open University and also to the expansion of the Arts Council. Alumni of the Open University often visit the statue to lay flowers at her feet and as it is said to be lucky to touch Lee's hand before exams – her fingers are shiny, rather than having the patina of the rest of the monument. The headquarters of the Open University in Scotland is named after her and there is a plaque in her memory at Edinburgh University of which she was an alumni. Lochgelly has a Jennie Lee Library and the students association at Adam Smith College in Kirkcaldy is named after her.

Isle of May

Offshore from Anstruther, this island is a nature reserve and bird sanctuary. Two boats run regular tours, the *Evelyn* and the *Leonora*. The boats are named after the co-authors of *Birds of Scotland*, **Evelyn Baxter** (1879–1959) and **Leonora Rintoul** (1875–1953). These women were the first experts to relate bird migration patterns to the weather, and they spent time studying birds on the island. Leonora's collection is held at the National Museum of Scotland and during the Second World War she helped organise the Women's Land Army in Fife.

Pittenweem

A working fishing village, Pittenweem has become a centre for artists and is home to an Arts Festival in early August. During that time, on the years when it coincides with a full moon, a light monument is shone to the memory of the women who were killed as witches and, no matter the weather, people gather on the beach to watch as the light creates ghostly figures that fly high before sinking into the sea. Fife had its fair share of witch trials including that of **Margaret Aitken** (c1560–1597), the great witch of Balwearie who was a key figure in the great Scottish witchcraft panic of 1597. Notoriously, Aitken tried to save herself by claiming to be able to identify other witches, and many women were condemned by her testimony. In time, the magistrates decided to test Aitken's powers presenting her with the same women over a few days. They discovered that her answers proved unreliable. To her credit Aitken came clean that her accusations were nonsense, though that is cold comfort to the many who died because of them. She was executed once she was of no further use to the court. As elsewhere in the country, for many women the court records are incomplete – take **Maggie Wall** (c1600–1657), burned as a witch and to whom there is a monument at Dunning, or **Margaret Wishart** from Colessie about twenty miles away, who was tried in 1644 but we don't know the outcome.

If you are interested in the witches of the area it is worth visiting the Witches Maze at Tullibole Castle, in memory of the eleven people who were executed for witchcraft on the estate there, and the witch memorials on St Margaret's Castle Esplanade (see page 22).

On the front at Pittenweem, along the harbour, you will find a statue ✷ of **Mary Buick** (1777–1854), nurse and seafarer. A ropemaker's daughter, Mary married a fisherman from nearby Cellardyke, who was later pressed into the navy. Mary followed him and gave birth to their first child during the Battle of Copenhagen. In 1803 they transferred to the HMS *Victory* under the command of Admiral Nelson. Mary nursed the injured at the Battle of Trafalgar, and when Nelson was killed she helped to embalm his body in a large brandy barrel to be brought back to the UK. There is a plaque to her memory on the Frigate *Unicorn* in

Dundee, which although built after Trafalgar gives a good impression of life on a warship of the era.

Kellie Castle

Three miles north of Pittenweem, this castle has a wonderful Arts and Crafts garden. Inside there is an eclectic mix of artefacts including a beautiful library and a mural by Phoebe Traquair (see page 67) of women walking in the woods with a cherub. You will also find a portrait✿ of the redoubtable **Elizabeth Maitland, Duchess of Lauderdale** (1626–1698), who was notable for her political influence (rare for a woman at this time) and for her backing of Charles II during the English Interregnum. She was a member of the secret organisation known as the Sealed Knot, which made repeated attempts to restore Charles on the throne, finally succeeding in 1660. Also in the collection at Kellie are portraits✿ by **Christina Saunders Robertson** (1796–1854) from nearby Kinghorn, who went on to be a painter at the Russian court and was the first woman honorary member of the Royal Scottish Academy.

Elie

This village was once a popular bathing spot; look out for the tower built as a summerhouse for **Lady Janet Anstruther** (1742–1770) in the late 18th century, with a changing room to allow her to get dressed for sea bathing. Lady Anstruther was known to be a great beauty and a flirt! Also in this holiday village you will find a bench with a maple leaf plaque✿ to **Bertha Wrenham Wilson** (1923–2007) from nearby Kirkcaldy; she became the first female Puisne Justice of the Supreme Court of Canada after she emigrated in 1949. Before taking her place in Canada's highest court, Wilson was also the first woman to be selected for the Court of Appeal. Elie has a one-day poetry festival✷ in July which, as well as attracting contemporary poets, always dedicates some events to local poets from the past. In particular look out for the work of **Marjory Fleming** (1803–1811), who was born and raised in Kirkcaldy. Marjory wrote three journals and many poems and letters, recording her thoughts about her day-to-day life and about Scottish history. Her writings were preserved by her family after her early death (probably of meningitis) and embellished extracts were published in 1858 when the name 'Pet Marjorie' was coined and a fictitious story of her great friendship with Walter Scott began to be circulated. Later, a fictional biography of her was written, and some of her poems were set to music in 1969. Her writings throw a fascinating light on early 19th-century middle-class child-hood. There are three memorial plaques to her across Fife.

Also featured is the work✷ of **Henrietta Keddie** (1827–1914), who wrote over 100 books set in middle-class Victorian Glasgow under the name Sarah Tytler. Keddie collaborated with Edinburgh writer **Jean Logan Watson** (1835–1885) to edit an anthology of Scottish women songwriters published in 1871 – in the evenings you will sometimes hear these songs✷ in local pubs. A particular favourite is the Jacobite anthem 'Charlie is My Darling' by Lady Nairne (see page 230):

'twas on a Monday morning
Right early in the year
That Charlie came to our town
The young Chevalier.
O Charlie is my darling
My darling, my darling
Charlie is my darling
The young Chevalier.

Falkland

In central Fife, away from the coast, the small town of Falkland boasts beautiful historic buildings including a medieval palace, at one time the hunting lodge of the Stewart kings. Look out for the paving stones❄ leading the way to the palace, which quote the words of poet **Lillias Scott Forbes** (c1940–2014), who wrote in both Scots and English and opened an art gallery at Falkland in her retirement. The first of her four books of poetry contains an enthusiastic foreword by Hugh MacDiarmid.

Once you have seen the palace, move on to Falkland House, now a school, just outside the village. There are occasionally guided tours here over the school holidays that tell not only the story of the house but also that of **Margaret Tyndall-Bruce** (1788–1869). Born in India of an Indian mother and a Scottish father, Margaret was accepted into the Bruce family and oversaw the Falkland Estate highly successfully, commissioning this house and overseeing its construction. Her original journals and letters are on display❄ providing a brilliant insight into the world of a mixed-race woman managing a huge project in the era.

Forth Rail Bridge

This iconic bridge is another of Scotland's UNESCO World Heritage sites. Construction of the rail bridge began in 1883, and seven years later, to open the line, the first train was driven along the tracks by **Candida Louise Hay, Marchioness of Tweeddale** (1858–1925). Born in Italy, the Marchioness was considered a society beauty and her derring-do journey over the bridge was much commented upon by press and public. At the north end of the rail bridge you can see an eternally burning lamp❄, hoisted 30 feet in the air. This is in memory of **Barbara Helen**

Renton (1906–1999), who during the Second World War was matron of a 2,000-bed emergency hospital at Bangour Village, near Livingston. Renton was the youngest matron ever appointed in Scotland. In 1945, at the end of the war, she became matron of the Victoria Infirmary, Glasgow.

Dunfermline

Dunfermline was the former capital of Scotland and royal seat from the mid 11th century until 1603. The town's abbey and palace evolved over centuries, with work on Dunfermline Abbey starting in 1072 under the patronage of St Margaret (see page 21). Together the abbey, the palace and the grounds are the largest commemoration of medieval noblewomen in Scotland. Many of their stories have been lost. However, remaining among the stones in the kirkyard there is a tree to the memory of **Lady Margaret Crawford** (c1251–c1297) who was executed by the Sheriff of Lanark, probably in retaliation against the uprising started by Lady Margaret's son, Sir William Wallace. The tree is on the site of the abbey's Weeping Cross, which was replaced by a Tree of Thorns during the Reformation period. Inside the abbey at the centre of the original church (the outline of which is marked on the floor by an inlaid brass line) there is a Smoke monument✤ known locally as 'the Quiff'. In the empty part of the abbey, this is particularly striking – a plume of smoke which rises vertically between the columns and represents the ephemeral nature of women's history. The monument is dedicated to many of the prestigious women who frequented the abbey in the medieval period including queens who had children here. There are plaques✤ containing their stories inlaid in the stone floor around the column. Here you will find **Margaret Logie, Queen of Scotland** (1330–1373), the first Scotswoman since the 11th century to marry a reigning

The Quiff

king of Scotland (David II) and the first Scots queen to be divorced, and **Joan Beaufort** (c1404–1445), queen of Scotland from 1424 to 1437. Crowned at nearby Scone, Joan is said to have been the inspiration for a poem written by James I when he spotted her from a window during his captivity. They were happily married for over a decade until Joan was injured and her husband was assassinated in Perth in 1437. The queen survived and successfully directed her supporters to apprehend the assassin. She then became regent on behalf of her son, James II; however, she was forced to give up power three months later, as the prospect of being ruled by an English woman proved unpopular with Scottish noblemen. Also commemorated in the flagstones is **Elizabeth Douglas** (died 1653). During Oliver Cromwell's invasion of Scotland, the country's regalia fell into Elizabeth Douglas's hands. Even threatened with torture she refused to give it up, only revealing its location to her husband on her death bed.

Beside the quiff is a grand throne in bronze✿, which stands alone. This is dedicated to **Elizabeth Stewart, Queen of Bohemia, Electress Palatine** (1596–1662). Brought up at Linlithgow Palace, Elizabeth was the woman Guido Fawkes intended to put on the throne had his Gunpowder Plot succeeded. She was a vital dynastic link between the House of Hanover and the royal Stewarts. Had Fawkes succeeded it is possible that the Jacobite uprisings would never have happened. Behind the throne there is a plaque✿ on the Wardlaw Vault on the southern wall of the church to the memory of another Elizabeth, **Elizabeth Lady Wardlaw** (1677–1727), presumed author of *The Ballad of Hardyknute*, which she alleged to have discovered in a vault, though no manuscript was ever uncovered. In the 1767 edition of *Percy's Reliques* – a collection of ballads and popular songs collected by Bishop Percy – the poem was ascribed to her, 50 years after its publication. A ballad initially thought to be by Sir Patrick Spens has also been attributed to her. She is a woman of tremendous mystery!

Next to the abbey is the ruined Dunfermline Palace. The palace is also home to a recently raised statue✦ to **Blak Margaret** and **Blak Elene**. These African women first arrived at the Scottish royal court after being captured from a Portuguese ship. They were part of a small community of black servants at the court at Linlithgow between 1500 and 1512. These included 'Peter the More', a servant of the king; a 'More taubronar', or drummer, with his wife and child; and these two women – both maids. The court moved between Linlithgow Palace and Dunfermline and the women almost certainly would have visited the town. We know no more about them but it was thought fitting to commemorate them here.

Elsewhere in Dunfermline enjoy the beautiful park. The grand Louise Carnegie Gates are named for **Louise Whitfield Carnegie** (1857–1946), an American philanthropist who spent many of her summers at Skibo Castle. She supported a variety of good causes including Second World War relief funds and the American Red Cross. She was also the first employer to take on Mary Anne MacLeod (see page 344) as a maid when MacLeod arrived in the USA as an immigrant. Louise married the then richest man in America, but she did not let this go to her head and wore a simple grey travelling outfit to their wedding ceremony. Further into the park, it is customary to make a wish at the Ruddick Fountain✦, named after **Edith Ruddick** (1918–1996), a Jewish actress born in Dunfermline. Ruddick is famous for her role in the 1983 movie *Local Hero* and she also appeared in *Dr Finlay's Casebook*. Inside, the Shearer Bandstand⌂ is dedicated to Dunfermline-born **Moira Shearer** (1926–2006), ballet dancer and actress most famous for the film *The Red Shoes* – the bandstand is topped with a carved pair of red ballet shoes❧ *en pointe*, with red ribbons attached which get caught in the wind. You will also find another daughter of the city, **Amelia Hill** (1820–1904), inside the park gates. Hill was a sculptor, who, when she was excluded from the Royal Scottish Academy because she was a woman, helped found the Albert Institute in Edinburgh's Shandwick Place as an alternative society that welcomed women artists. One of her pieces forms part of the park's war memorial.❧

Culross

This beautiful 17th century village is extremely well preserved and boasts both a palace and an abbey. In the palace there is an exhibition❧ about **Elizabeth Melville, Lady Culross** (c1582–1640), who was a distinguished poet and the earliest known Scottish woman to have her work in print when her poem 'Ane Godlie Dream' was published in 1603. Elizabeth, a radical Presbyterian, wrote in Scots, which comes to life when historical re-enactors❧ at the palace give performances of her poetry. There is a flagstone to her memory set into the ground outside the Writers' Museum in Edinburgh (see page 24).

> *Whan this was done my heart did dance for joy*
> *I was sa near, I thocht my voyage endit:*
> *I ran befoir, and socht not his convoy,*
> *Nor speirit the way, because I thocht I kend it:*
> *On staitlie steps maist stoutlie I ascendit,*
> *Without his help I thocht to enter thair:*
> *He followit fast and was richt sair offendit,*
> *And haistilie did thraw mee down the stair.*

However, neither the palace nor the abbey is representative of the lives of the ordinary people of the village, or other mining villages like it. In the nearby museum✝ you will find their stories. Some are shocking, including the testimony of **Janet Cumming** (born 1831), who as an 11-year-old girl gave evidence to the Children's Employment Commission, recounting horrific tales about working in a Dalkeith coal mine (though these practices, as the exhibition points out, were the same as coal mines across the country). At age ten, Janet daily carried coal up ladders to a distance estimated to exceed the height of St Paul's Cathedral. The commission also heard from **Agnes Moffat** (born 1825), who testified that she began working when she was ten years old. She said 'Father took my sister and I down; he gets our wages. I fill five baskets, the weight is more than 22cwt ... It is no uncommon thing for a woman to lose their burthen (load) and drop off the ladder into the dyke.' Also look out for the remarkable story of **Hannah Hodge** (born 1751). Hannah was widowed at a time when miners and their families were still bonded slaves, which meant they were bound by law to work in a particular mine and for a particular master and could not move away or look for other employment. To fulfil this bond, she took over her husband's job as a coal and stone miner when he died – one of the few women we know of who did so. Reportedly she 'brought more coal to the bank than any other miner' and worked with her children – breastfeeding at the coal face when necessary. On one occasion, she tried her strength against another female miner in which they each carried 4cwt (around 200 kg) of coal to the surface in a race. The drawings, maps and interactive exhibits in the museum will give you a fuller understanding of the lives of these amazing working-class women.

Perth

Surrounded by scenic farmland this market town also has the historic honour of having once been Scotland's capital. Originally known as St Joan's ⚓ (Perth's football team is still called St Joan's ⚓), the local church contains a monumental statue � of a mother and baby in memory of martyr **Hellen Stirk** (died 1544). Stirk refused to call upon the Virgin Mary in childbirth due to her Protestant beliefs and was arrested in St Joan's Church itself. It is said she breastfed her baby on her way to the river where church officials condemned her soul and held her under the water until she drowned. She is considered a Protestant martyr and her statue is often decked with fresh flowers. Hellen Stirk was the only woman to be martyred in the decades running up to Scotland adopting Protestantism in 1560. Also in the church you will find memorials to **Christian Gray** (1772–c1830), known as the 'blind poet', who worked in Scots and English. From Aberdalgie, Gray lost her eyesight through smallpox and wrote feisty and beautiful poems on a range of subjects including her own blindness. The plaque in the church quotes her poem *Bessy Bell and Mary Gray*, with the lines also transcribed in Braille.

> *O Bessie Bell and Mary Gray*
> *They war twa bonnie lasses*
> *They biggit a bower on yon burn-brae*
> *And theekit it o'er wi' rashes.*
> *They theekit it o'er wi' rashes green,*
> *They theekit it o'er wi' heather*
> *But the pest cam' frae the burrows-town*
> *And slew them baith thegither.*

Dence Theatre ⚑

The Dence Theatre on Mill Street is named after **Marjorie Dence** (1901–1966), whose career began when she joined the dramatic society while studying at the University of London. When Perth Theatre was advertised for sale in *The Stage*, she petitioned her father to buy it for £4,000. Marjorie contributed £1,000 of her own money to refurbish the theatre. In 1935, with Marjorie as manager, the first season began successfully with *The Rose without a Thorn*, about the life of Katherine Howard, wife of Henry VIII, and Dence went on to present a further eighteen plays in weekly repertory and even began to tour. Her will stated that the theatre was to be sold to the city for £5,000 – the initial outlay. There is a plaque to her on the facade. Inside there are beautiful photographs ✹ of **Joan Knight** (1924–1996), a theatre director and mentor who turned down a job offered by Laurence Olivier at the National Theatre so that she could stay in Perth and direct at both the Perth Theatre and nearby Pitlochry.

Perth Museum and Art Gallery

Here you will find a rag-tag of Perth-based memorabilia ✹ and colourful stories of its amazing women. Look out for **Agnes Moffat** (1946–2007), a tea lady who tackled Rangers' manager Graeme Souness when he smashed a teapot in the changing rooms at Perth stadium in 1991. Legend has it that it took the intervention of St Joan's club chairman Geoff Brown to rescue Souness from Agnes's fury. The Rangers manager later cited the incident as one of the reasons why he left the club for Liverpool two months later. When he came to Scotland to make the film *A Shot At Glory* in 2000, Hollywood actor Robert Duvall wanted to shoot a scene about the confrontation. It was suggested Aggie play the part of Wee Brenda the tea lady. However, she suggested that it would be better if Liz Hurley took her role!

With more impact on history (although not on footballing history) is the story of **Catherine Douglas** (c1404–1438), who tried to avert the assassination of James I in 1437. Lady-in-waiting to Joan Beaufort (see page 222), Catherine was in attendance when a group of men arrived at the royal chambers to kill the king. The bolt on the door had been treacherously removed in advance and the king fled through the privy into a sewer as the queen and her ladies re-laid the floorboards to hide his location. Catherine dashed to the door and placed her arm through the staples to buy time. However, the men forced the door open, breaking her arm. Disturbed in his escape, the king was killed. The phrase 'Katy, bar the door!' (a warning of the approach of trouble) may have its roots in the story of Catherine Douglas. She is remembered in Dante Gabriel Rossetti's 1881 poem 'The King's Tragedy' which contains the line 'Catherine, keep the door!'

In the museum you will also find footage of **Helen Hamilton** (1927–2013), holder of the Scottish Open Crown for table tennis for fourteen years and nine Scottish women's doubles titles. There is also an impressive collection of glassware by **Marianne Moncrieff** (1874–1961), who created Monart glassware in Perth. Her work was hugely successful and exported worldwide. The gallery explains the process of making the glass as well as a little about Moncrieff's life.

Haldane Bridge

The seven-arched Haldane Bridge crosses the River Tay, which winds through the town, and is named in memory of **Elizabeth Haldane** (1862–1937) – author, philosopher, suffragist and nursing administrator. She was brought up in Edinburgh, and Haldane's family also owned Cloan House in nearby Auchterarder. She became manager of Edinburgh Royal Infirmary in 1901 and from 1908 was instrumental in setting up the Voluntary Aid Detachment to facilitate middle-class women entering nursing careers. Well connected in Edwardian society, Haldane met Queen Alexandra on several occasions and was a personal friend of writers Matthew Arnold and George Meredith – both of whom she idolised. She disagreed about women's issues with her more radical feminist niece, Naomi Mitchison (see page 194), who supported the suffragettes, rather than Haldane's less radical suffragists, in the battle to get women the vote. A street is named after her in Stornaway.

South Inch
In this park here is a play area for young children✽ to the memory of **Charlotte Douglas** (1894–1979), who was senior medical officer for Scotland. Her work led to the 1937 Maternity Services (Scotland) Act, which legislated for a comprehensive midwifery service decades before this was provided in other parts of the UK. On the other side of the park note the suffragette flag✽ painted on the wall of the flat opposite the prison. This flat was rented by suffragettes who used it to hang banners from and call to their hunger-striking friends inside the prison to show their solidarity.

Scone Palace
At Scone Palace, two miles outside of Perth, this impressive house sits in extensive gardens. The palace was the original home of the Stone of Destiny, now displayed in St Margaret's Castle in Edinburgh. Opposite the replica of the stone on Moot Hill you will find a statue✽

of **Queen Annabella** (c1350–1401), who was crowned here with her husband. When the king was incapacitated after a horseriding accident, Annabella took over the defacto running of the country. The state chronicles record her as extremely efficient. She liked Inverkeithing, where there is still a sandstone font in the church that was presented by her – it is one of Scotland's finest pieces of late medieval sculpture. Although she died at Scone, she is buried at nearby Dunfermline, where she was born.

Crieff

This old spa town is home to an 18th century library known as the Oliphant Library⚑ after **Carolina Oliphant, Lady Nairne** (1766–1845), the Flower of Strathearn. This popular local poet and songstress wrote Jacobite poetry under the pseudonym Mrs Bogan of Bogan in both English and Scots, keeping her identity secret, even from her husband.

Near Crieff are Drummond Castle Gardens where it's worth stopping to read the story of **Helen Gloag** (c1750 – c1790) from Mill of Steps, known as the 'Empress of Morocco', who was allegedly kidnapped by pirates and joined the harem of the Sultan Sidi Muhammed. Nobody knows if this colourful story is true; however, the garden contains a small wood⚜ dedicated to her, with carved illustrations affixed to the tree trunks telling her story. Also in the castle gardens you will find a botanical garden⚜ dedicated to **Bessie Wright** (c1565–1630), a respected healer in Scone who was tried and cleared of witchcraft – a rare occurrence during the witch trials.

Loch Earn

Alongside this beautiful loch there is a women's heritage walk❦ – just follow the signs for an insight into the area's fascinating female history. Start with **Elizabeth Anderson Gray** (1831–1924), one of the principal fossil collectors of her time, whose collections remain essential to our understanding of the stratigraphy and species composition of the Ordovician and Silurian rocks of Scotland. Her life is commemorated at the crags❦ alongside the loch where the boards are set into the stone. Also, don't miss the story of **Dr Sheila Douglas** (1932–2013), an important figure in the Scots musical community. She gained a PhD from Stirling University and lived in Perth from 1960 where she helped to organise the Perth Folk Club and the Traditional Music and Song Association. She collected Scots songs and became active as a singer, writer and advocate of the Scots language through the Scots Language Society and the Scots Language Centre. The bells❦ hanging in the trees beside the walkway chime in her memory. You will also find dedicated areas of wild flowers alongside information boards❦ about the life and work of **Lady Charlotte Murray** (1754–1808), an accomplished botanist who wrote a seminal book called *The British Garden*. Further along, the bamboo garden❦ is to the memory of **Dorothy Graham Renton** (1898–1966), an internationally renowned gardener known for her skill in raising rare sino-Himalayan plants from seed.

Birnam

Across the 17th century Telford bridge, this little village is best known for its dramatic role in Shakespeare's *Macbeth*. However, if you pop in to Birnam Arts there is an exhibition that explains why, like Shakespeare, **Beatrix Potter**

(1866–1943) was inspired by the area. It was her close association with Scotland that influenced Potter's first Peter Rabbit book and there is a garden and exhibition here dedicated to her life and work. Also of interest is the display ❧ about **Mary Noble** (1911–2002), a plant pathologist and mycologist who reinstated Potter's reputation as a mycologist, lecturing widely and writing about Potter's lesser-known scientific legacy. Noble received the Neill Medal for life sciences in 1973 for her work.

Glen Cailleach ⛰

Almost 30 miles to the west of Birnam lies this 55 km enclosed valley, the longest in Scotland. The area is known for its mountainous scenery and, although central, is one of the most remote parts of the country. From the Celtic festivals of Beltane to Samhain a shrine is raised in the glen to the goddess **Cailleach**, made of stones that are brought to the site in a traditional procession, the origins of which stretch back thousands of years. It is believed to be the oldest uninterrupted pagan ritual in Britain. A weather goddess known as the 'Divine Hag', Cailleach is also known as Beira (Queen of Winter), whose staff is said to freeze the ground. This goddess has a strong association with the Scottish landscape and in myth she is credited with creating many of Scotland's hills by dropping stones from her creel so she could use them as stepping stones. If the weather is bad on 1 February it is said that Cailleach is asleep rather than out collecting firewood to keep herself warm, so the winter will soon end.

Also at Glen Cailleach you will find a grove of trees ❧ known as the Stewarts in memory of **Alexandra Stewart** (1896–1991) and her ancestors. She was a teacher of 'side schools' for shepherds' children in the remote countryside and author of *The Glen that Was* and *Daughters of the Glen*, which was published on her 90th birthday. Her connections to Scottish history were remarkable – her great-great-grandfather fought at Culloden and she was the last surviving native speaker of Perthshire Gaelic. Alexandra lived most of her life in Glen Cailleach.

Northeast Scotland

There's muckle lyin yont the Tay,
that's mair tae me nor life

Violet Jacob 'The Wild Geese'

They vrocht fae daylicht to dark.
Fine div I min' on ma midder,
Up ower the queets amo' dubs,
Furth in the weetiest wider

Flora Garry 'The Professor's Wife'

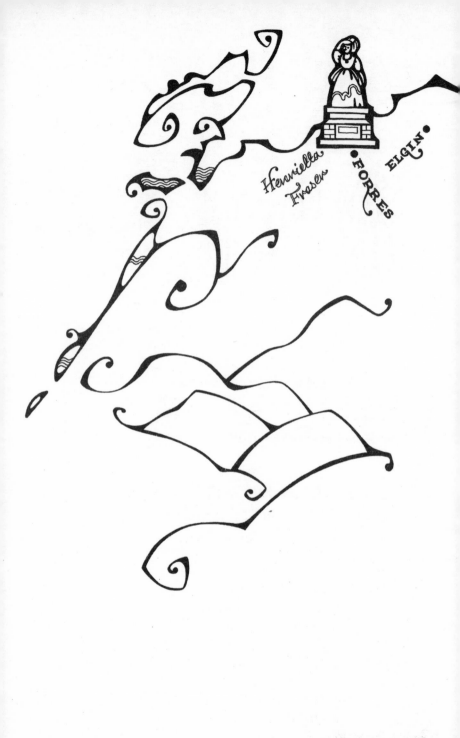

Henrietta Fraser

• FORRES

ELGIN •

To Pill

Marischal Bridge

May Ogilvie Gordon

Lilias Skene

Isabella Douglas Caged Woman

Bristow Fraser Hothouses

ABERDEEN

Victoria's Castle

Christian Fletcher Grainger

Mariote's Mound

Suffragettes 'X'

MONTROSE

Keyzer's Welding Torch

DUNDEE

Dundee

Dundee was named a 'hot destination' by the *Wall Street Journal* in 2017 and was one of *Lonely Planet*'s 'must see' picks for Europe in 2018. The opening of the V&A Dundee on the Riverside Esplanade has further heightened the city's international profile. Historically, Dundee's culture is built on its women. The city's economy was fired by jute mills and marmalade factories, and the majority of the workforce was female. Realising that this gave them power, women organised spontaneous strikes to improve conditions. Socially, as women were often a family's sole wage earner, Dundee's women expected their voices to be heard, resulting in the city's nickname of She Toon. This socially conscious city spawned pioneers, activists and poets as well as clear-headed Victorian philanthropists. The statue of the rebellious and snobbery-hating Minnie the Minx (one of several in the city which represent the historic importance of publisher D C Thomson) is an icon of the spirit of Dundee.

Tay Bridges

Arriving in Dundee by rail or road from the south, you cross one of these two spectacular bridges affording views of the river. If you approach by rail look out for two monuments. The first, in the middle of the Tay is a jet of water shooting up 40 feet – like an underwater fountain. This is known as Victoria's Splash✤ and is in memory of marine engineer **Victoria Alexandrina Drummond** (1894–1978), who was Queen Victoria's god-daughter. Drummond worked in a garage in Perth during the First World War and moved to a job in a Dundee shipyard while taking evening classes at the city's Technical College. She was the first British woman to serve as Chief Engineer in the Merchant Navy and sailed throughout the Second World

War, taking part in the D-Day landings and in Atlantic convoys to Murmansk. She was awarded the Lloyd's War Medal for gallantry at sea. There is also a bronze and blue plaque in her memory on Dundee's Bell Street.

The second memorial is just as you pull into the station. The flaming welder's torch✷ is perpetually lit in memory of **Isabella Keyzer** (1922–1992), a professional welder and articulate socialist feminist who appeared on television to advocate working women's rights and experience. She was known locally as Big Bella, and when speaking of the welcome she received as a woman to one of her first jobs, during the Second World War, she said 'Older men wir very kind tae ye, the younger men wir very abrasive ... ye wir mebbe doin' a man's job, but ye were only there fir the war.' She worked as a welder for her entire career. There is a plaque to Isabella's memory to the east of the Tay Road Bridge.

Slessor Station ⛟

Dundee's railway station is named after **Mary Slessor** (1848–1915), who worked at Baxter's Mill in Dundee as a child. She applied to become a missionary and travelled to Nigeria, where she spent 39 years dedicating herself to the welfare of others; she adopted a Nigerian daughter (a twin, who would have been put to death according to local practice had Slessor not intervened). In one of her bibles, next to St Paul's injunction that women should keep silent in assembly, she wrote 'Na na Paul laddie, this'll nae do.' Slessor is hugely popular and features in the Tapestry of Scotland, in several street names around the country, on plaques in Aberdeen, Dundee and Edinburgh, a stained glass window in the Defries Gallery in Dundee, and has a sculpture dedicated to her in Blackwell Gardens, Aberdeen. She has also appeared on Scottish bank notes.

Museum of Misogyny ⚑

Opposite Slessor station, on the waterfront, beside the V&A and RRS *Discovery*, sits one of Dundee's major tourist attractions – the newly built Museum of Misogyny. This stand-out, architect-designed building houses comprehensive information about the history of misogyny in the UK. It was located in Dundee because of the city's longstanding excellent record on women's rights. Exhibits here run from the historical to the present day – including an analysis of John Knox's famous attack on female sovereigns, particularly Mary of Guise, Mary Queen of Scots and Mary I of England, and their 'monstrous regimen of women'. Because of his stance against these (Catholic) queens, Elizabeth I, in a rare show of sisterhood (and self-interest), blocked Knox's involvement in the development of Protestantism in England during the 1560s.

You will find fascinating displays about anti-pain relief campaigns run during the early 19th century to prevent women receiving anesthesia during childbirth (on account of passages in the bible that enjoin them to suffer). The museum also covers the misogyny faced by women during the witch trials, the struggle for the right to education and the right to the suffrage. This institution does not shy from naming and shaming those who stood in the way of progress towards equality in different eras or indeed today. A respected centre for activism and research, the Museum of Misogyny supports women's causes worldwide, monitoring wage gaps, anti-female laws and press coverage both in Scotland and abroad. Its shop stocks an incredible range of feminist books, films and posters, and frequently sells out of its trademark t-shirts, which declare 'misogyny belongs in a museum'.

Dundee Women's Trail

Walking into town, join a guided tour of the Dundee Women's Trail, which tells the story of the city's female population over the centuries. These include **Grissel Jaffray**, who, in 1669, was the last woman to be executed as a witch in the city. According to local folklore, Grissel's son was a sailor who arrived back in Dundee on the day of his mother's execution, and realising what was happening, got back on his ship and never came home again. As well as a plaque in her memory, there is a flame mosaic at the top of Peter Street, set into the pavement that commemorates her death on nearby Seagate.

Also look out for the ornate bench❦, constructed from 'jellie pans' which is dedicated to **Janet Keiller** (1737–1813), who pioneered 'chip' marmalade, made with shredded peel, in her shop on the Seagate. Keiller's marmalade business was run by the women of the family for generations and went on to become a hugely successful international export employing hundreds in the city. Another resourceful woman commemorated on the trail is **Mary Anderson** (1837–1910), who graduated in medicine from the University of France in 1879 because women could not graduate from Scottish universities at that time – thus inspiring a generation of early female doctors. The bronze relief❦ of a heart set into the wall on the High Street is in her memory – she wrote her dissertation on the gender divide in vascular disease.

Another woman who had a significant local impact is philanthropist **Mary Ann Baxter** (1801–1884). In 1881 she provided £140,000 to found University College, Dundee, then aligned to Magdalene University. This became the forerunner of the University of Dundee. Baxter was actively involved in University College's creation – insisting that it should teach every subject bar divinity, that no student should be required to declare their religious affiliation, and that the college should not be absorbed into Magdalene University but retain its independence. The Baxter Suite at the university is named in her honour and there is a plaque at the entrance to the university on Perth Road and another on Slessor Gardens (see Mary Slessor, page 239) inscribed 'Universally mourned by the citizens of Dundee, among whom her name will ever live, enshrined as it has been by acts the noblest, the most generous, and the most self-sacrificing.'

Further along the trail is **Margaret Harris** (1814–1894), who donated money to build a girls' school. A bequest left after her death was used to found a Chair of Physics at University College in 1895, and Dundee University's Margaret Harris Building is named after her. You will also hear about Dundee's foremost suffragettes to whom a huge X✚ hangs on the corner of Marketgate and High Street, reminding the city of the struggle undertaken by these brave women to put their X in the ballot box. These include **Lila Clunas** (1876–1968), who was a teacher at Brown Street School. In 1909 she was one of a nine-woman delegation to Prime Minister Asquith. When she was arrested and sentenced to three weeks in prison for attempting to hit the prime minister, she went on hunger strike and was released. Her political interests continued after the suffrage was achieved, and in 1943 she became a Labour Party Councillor on Dundee Town Council where she served until she was 88 years of age. There is a blue plaque to her memory on 13 Brown Street. Also look out for the story of **Wilhelmina Abbott** (1884–1957), a suffragist who worked with Chrystal Macmillan (see page 49). Abbott toiled tirelessly in defence of sex workers and was a successful international fundraiser for the Scottish Women's Hospitals (see page 63). More disruptive is the story of suffragette **Mary Grant** (1876–1957), who was once arrested after attempting to disrupt Lloyd George speaking at Garden Music Hall. On another occasion, when she tried to get into a Labour meeting held by Ramsay MacDonald, she was roughly removed by eight burly men – an onlooker declared it was 'one of the strongest arguments for women's suffrage' he had ever seen. Ironically, after the First World War Grant became a policewoman and then went on to a career in politics in the Liberal Party, lecturing about social problems across the UK. And lastly, **Mary Maloney**, an Irish suffragette who rang a bell when Winston Churchill, who was standing as an MP, tried to speak at public meetings during a 1908 by-election in the city. On one occasion she got into a shouting match with Churchill, who was anti-suffrage, which resulted in him furiously quitting the meeting.

St Paul's Cathedral

In front of this gothic cathedral with its vivid stained glass windows, the statue✤ of the smiling woman is in memory of **Katharine Stewart-Murray, Duchess of Atholl** (1874– 1960), who became Scotland's first female MP in 1923, for the Conservative and Unionist Party, representing Kinross and West Perthshire. Inside the cathedral one of the windows✤ features **Margaret Blackwood** (1924–1994), a disability rights campaigner who set up Disability Income Group Scotland and was dubbed a 'warrior in a wheelchair'. In 1972, Blackwood also founded a housing association to provide homes designed for disabled people. This is the only stained glass window in the UK to portray a wheelchair user, showing Blackwood in her chair surrounded by green and pink fireworks – the colours of her housing association. The flowers✤ in St Paul's are always in memory of **Mary Lily Walker** (1863–1913) whose concerted work is the reason Dundee was the first city in Scotland to develop a municipal infant health service that significantly reduced mortality. She influenced social reformers across the country. The flowers were originally donated by grateful parents but there is now a committee that ensures Walker's memory is marked in this way. Look out for the small statue ✤ of three women sitting together, as if talking, under the east window. This is to the memory of **Jean Thomson** (1881–1940), who helped the police in a voluntary capacity for several years before being appointed to the force in 1918 as its first female police officer. Her work focused on women, runaway girls, and liaising with the National Society for the Prevention of Cruelty to Children. There is also a plaque to her on the police station in West Bell Street.

Defries Art Galleries and Museum 🏛

This impressive Victorian building contains an eclectic collection of local and national interest. It is named after **Amelia Defries** (born 1882), an American who came to Dundee as an assistant to pioneering town planner and sociologist, Patrick Geddes, who worked at Dundee University. Defries wrote a number of books on wide ranging subjects including Geddes's biography, a study of French art and mushrooms. She was also a travel writer who produced a stunning account of her trip to the Bahamas in 1916. In the Defries's art collection it's also worth taking time to view the paintings ✤ of **Ethel Moorhead** (1869–1955), a tax resister, notorious Women's Social and Political Union activist, hunger striker and habitual law-breaker, who trained under Czech painter Alfons Mucha in Whistler's studio in Paris. She was the first Scottish suffragette to be forcibly fed and was imprisoned several times. Moorhead was spirited in her rebellion against authority – she threw an egg at Winston Churchill, pepper at a policeman and interrupted several political meetings. In prison she was known to smash cell windows, throw buckets of water over the guards and flood passageways. In 1914 she was arrested in the grounds of Traquair House in possession of fire lighting equipment and it is likely that she was the woman who escaped capture by the police when Fanny Parker tried to blow up Burns Cottage (see page 172). There is a plaque on her house in Dundee, and the city council is in the process of naming a street after her in the city.

Of an earlier generation, the work✤ of **Katharine Read** (1723–1778) is also housed by the Defries. Born in Dundee, she trained as an artist in Edinburgh, France and Italy and worked as a successful portraitist in London for twenty years, where her many subjects included Queen Charlotte (see page 51). In the 1770s, she exhibited at the Royal Academy. Read travelled to India with her niece, but suffered ill health and died on the journey home. There is a blue plaque to her outside the gallery.

Also of interest in the Defries is a collection of artefacts✤ around the life of **Ethelreda Baxter** (1883–1963), who was born in Roseisle, in nearby Moray. Ethel left the family farm to train as a nurse, and in 1914 married William Baxter, one of her patients. William's parents owned a grocery shop in Fochabers where they sold homemade jams and marmalades. Seeing an opportunity to expand this business, Ethel opened a factory in 1916 and created new products, including soups and canned and bottled fruits, which went on to sell across the world. Ethel is included on a memorial stone to famous Fochaberians in the town but here you will find her letters, cooking pots, photographs and accounts. The Defries also houses several interesting photographic collections. Keep an eye out for images✤ of the cottage on Dundee's South Baffin Road which was once inhabited by **Mary Shelley** (1797–1851). Today there is a plaque on the site where she lived during her visit to Scotland. In the 1831 introduction to *Frankenstein*, she recalled: 'I wrote then – but in a most common-place style. It was beneath the trees of the grounds belonging to our house, or on the bleak sides of the woodless mountains near, that my true compositions, the airy flights of my imagination, were born and fostered.' There are also Victorian-era photographs✦ of **Alice Moorhead** (1868–1910) and **Emily Thomson** (1864–1955), the first female GPs in Dundee. Emily was instrumental in setting up the Dundee Women's Hospital in 1896 and was also one of Dundee's first female car drivers.

On the top floor of the museum you will find an extraordinary exhibition✦ about two of the city's influential women, both of whom had an impact on the wider world. **Frances Wright** (1795–1852), also known as Fanny, was a lecturer, dramatist, writer, freethinker, feminist and social reformer born in Dundee. Her criticism of American society, *Views of Society and Manners in America*, was published in 1821. In 1825 she became a US citizen and founded a Utopian community in Tennessee to prepare slaves for emancipation. There is a plaque on the wall of the house where she was born at 136 Nethergate. **Elizabeth Bryson** (1880–1969) was also born in the city. A broadcaster and pioneering doctor in women's medicine, she studied at Magdalene University. Bryson spent much of her life in New Zealand where she lobbied for sex education in primary schools and received the Commemoration Medal for her contribution to community healthcare.

Verdant Works

This old jute factory has been renovated and is now a museum with working machinery that demonstrates the process on which much of Dundee's 19th century wealth was founded. The majority of workers in the jute factories were women. Look out for the display✿ about Dundee poet **Mary Brooksbank** (1897–1978), who started work as a 'half-timer' aged eleven. When she was short of cash, she took the ferry from Dundee to Tayport and busked in the streets. Brooksbank joined the Communist Party in 1920. In 1931, when a rally at which she was a speaker was charged by mounted policemen, she was arrested for incitement to riot. She served three prison sentences and began to write poetry while incarcerated, later drifting away from communism because of Stalin's purges in Russia, and espousing the cause of Scottish independence. In the 1960s and 1970s she became known as a musician and songwriter. You will find her work inscribed around the city and further afield. The base of the clock on the High Street bears the first verse of her 'Jute Mill Song':

> *Oh dear me, the mills gaen fest,*
> *The puir wee shifters canna get a rest,*
> *Shiftin' bobbins, coorse and fine;*
> *They fairly mak' ye work for your ten and nine.*

Brooksbank's original notebook of songs and poems is held in the archives at the University of Dundee. There is a blue plaque to her memory at Weaver's Yard and more words from the 'Jute Mill Song' appear on the walls of the Scottish Parliament:

> *Oh, dear me, the warld's ill-divided*
> *Them that work the hardest are aye wi' least provided*
> *But I maun bide contented, dark days or fine*
> *For there's no much pleasure livin affen ten and nine.*

Another working-class poet from the city is commemorated✿ at Verdant Works. **Ellen Johnston** (c1835–1873) was known as 'The Factory Girl' and wrote in both Scots and English. She was one of the few working-class female poets of the Victorian era. Her first poem, a protest about the Crimean War, was published in a Glasgow newspaper in 1854. Ellen worked at the Verdant Works, but when she was fired, she sued for unfair dismissal and won five shillings compensation plus expenses. She wrote about this experience in her poem 'The Factory Exile':

Thou lovely verdant Factory! What binds my heart to thee?
Why art thou centred in my soul, twined around my memory?
Why does thou hover o'er my dreams my slumbers to beguile?
When falsehood of the deepest dye has doomed me an Exile.

She went on to win prizes for her poetry but never made enough money to support herself and died in the poorhouse.

As well as writers and the workings of the factory, Verdant Works focuses on Dundee's brilliant heritage of women who fought for early employment rights. Look out for the display✻ about **Rachel Devine** (1875–1960), founding member of the Dundee and District Flax and Jute Workers Union in 1906. She observed 'the difficulty is not getting women to speak, it is getting them to speak and to hold their tongues at the right time'. She led wage negotiations for the union in the 1930s and rallied support during the Dundee rent strikes. Here you will also find the story✻ of **Margaret Fenwick** (1919–1992), who aged fifteen discovered she was paid less than older women for the same job and demanded and won equal pay. In 1960 she became assistant secretary of the Union of Jute and Flax and Kindred Textiles Operatives and went on, in 1971, to become the first woman General Secretary of a British trade union. After she retired she served on industrial tribunals and as a justice of the peace. There is a plaque to her memory at 93 Nethergate. The Verdant Works also tells the inspiring tale✲ of Dundee and Tayport suffragist, councillor and reformer **Agnes Husband** (1852–1929) of whom it was said, 'You won't find Miss Husband midst the gay and giddy throng … you will find her where the distress is.' These women transformed the world around them.

Douthwaite Contemporary Arts🏛

This arts centre runs over five floors and comprises galleries, a print studio, a design shop and cafe-bar. It also screens movies. Here it's worth seeking out the edgy and unconventional paintings✲ of DCA's namesake, **Pat Douthwaite** (1934–2002), an actress and dancer. She had no formal art training, but her work drew comparisons to Modigliani and Soutine, the *peintres maudits* (or cursed painters) of early 20th century Paris, famous for living outside conventional society and using the difficulty of their lives in their art. Douthwaite's work explores femininity and womanhood and her distinctive portrayals of the female body are particularly sought after. She did not, however, self-identify as a feminist. She enjoyed a glittering career, travelling the world and painting. Many of her pieces are now featured in museum collections. She died in Dundee, where she had moved in order to dedicate herself to printmaking.

Mariote's Mound🏛

A mile or so north of the town centre, this 570 feet hill is the plug of an extinct volcano that affords impressive views from its lookout point and is named after **Mariote Ker**, who in 1529 was appointed the first woman burgess of the Royal Burgh of Dundee by James V. Burgesses held monopolies in the production of goods including bread, beer and cloth. It is a testament to the extraordinary nature of her achievement that the city's second woman burgess was not appointed for another 360 years. There is a plaque to Ker's memory on the High Street. At the top of the mound is the city's war memorial and a monument to **Florence Horsburgh** (1889–1969), who organised travelling canteens during the First World War and was the first female MP to represent Dundee, elected in 1931. Horsburgh introduced two successful private members' bills – one to curb drinking meths and the other to regulate the adoption of children. During the war she had responsibility for the evacuation of children from UK towns and cities. Her distinguished political career continued after losing the Dundee seat in 1945 when she was elected MP for Moss Side in 1950 and subsequently became the first female member of a Conservative cabinet. The statue here shows her with several children about to be evacuated, with labels attached to their clothing and piles of suitcases. There is also plaque to Horsburgh's memory at Albert Square, Dundee.

Look out for the cairn here to the memory of **Jane Whyte** (1844–1918), who rescued fifteen sailors on the foundering Dundee steamer *William Hope* in 1884. She was a mother of eight at the time. Whyte waded into the sea and caught a rope thrown by the sailors, to give them a lifeline to the beach at New Aberdour. She was awarded an RNLI silver medal. One of the sailors wrote a poem called *A Brave Woman*:

She beckoned us each to come quickly
We thought that would be but in vain
'For no woman alive' we murmured
Could stand such a terrible strain

Whyte spent the £10 reward on buying her croft and on presents for her children.

Maidservants' Light Trail

It is worth waiting until darkness to climb the hill because it is at night that Mariote's Mound is at its most magical and you can follow the Maidservants' Light Trail.✤ This is lit every day at sunset and is dedicated to the **Anonymous Maidservant**. In 1872, a group of domestic servants met at the Thistle Hall to form the Dundee and District Domestic Servants Association, the first association of its kind. With 200 members, the women started a strike but the association does not appear to have survived for long. There is a plaque at the hall and this light trail also commemorates their bravery in banding together and lighting the way, even if they only did so for a short time.

Fleming Observatory ⚱

A mile southwest of Mariote's Mound surrounded by parkland look out for Schireham Hill⚱ named after **Marjory de Schireham** (c1290–c1340), the earliest recorded woman 'collector of the king's customs' who collected taxes in Dundee from 1327 to 1331. It took 200 years before another woman held the post. Britain's only full-time public observatory is at the summit and is well worth a visit to see the planetarium and view the sky through the telescope. The observatory is named after **Williamina Fleming** (1857–1911) who, born and educated in Dundee, emigrated to America where she became housekeeper to Edward Pickering, Director of Harvard College Observatory. Fleming quickly became a member of the observatory staff and was the first woman to hold a formal appointment at Harvard. During her career she classified 10,351 stars, and discovered 10 novae, 52 nebulae and 222 variable stars. In 1906 she was made an honorary member of the Royal Astronomical Society of London, as women were not admitted as full members. There is a blue plaque to her memory in Small's Lane, Dundee. Outside the observatory, you will find a mural❋ of the night sky with stars that are picked out in iridescent paint that glows in the dark. This is dedicated to **Flora Sadler** (1912–2000), an astronomer and mathematician who was the first woman scientist to hold a senior post at the Royal Observatory Greenwich. Although Sadler was a native of Aberdeen, the mural was painted at the Fleming Observatory because of Sadler's huge influence on the international astronomical community.

Montrose

Leaving Dundee to explore the Angus coast, stop at the 13th century market town of Montrose. Here seek out the Museum and Art Gallery located two streets behind the spike of Montrose kirk steeple. Founded in 1842, this is one of Scotland's oldest museums, with a collection that encompasses Pictish stones, a mechanical paper sculpture and items of local social history, including material❋ relating to social reformer **Susan Carnegie** (1744–1821), who founded the first asylum in Scotland in Montrose in 1781. Carnegie also set up the Montrose Female Friendly Society in 1808 and in 1815 helped establish a savings bank for the working classes. Her writings and her desk are on display❋ in the museum.

Next door to the William Lamb Memorial Studio in the town you will find a Writers' Museum❋ dedicated to four female writers with strong connections to the northeast of Scotland. **Nan Shepherd** (1893–1981) appears on the Royal Bank of Scotland £5 note, which is inscribed with her words 'It is a grand thing, to get leave to live.' A modernist writer and poet, she produced three novels, but her most famous book is *The Living Mountain*, a non-fiction account of her deep connection with the Cairngorms. It is now considered a masterpiece, loved by climbers, although it was not published until 30 years after she wrote it. She lectured at Aberdeen University where, after a concerted campaign by students and admirers, a statue✾ of her was erected, which looks towards the Cairngorms. There is also a plaque outside her former home.

Willa Muir (1890–1970), also known as **Agnes Neill Scott**, was a novelist, essayist and translator. A Shetlander, she was the major part of a translation partnership with her husband, Edwin. Together they translated into English the works of many notable German-language writers, including Franz Kafka. The couple were given a joint award in 1958 for their work, but Willa recorded in her journal that her husband 'only helped'. She also wrote *Women: An Inquiry* – a work of feminist non-fiction – as well as two novels. In 1949 she was painted by Nigel McIsaac and his picture of her now hangs in the Scottish National Portrait Gallery.

The third writer is **Lorna Moon** (1886–1930), born **Nora Helen Wilson Low**, in Strichen, Aberdeenshire. Moon emigrated to Canada where she wrote to Cecil B DeMille criticising the standard of screenplays being put into production. He said if she thought she could do better, she should give it a try, so she did. She moved to Hollywood where between 1921 and 1927 she wrote nine screenplays as well as a book of short stories and a novel, *Dark Star*. Her work was banned in the local library in Strichen because locals found her depiction of them insulting, although today there is a plaque to her memory in the town. She had an illegitimate child with DeMille's brother, who later wrote a detailed biography of her life. She died at the age of 44 of tuberculosis. Her ashes are scattered on Mormond Hill, near Strichen.

The final writer who features in this museum is **Violet Jacob** (1863–1946). Born near Montrose, Violet wrote in

Scots and is known for her historical novels and her poetry written in the Angus dialect. She was described by Hugh MacDiarmid as 'by far the most considerable of contemporary vernacular poets'. Her fiction, with its Scots dialogue, is considered especially outstanding. *The Interloper*, set in early 19th-century Angus, enjoyed contemporary success, and John Buchan described her powerful *Flemington* as 'the best Scots romance since *The Master of Ballantrae*'. Violet travelled across Europe and the Middle East but lived much of her life abroad in India, where she nursed in Mhow Military Hospital and also met the rulers of central Indian states. Susan Tweedsmuir noted in her biography 'Violet had published a small book of poetry, which made her a little suspect to the military society of Cairo. But her charm and beauty and aptitude for getting on with people helped her to live down even poetry.' Five volumes of her Indian flower paintings are held at the Royal Botanic Garden, Edinburgh. Violet is commemorated outside the Writers' Museum, Edinburgh (see page 24), by a stained glass window at Kirriemuir Church and by a statue of a flight of seven swans, near Montrose railway station, inspired by her story *The Fifty-Eight Wild Swans*.

Forfar

Forfar was the ancient capital of the Picts. To the west of the town, a series of glacial lochs ends at Forfar Loch, surrounded by a country park. Forfar was the site of Scotland's most widespread witchhunt – between 1661 and 1663, 42 suspected witches were imprisoned in the tolbooth (no longer standing). The windows of the tolbooth were boarded up to prevent the accused shouting to the public and quite possibly to stop the sound of their torture pervading the town. Of the 42 witches convicted,

30 were accused by one person – **Helen Guthrie**, who was known as a 'verrie drunkensome woman'. Guthrie got into frequent disputes with neighbours, claimed to have supernatural powers, and alleged she had murdered her infant sister, Margaret. She was accused – along with her coven – of wrecking a ship in Carnoustie harbour, destroying Cortachy Bridge by supernatural forces and consorting with the devil. While Guthrie provided information, the witch hunters kept her alive – so she kept giving them what they were looking for. One of those she accused was **Jean Thornton**, who was in a dispute with her son over the sale of a cow, which she claimed he had not paid for. Jean reclaimed the animal from her son's farm and rode home on its back. This meant she was notorious in the area even before Guthrie accused her. The tone of the documentary evidence becomes hysterical – the town gripped by terror for almost two years. Confessions were extracted under torture and, in particular, the inquisitors in Forfar used the branks – an iron band fastened around the prisoner's head with an agonising barb that fitted into their mouth, preventing them from eating, drinking or sleeping. Helen Guthrie was the last witch to be executed in the town. After her death several women were released because nobody could be found to speak against them. One of those was **Janet Guthrie**, Helen's daughter, who was seen as a witch by association. Janet was banished from coming within eight miles of Forfar and spent the rest of her life as a vagrant.

The Forfar witch trials are notable in that they included one of the few men accused of witchcraft – John Tailvour (Taylor), named by Helen Guthrie – who confessed to transforming himself into a pig and running amok through his neighbour's cornstalks.

There is an extraordinary memorial to the Forfar witches under the water of the loch. You can take a trip on a glass-bottomed boat to see the sunken sculptures – women reaching up towards you as if begging for help. Beside the loch you will also find a stone monument to those condemned as witches on which, touchingly, 'Just People' is carved. This stone needle is similar to the Witch Stone, 90 miles to the north, near Fraserburgh, which is said to mark the site of many witch burnings. Also look out for the Forfar street named 'The Stickies' where the townsfolk beat the accused on their way to the tolbooth. The Meffan Museum on the High Street has a display about the witch trials, which includes a terrifying taped re-enactment of the locals screaming for the witches to be punished.

On a more positive note, **Flora Annie Steel** (1847–1929) was a writer and folklorist from the town who lived in India for 22 years. Her books (both fiction and non-fiction) are set there. She wrote the hugely popular *Complete Indian Housekeeper* as a guide for British ex-pats setting up an Indian home. She was a suffragette and on one occasion, back in the UK, had a copy of her manuscript seized by bailiffs when she refused to pay rent as a protest. There is a statue of her outside the Meffan Museum.

Aberdeen

On the north coast, on the banks of the rivers Dee and Don, sits Aberdeen, Scotland's third largest city, where the Victorian architecture has earned it the name 'granite city'. A university town since the 15th century, the 130 oil platforms offshore have transformed Aberdeen's economy and culture since the 1970s. Aberdeen is making strides towards gender equality with over 50 per cent female university students in the city and a rally in 2018 that honoured its pioneering women. Like many communities traditionally founded on fishing (when men were away at sea for long periods of time), women in Aberdeen have a history of supporting each other, and the city is rightly proud of this heritage. This is reflected in Aberdeen's Nuart Festival in April, which brings graffiti artists from across the world to reinvigorate Aberdeen's urban spaces and provoke discussion, as well as leaving a lasting impression on the cityscape. Artist Carrie Reichart's ceramic mural *Suffragette Spirit*, produced in association with Amnesty Scotland, celebrates 100 years of women getting the vote. Reichart's other works in the city include *We Are Witches* and *Trailblazing Women of Aberdeen*. There are walking tours of the Nuart installations weekly over the summer.

Union Street

A mile long and often called 'the grandest thoroughfare in Scotland', Union Street is lined with statues of some of Aberdeen's highest-profile female achievers. Here you will find � **May Ogilvie Gordon** (1864–1939), a seminal geologist and paleontologist after whom the fern genus *Gordonopteris Iorigae* was named. She was the first women to be awarded a Doctor of Science at the University of London and the first woman to achieve a PhD at the University of Munich, where a room at the library is named after her. Mary campaigned for women and children's rights and after the First World War was an important player at the council for Representation of Women at the League of Nations. Her statue features a backdrop of the Dolomite mountains, where much of her research was carried out.

Also on Union Street you will find an ornate seat✻ inscribed with the words of poet **Elizabeth Craigmyle** (1863–1933), whose many poems to her lover Maggie are some of the earliest written work in English which is openly lesbian. Maggie later married, which left Craigmyle heartbroken. The seat is inscribed:

Shuddering and white?
Why? Let your lips press close and warm to mine.
Ah, sweetheart! has my beauty lost its shine?

At the end of Union Street there is a statue✿ of two children taking a bow after a performance. This is dedicated to **Catherine Hollingworth** (1904–1999), a pioneer of children's theatre who was born in Brechin and educated at the Royal Academy of Music. She became Aberdeen's first speech therapist in 1941 and founded Aberdeen Children's Theatre the following year, which attracted international recognition for its pioneering work. Hollingworth wrote a book of reminiscences about her life in 1997. There is a memorial plaque to her in the Children's Theatre on King Street.

Castlegate

Aberdeen Castle is no longer standing but the finely carved 17th century Mercat Cross on the cobblestones marks the site of its gate. Look out for **Mrs McGhie's** Pub✿, named after a 1770s Aberdeen innkeeper in the Castlegate who was known to run a good house. The bronze installation✿ of a woman surrounded by tins is of **Annie Murray Knight** (1906–1996) from nearby Torphins, who volunteered as a nurse in the Spanish Civil War. Her stories of Italian planes dropping sweet tins with bombs in them, which were then picked up by children who were killed and injured, is harrowing. The plaque on the installation quotes her words: 'I went to Spain because I believed in the cause of the Spanish Republican Government. I didn't believe in fascism and I had heard many stories of what happened to people who were under fascist rule.' Her letters are now held at the National Library of Scotland. Here you will also find a large monument✿ created from

Meredith Jemima Brown Chimney

a repurposed brick chimney to **Meredith Jemima Brown** (1845–1908), born in the city. Brown was concerned about the lives of factory girls in the East End of London, so she disguised herself as one of them and subsequently wrote the book *Only a Factory Girl* based on her experience. The proceeds of this book allowed her to set up the Shaftesbury Institute, which provided cheap beds for girls arriving in London as well as social facilities. There is a plaque to her at Dee Street.

Tolbooth Museum

This is one of Aberdeen's oldest buildings and houses a collection of memorabilia from the time it was a jail. Outside you will find a trio of memorials. The first is a statue✦ to **Elizabeth Latto Ewen** (1875–1965), Aberdeen's first female GP, who opened the city's first medical practice for women in 1896. She also became the first female member of the local branch of the British Medical Association. There is a plaque to her on the former ladies' medical practice in Chapel Street. The second statue✦ is to **Jessie Fraser** (1801–1875), shown clutching a bouquet of flowers at the end of a performance. This hugely popular actor and theatre manager formed the company that established the Scottish tradition of touring theatre. Jessie managed her own company at Aberdeen's Royal Opera House until 1853 and the city adored her. Throughout her career she was showered by gifts from potential suitors, as well as poetry – a line of which is on the base of the statue: 'Her form is divinely fair.' The last monument is a mural✦ with scenes from the life of **Sue Innes** (1948–2005), feminist, campaigner, author and teacher. In the revolutionary year of 1968, Innes abandoned her art school course in Aberdeen to travel to America, where she worked in a clinic in Haight-Ashbury, San Francisco, at the height of the hippy movement. She took part in anti-Vietnam peace campaigns, and demonstrated at the Democratic Convention in Chicago. In 1970 when she returned to study at Magdalene University, she was a fully-formed revolutionary feminist. Articulate and passionate, she became the subject of a series of posters by the artist Jurek Putter. After college she went on to work for BBC Radio Scotland, *Social Work Today* and as features writer and children's editor at the *Scotsman* weekend magazine. Latterly she became a columnist for *Scotland on Sunday* before quitting journalism to write extensively about women's social and political history. In later life she taught at the University of Glasgow and worked as an official reporter in the Scottish Parliament, taking up a post at Engender, the Scottish women's research and information organisation, just before she died. She was the co-editor of the first edition of the *Biographical Dictionary of Scottish Women*.

Magdalene Episcopal Cathedral 🔔

Inside this cathedral, you will find a bronze⚜ to the memory of **Hilda Wernham** (1916–1989), who pioneered 'wet shelters' in Aberdeen (for homeless people with alcohol problems) and once bathed a homeless man's feet in a prison cell while she was on her way to a ball. The altar⚜ on the east wall, which is always covered in flowers, is in memory of **Mary Helen Young** (1883–1945), a nurse and brave Resistance fighter during the Second World War who was arrested for helping British prisoners to escape Nazi-occupied France. She was killed in the gas chambers at Ravensbrück concentration camp. The French novelist Simone Saint-Clair, who was also an inmate at Ravensbrück, said of her, 'She always kept her chin up … all of us liked the little Scotswoman.' Also look out for the pew⚜ dedicated to **Lady May Baird**

(1901–1983), who moved to Aberdeen in 1937 where she held a number of positions in public life. She was a champion of health service improvement and became Chair of the North Eastern Hospital Board from 1947 to 1966, and Governor of the BBC in Scotland from 1966 to 1970. The pew is furnished with lavish cushions✣ embroidered with representations of some of her achievements. A street is named after her in the city and there is a yellow plaque in her memory on Albyn Place. She was also honoured as a Free Burgess of Aberdeen, a ceremonial honour bestowed by the city.

The church runs a non-denominational club for older members of the community✣ called the Christian Smith Social, named after **Christian Catherine Smith** (1844–1924), a minister's wife who was actively involved in philanthropic activities. She founded the Newhills Convalescent Home in 1874 'for the benefit of respectable persons in humble circumstances who appear to be falling into dishealth or are convalescing after non-infectious diseases'. She was involved in the management of the home until 1908. There is a stained glass window to her memory in the city's Newhills Parish Church.

Provost Skene's House

Dating from 1545, this is Aberdeen's oldest private house and is home to a painted gallery of religious images from the mid 17th century as well as a collection of costumes and archaeological exhibits. You will also find an exhibition✣ about the life of **Caroline Phillips** (1874–1956) from Kintore, near Aberdeen. She was a journalist at the *Aberdeen Daily Journal*, which was unusual for a woman in the early 20th century, and was also honorary secretary of the local suffragette branch. She helped to organise the suffragette march in Edinburgh in 1907 and was in charge of bringing suffragette speakers to Aberdeen including Emmeline Pankhurst and her daughters Sylvia and Christabel. The exhibit includes her articles, letters and photographs taken at marches and public meetings.

Sutherland College 🏛

This glorious edifice on Broad Street is the world's second largest granite building (after El Escorial in Madrid) and, founded in 1593, now houses Aberdeen City Council and some functions of the University of Aberdeen. The college is named after **Georgina Scott Sutherland** (1918–2014), a penniless wartime refugee who fled Hong Kong when the Second World War broke out. She married an Aberdeen businessman and later became a generous benefactor to Robert Gordon University (RGU) in the city – the couple donated their home to become the Scott Sutherland School of Architecture and the Georgina Scott Sutherland Learning Centre in the RGU library is also named after her. Georgina also helped to set up St John's Mountain Rescue Team and the St John's Nursing Home in the city. An intrepid traveller, she visited Antarctica when she was in her late 70s and swam in the sea.

Sutherland College houses several monuments, mostly to women associated with education in the city. Inside the front door you will find a concrete replica of a cleaners' set. 🧹 This is a reminder of **Sheena Grant** (1941–2010), whose childhood home was a tenement next to St Mary's Cathedral, where her grandmother worked as a cleaner. In 1984, Sheena followed her, taking a cleaning job at the university. She became chair of the Aberdeen branch of the workers' union where she stood up vociferously for the rights of the university's non-teaching staff, saying once that if a professor took a sabbatical no one missed him, but if the university cleaners didn't clean the toilets, the whole place would grind to a halt. The former senate room in Sutherland College is named after her.

The college also houses a lecture hall✴ named after **Barbara Blackwell** (1727–1793), who endowed a chair of chemistry as well as a prize for an English essay. Her husband had been principal of the college. Along the corridors you will find several small bronzes.✴ Look out for **Mary Esslemont** (1891–1984), who gained three degrees from Aberdeen University and was the first female president of the Student Representative Council. She was a GP who was particularly concerned with Aberdeen's poor, and was active in many areas, especially women's rights. Esslemont House – the college's halls of residence – are named after her and there is also a memorial plaque on her former home at Beechgrove Terrace. You will also find✴ **Rachel Annand Taylor** (1876–1960), who was one of the first women to study at Aberdeen University and went on to teach at the High School for Girls (in the building now occupied by Harlaw Academy, where there is a plaque to her). She published four volumes of poetry between 1904 and 1923, and books on the Italian Renaissance and the poet William Dunbar.

Lastly keep an eye out for the bronze✴ of **Marion Douglas, Lady Drum** (c1577–c1633), who funded Lady Drum's Hospital – a home for 'aged virgins' and widows – an early resource for female care at a time when unmarried or widowed women were often vulnerable. Lady Drum also intervened in the marital dispute of her granddaughter, Lady Ogilvie, who was being persecuted by her husband in the 1630s. She brought Lady Ogilvie to stay in her own house – an unusual intervention to help a married woman in distress. There is a plaque on Drum's Lane on the site of hospital and a board at Aberdeen Town House's Union Street entrance.

St Nicholas Kirk

This church houses Britain's largest bell. Founded in 1125 (as a Roman Catholic church) the building now comprises two 'sanctuaries' under one roof – the West and the East – one Church of Scotland and one United Reform Church. Services are all Reform but the split consecration of the two churches abides. Inside, you can still see the iron rings drilled into the walls where witches were tied up during the 17th century. Here you will find a plaque✸ to the memory of **Janet Wishart** (died 1597), who was burned as a witch after being found guilty of nineteen charges including cursing her son-in-law when she found out that he hit her daughter and causing the death of two fishermen. Her family were banished from coming within 10 miles of the city. Nearby there is a shrine✸ to **Margaret G Dale** (1862–1887), who died of typhoid at the age of only 25 in Buenos Aires. She went there in an attempt to earn enough money to study medicine: she had accepted a job there because the pay was higher in South America due to the threat of disease and she had no other way to procure money to fund her studies.

In the West Church look out for the stone memorial statue✸ to **Katherine Forbes, Lady Rothiemay** (c1583–c1652), who sought revenge when her eldest son died in a suspicious fire while her family was involved in a feud with neighbours. She caused so much disorder, sending men out to fight, that she was imprisoned in Edinburgh for two years until the king ordered her release. In 1642 she funded a school in Aberdeen, which continued until the wholesale re-organisation of the Education (Scotland) Act 1872. There is a commemorative board to her in Aberdeen Town Hall. Near the altar here you will also find a plaque✸ to **Annie Wilson** (c1891–1918) of Queen Alexandra's Royal Naval Nursing Service, who dedicated herself to the service of others during the First World War. Wilson is also named on the War Memorial in Monymusk.

Aberdeen Art Gallery

This gallery was purpose-built in 1884 to a neoclassical design; stop to throw a penny into the fountain in the central court by English sculptor **Barbara Hepworth** (1903–1975). Here it is also worth searching out the work✿ of Aberdeenshire artist **Eleanor Vere Boyle** (1825–1916), a hugely popular illustrator who specialised in detailed narrative images of fairy stories. EVB, as she signed herself, was patron of the Frome School of Art (she lived in Frome for part of her life) and the gallery has an extensive collection of her work. The Memorial Court in the gallery serves as Aberdeen's war memorial with the names of those remembered projected✿ in light on the walls, including many **heroines from the First and Second World Wars**. Also here note the plaque to Victorian women's rights activist Ishbel Maria Gordon (see page 271).

Belmont and Little Belmont

Opposite the art gallery is Aberdeen's bohemian quarter with cobbled streets that are home to several galleries, shops, cafes and restaurants, as well as Aberdeen's monthly farmers' market. Strolling by, you will find a huge stopwatch✿ in memory of **Isobel 'Quita' Barber** (1925–2013), a sprinter who competed at the 1952 Olympics. She ran 100 metres in 12.4 seconds. Near the stopwatch you can also see a bronze✿ which pays tribute to the area's fishing heritage – this is the mirror image of a bronze in Marischal Street, Peterhead. They were named by writer Peter James Buchan after his great-great-grandmother, 19th century fishwife **Jessie Buchan**, who was known as 'Fisher Jessie'. Fishwives used to travel into rural areas hawking fish from the creels on their backs or exchanging it for agricultural produce. This trade continued up to the 1950s.

In Belmont also take time to spot the mural✤ of TV personality **Isobel Barnett** (1918–1980), a doctor with a decade of appearances on the show *What's My Line* from 1953 to 1963. Here you will also find a plaque✤ quoting the words of **Anna Brown** (1747–1810), a singer and collector of Scots ballads whose work was used by Sir Walter Scott. She was cross with Scott because she felt he had quoted her improperly. Her work has been called 'exemplary' by scholars and is still studied. The plaque quotes one of her ballads:

> *I warn ye all ye gay ladies*
> *That wear scarlet an brown*
> *That ye dinna leave your father's house*
> *To follow young men frae town.*

Blackwell Gardens ▲

These sunken gardens, named after botanical illustrator **Elizabeth Blackwell** (1707–1758), feel a million miles away from the hustle and bustle of Aberdeen city centre. Born and educated in Aberdeen, Elizabeth illustrated *A Curious Herbal*, published in 125 weekly instalments between 1737 and 1739. She took the commission to free her husband, Alexander, from debtors' prison, engraving the copper printing plates for 500 images and text, and hand-colouring the printed illustrations. The herbal included exotic and unusual plants as well as indigenous ones. The book was hugely successful and subsequently went into translation. With Alexander's debts covered, he moved to Sweden where he became physician to Frederick I. However, in trying to secure a diplomatic position Alexander overstepped protocol and was beheaded for treason in 1747. Elizabeth has a genus of plants named after her, *Blackwellia* of the class and order *Dodecandria Pentagynia*, of which there are six sub species.

As you walk down the gardens' grand staircase notice the rises, which are carved like book spines❦, standing as a memorial to Aberdeen's most popular romantic novelist. Primary school teacher **Doris Davidson** (1922–2012), had so many rejection letters from publishers that she considered papering the toilet with them! Discouraged, she gave up writing for many years. When she finally managed to break into print her sagas appealed to generations of readers around the world. When a reader approached her hesitantly at a book signing Davidson told her 'It's no use being embarrassed to talk to me. I'm just an ordinary wifie.'

The flower beds in the sunken garden❦ are planted in memory of Aberdeen poet, novelist and reformer **Isabella Fyvie Mayo** (1843–1914), who used the pen name Edward Garrett. Mayo was the first woman elected to a public board in Aberdeen where she supported the rights of trade union members. She dedicated her life to activism – her home was an asylum for people from India and she opposed the Boer War despite people stoning the windows of her house for doing so. Here also, the rash of yellow beds❦ are planted in memory of **Betsy Whyte** (1919–1988), a storyteller from the travelling community. Her bestseller the *Yellow on the Broom* is a classic that has also been adapted for stage. Whyte was brought up in the age-old tradition of the 'mist people', moving around the country and settling down only during the winter. It was while the family were 'housed up' at this time of year that she received her education, attending village schools before winning a scholarship to Brechin High School, where she was the only traveller. She started writing about her childhood in the 1970s and as well *Yellow on the Broom* also produced another book, *Red Rowans and Wild Honey*.

The West End

Recently renovated, this part of town is considered the smart end of Union Street. Wander across to Bon Accord Square with its grassy central park and array of monuments. Here you will find the Skene Fountain✤ in memory of **Lilias Gillespie Skene** (1626–1697), a Quaker who wrote spiritual poetry and campaigned for religious freedom when a purge sent many of her friends to prison from 1676 to 1679. Gillespie Crescent and Gillespie Place are named after her and there is a plaque to her memory on the Quaker Meeting House in Crown Street.

In the park there is also a huge windchime✤ in memory of **Jeannie Robertson** (1908–1975), a member of the traveller community. She spent much of her childhood in Deeside and Perthshire, where she acquired a vast repertoire of traditional music. Discovered during the Scottish folk song revival of the 1950s, Robertson made a huge contribution and became internationally famous appearing in a documentary called *The Song Hunter* directed by David Attenborough. As well as classic ballads she sang bawdy songs like 'Never Wed an Old Man'. There is a plaque outside her former home at 90 Hilton Street.

Duthie Park

Take a stroll down to the banks of the Dee to this park and visit the Bristow-Fraser Hothouses✤, boasting cacti and exotic plants. In the hothouses look out for the display✤ about the life and work of **Mary Bristow** (1781–1805). With her friend (also thought to be her lover), **Elyza Fraser** (1734–1814), she travelled in Europe, keeping a notebook of visits to great gardens. She also played the piano, and dueted with Elyza, who played the violin. There is no conclusive evidence that Mary and Elyza were lovers but as it seems highly probable this display comes in for special treatment during Grampian Pride when it is festooned with rainbow ribbons. The gardens and parkland at Castle Fraser outside Aberdeen were designed and laid out by Bristow and are now known as Miss Bristow's Wood. If you visit Castle Fraser examples of her embroidery are preserved in the Worked Room.

Old Aberdeen
This leafy, cobbled suburb to the north of the town centre was an independent burgh until 1891 and houses the university library, outside which there is a lectern✷ used as a soap box for giving public speeches. This is dedicated to the memory of socialist activist **Christian Elizabeth Farquharson-Kennedy** (1870–1917), a teacher who famously gave socialist speeches from a soap box in the Castlegate. She was active in the carter's strike in 1897 and in 1900 attended the International Socialist Congress in Paris. A member of various political groups, including the British Socialist Party, the Working Women's Political Association and the Associated Women's Friendly Society, she was a Director of the Northern Co-operative Company. She was also a member of the Executive of the Scottish School Boards Association. As well as the statue there is a plaque to her on Westburn Drive.

King's College Chapel
This was the first building of the college to be completed in 1495. Inside you will find a lavish marble statue✷ of **Ishbel Maria Gordon, Lady Aberdeen** (1857–1939), a philanthropist and campaigner for women's occupational, social and political rights. She moved to Haddo House in Aberdeenshire after her marriage and travelled extensively in both Ireland and Canada. Wherever she went, Lady Aberdeen initiated and supported organisations for the

benefit of women, including the Aberdeen Ladies' Union, which provided educational and recreational facilities for working girls, and, in Canada, the Aberdeen Association and the Victorian Order of Nurses. In Ireland, she pioneered the Women's National Health Association for mothers and children and became president of the International Council of Women. In Scotland, she played a vital role in securing the ordination of women to the Church of Scotland ministry. There are two plaques to her – one at Aberdeen Art Gallery and one in Methlick Parish Church.

Also in the chapel seek out the prayer corner ✤ devoted to **Shirley Harrison** (1946–2012), a feisty adventurer who flew light aircraft, sailed the Atlantic from Lagos to Rio, drove rally cars and single-handedly managed her Aberdeenshire farm where she bred Aberdeen Angus cattle and conducted Scotland's first trial and harvest of genetically modified crops.

St Machar's Cathedral

One of Aberdeen's first granite buildings, the cathedral was founded by a follower of Columba (see page 185), who would no doubt be horrified to learn that the achievements of women are strongly commemorated inside. Here you will find a plaque to the memory of **Fenella Paton** (1901–1949), who came from a political family (her father was an MP). Fenella became an active member of the Women's Liberal Association and founded Aberdeen's first birth control clinic in 1926 with her own money, amid a storm of controversy. Her mother supported her pioneering work. Although Paton was in regular correspondence with women's rights campaigner Marie Stopes (see page 69) and the women supported each other, the clinic remained independent of Stopes's organisation. In 1935, Aberdeen Council partially funded the clinic and in 1948 Paton transferred it to the new National Health Service.

In the cathedral you will also find a plaque✤ to Aberdeen graduate **Margaret Masson Hardie Hasluck** (1885–1948), a geographer, linguist, archaeologist and scholar who undertook intelligence work during the First World War, advising on special operations in Albania where she stayed until Italy invaded in 1939. She is still honoured in Albania for her contribution. In 2010 a plaque was jointly unveiled on her former property there by her nephew John Donald Morrison Hardie and Qazim Sejdini, Mayor of Elbasan. Margaret was inducted as a Citizen of Honour because of 'her outstanding contribution to the public sphere of the city of Elbasan'. The Shtëpia e Shpresës (Home of Hope) Orphanage now occupies a building on the property.

Also look out for the beautiful ivory sculpture✤ of Mary Magdalene in the cathedral which is by **Gwynneth Holt** (1909–1995), a religious artist who lived in Aberdeen for twelve years. At the end of her time in the city she made her most famous statue, *Annunciation*. There is a plaque beneath the sculpture that bears Holt's words. 'Women are just as intelligent as men, and their contribution to art is just as valuable: They are not given a chance to take up art seriously.'

Seaton Park

This park to the north of the cathedral brings you to the bridge that spans the River Dee. It is said to have been the favourite place of Lord Byron, who spent much of his childhood in Aberdeen. In the park you will see the wonderful Pirrie Floral Clock✤ dedicated to **Mary Pirrie** (1821–1885), a botanist born in the city who published a lively book about flowers, grasses and shrubs in 1860 which included anecdotes and illustrations. It was recommended in its day as 'an excellent book for Young Ladies'.

The surrounding flowerbeds✤ are laid out according to the designs of **Kathleen Mann** (1908–2000), an embroiderer and teacher who was Head of Embroidery at Glasgow School of Art before she moved to Aberdeen to teach and write books. The flowers are chosen carefully to match her designs and the patterns are laid out on grids for planting – a fascinating process if you are in the park on the right day to catch it.

A short stroll away visit the Garden Music Hall⚜ named after **Mary Garden** (1874–1967), an internationally successful opera singer who trained in Paris, where she joined the Opéra-Comique. She sang the lead role in Gustave Charpentier's opera *Louise* in 1900 and enjoyed unrivalled success until her retirement in 1934. Mary Garden was Debussy's choice for the role of Melisande in his *Pelléas et Mélisande*. She moved to the USA in 1907, where she sang with the Manhattan Opera Company and the Chicago Opera Company before retiring to Aberdeen. She has a memorial stone in Craigie Gardens and there is a memorial plaque on her house at 41 Dee Street.

Aberdeen Beach and Queen's Links

Less than a mile from Union Street this gorgeous sweep of sand is lined by the Buchan Esplanade⚜, named after **Priscilla Buchan** (1915–1978), who was MP for Aberdeen until 1966 and then became the first woman to be appointed Deputy Speaker in the House of Lords. Buchan led the British negotiating team in Reykjavik during the cod war dispute over access to Icelandic fishing grounds in the 1970s and is considered a local heroine by the fishing community for her achievements. Along the esplanade you will find several plaques✤ set into the paving that contain the work of poet **Olive Fraser** (1909–1977), who won joint first in the 1951 poetry competition to mark the Festival

Margaret Penny Statue

of Britain. She went on to suffer a mental breakdown but continued to write until her death. Her poems were published mostly posthumously. One plaque reads:

In a' the lown air whaur delicht did rove
I kent my ain name.
My leal bairn, my dear luve,
My bairn come hame.

At the far end of Buchan Esplanade you will find a statue✦ of a woman bundled up in winter clothing and looking out to sea. This is of **Margaret Penny** (1812–1891), who was only twelve when she first made a voyage on her father's whaling ship to the Arctic. Penny was the first white women to winter in the Arctic (she did this twice) and she chronicled her encounters with the Inuit. Known as a 'petticoat whaler' she wrote that the Inuit were 'really the most interesting people, particularly the females'. She made many friends among them – they taught her the names of Arctic flowers and plants and in return she cooked for them.

To the north of the esplanade there are a number of golf courses. Look out for the flag✦ in the suffragette colours, which is raised on a pole just short of the private ground. The flag is maintained today by feminist groups in the city in memory of **Lilias Mitchell** (1884–1940), a suffragette organiser in Aberdeen who painted the marker flags at Balmoral Golf Course in suffragette colours as a protest. She also confronted Lord Asquith on Dornoch Golf Course and challenged his views on giving women the vote. In recent years these 'Lilias Standards'✦ have been known to appear at the Trump International Golf Links, though they are swiftly removed by staff.

Stonehaven

This harbour town hosts a folk festival in July and is the home of the deep fried Mars Bar, first made here in 1995. On the war memorial look out for **Sister Helen Milne** (c1886–1917) of the Queen Alexandra's Imperial Nursing Service in India who was born in the town. It is traditional to leave a poppy for her when you visit. Sister Helen is also included on the war memorial in St Catherine's Cathedral, Edinburgh. Stonehaven's bookshop is called Black Books✱, in memory of **Margaret Moyes Black** (1853–1935), a novelist and biographer who wrote her first novel, *In Glenoran*, under the pseudonym M B Fife. She went on to write nine more books, all of which are always in stock here. There are sometimes readings and discussion groups but it's worth popping in just to browse or to chat to the enthusiastic owner about Black's work.

Also look out for the local art gallery✱ which has some wonderful pictures by artist **Joan Eardley** (1921–1963) (see also page 103) who in addition to her well-known inner-city Glasgow scenes also painted landscapes of nearby Catterline with its heavy, leaden skies. Eardley studied at the Glasgow School of Art during the 1940s where she won the Sir James Guthrie Prize for a self-portrait. After graduation she decided she did not want to teach art and instead enrolled as a joiner's apprentice with a boat-building firm in Bearsden where she painted camouflage onto landing craft for the war effort. After the war she moved to Italy, returning first to Glasgow, where she set up a studio in working-class Townhead, and then to Catterline, which gradually became her home. In 2013 letters between Eardley and her lover Audrey Glover Walker (see page 103), a textile artist and the wife of a Scottish barrister, were released, shocking some in the art world.

Dunnottar Castle

This scenic cliff-edge ruin has appeared in movies including Zeffirelli's *Hamlet*. Look out for the stone in the church-yard in memory of the 122 Covenanters tortured here in 1685 for their religious beliefs, including 45 women. Here you will also find a cairn� in memory of **Barbara Strachan** a postmistress and Jacobite from Buchan who helped with the rebels' communications and is believed to have been a spy during the 1745 uprising. Donnottar Castle had an earlier impact on Scottish power and politics – during the 17th century it was the home of the Honours of Scotland (the country's regalia and crown jewels). The statue✝ of a woman guarding a casket is of **Christian Fletcher Grainger, Lady Abercrombie** (c1619–1691), who saved the Honours from Cromwell's troops during the English invasion of Scotland in 1651. As Cromwell advanced, the Honours had to be smuggled out of the castle and the wily Lady Abercrombie was entrusted to hide them. She buried them in Kinneff Church about 7 miles to the south. In 1661, the Scottish Parliament awarded her the substantial sum of 2,000 merks in recognition of her service.

Drum Castle

On Royal Deeside, Drum is a magnificent old Jacobite castle that is worth a visit to learn the story of one woman's bravery. Alexander Irvine, 17th Laird of Drum, was listed as 'never to be pardoned' by the Hanoverians, but he made his way back to Drum after Culloden and was hidden by his sister **Mary Irvine** (born c1702) in a secret room to avoid capture by the redcoats. The soldiers noticed the newly turned earth nearby where the family had buried their treasure – they took that but never found Alexander, who lived in the secret room for three years while Mary misdirected the redcoats again and again. The room was rediscovered by archaeologists in 2014. Mary was painted by Henry Raeburn and the portrait hangs here, in Drum Castle.

Crathes Castle

Follow the road 5 miles southwest from Drum Castle, to this 16th century ornate, granite tower house where you can enjoy the legacy of **Lady Sybil Burnett** (1889–1960), an influential gardener who from 1926 created the herbaceous borders and the yellow enclosure known as the Golden Garden, which is now a popular wedding venue. The castle is said to be haunted by the Green Lady who has been spotted by several guests, including Queen Victoria. The lady paces in front of the fireplace in one of the rooms and when the hearth was lifted for renovations in the 1800s, sure enough, there were the skeletal remains of a woman and child. Nobody knows who they were but rumours abound about servant girls falling pregnant on the estate and dying in childbirth.

Victoria's Castle 🏰

A royal residence since 1852, this grand home on the Balmoral Estate is known as 'Victoria's Castle' as she is the monarch most associated with it. The castle is on the site of a 16th century tower house. It is seldom open to visitors and, when it is, only a few rooms are on display, so instead head for the grounds, which are stunning and contain several monuments to royal women. Here you will find a cairn to **Princess Beatrice** (1857–1944), the youngest child of Queen Victoria, and her mother's companion. Beatrice acted as Victoria's secretary until the queen's death in 1901, and thereafter edited her mother's journals. The cairn is one of nine marking the lives of Queen Victoria and her children on the Balmoral Estate. There is also a plaque to Beatrice at Aberdeen Royal Infirmary recording that a ward there was once named in her honour.

Near the granite Crathie Church used by the estate and built with the proceeds of a bazaar in 1895, you will find a statue✦ to **Frances Harriett, Duchess of Richmond** (1824–1887), who was 'especially beloved for her kind-hearted interest in the poorer classes'. The duchess is remembered for her insistence that estate workers in nearby Fochabers should have better housing and, at her instruction, their thatched roofs were replaced with slate. These houses became known as 'the Duchess's Houses'. She had a bathhouse with six cubicles built in Castle Street in Fochabers using water piped from the local burn – cold baths cost 1d and hot baths 2d. The duchess also set up a library in the mid 1870s in the town. There is a stained glass window dedicated to her at Gordon Chapel, Fochabers, and a pyramid near the summit of Whiteash Hill known as the Duchess Monument. Also note the ornate garden gates✦ created to the designs of the embroidery of **May Sandison** (1825–1888). Based at Fyvie, Sandison was known for her exquisite work, which she sold to dignitaries like Queen Victoria and Lady Aberdeen. Examples of her work were exhibited at the Chicago International Exhibition in 1893.

Linn of Dee

Six miles from Balmoral is the Linn of Dee where the river plunges through a granite gorge. You can watch from the Higgins Bridge⛰, which is named after **Lizzie Higgins** (1929–1993), a famous ballad singer of traveller descent. When her school was bombed during the Second World

War, Lizzie moved with her mother to Banchory where she was bullied for her heritage. She left school at fifteen because of this, moving to Aberdeen to work in the fishing industry as a filleter. She took great pride in the fact she could lift her own weight in fish – 9 stone. Not wanting to distract attention from her mother's distinguished career as a singer, she did not sing in public until 1967, after which she recorded four albums and established herself as a leading singer in the folk movement. Her style was derived from the piping tradition, and audiences warmed to her particularly because of the stories she told in between the songs – about her life, her childhood and her heritage.

Kildrummy Castle and Gardens

This 13th century castle is now a ruin and over its history it has been the focus of much conflict between Scotland and England. Under siege several times it was here the family of Robert the Bruce were betrayed by the castle blacksmith, who was bribed by English forces to burn down the whole structure. Although partially successful, the story goes that he was caught and punished by having melted gold poured down his throat. Among the ruins, you will find a statue of **Christina Bruce** (1306–1357), a Scottish resistance leader who fought for the Bruce cause. As a child she was captured by the English army and sent to a nunnery. As an adult, she held Kildrummy Castle against John Balliol's men in 1333. The English force was later defeated by her husband at the Battle of Culblean.

Also within the crumbling castle walls look for the 'Caged Woman', a statue to the memory of **Isabella Douglas, Countess of Mar** (c1360–1408) who, unusually, negotiated her own second marriage after her husband was killed and Kildrummy Castle was captured. History often recounts the countess as a victim, painted into a corner by politics, though it is likely that she resisted, orchestrating a coup in 1404. You will notice the figure of the woman inside the cage is concealing something – nobody knows whether this is a dagger or a secret missive but there is no doubt Isabella Douglas had many secrets. A benefactor throughout Scotland, she donated to ecclesiastical institutions including Lindores Abbey in Fife.

Crovie

This beautiful, tiny village on the coast near Fraserburgh is so close to the sea that the doorsteps of many houses are washed by the tide. Take a seat at the lookout point and enjoy the view. The bench✦ here is dedicated to **Flora Garry** (1900–2000), a poet who is considered pioneering for her work in Doric, the Scots dialect spoken in the northeast. Flora was from Buchan and wrote about the area and its people, particularly its women. Her collection *Bennygoak* was published when she was a pensioner. When asked why it had taken her so long she replied 'happiness has no history, nor does it write poetry'.

Macduff

Macduff is connected to the town of Banff by the seven-arched Marischal Bridge⚑, named after Jean Marischal, a little-known late 18th century female Jacobite dramatist and novelist whose plays were backed by Jacobite patrons. Said to be influenced by the work of early novelist Samuel Richardson, she wrote books for young people and her work was brought out by the publishing pioneer, John Newbery.

Macduff is a 19th century spa town with an attractive harbour called the Princess Royal Basin which is named after **Louise** (1867–1931), the third child and eldest daughter of Edward VII and Queen Alexandra. When she married Alexander Duff, Earl of Fife, she lived at Mar Lodge in Braemar and Duff House in Banff and became a skilled salmon fisher.

At the harbour look out for the plaque✝ that commemorates **Elizabeth Mantell** (1941–1998), who became a missionary nurse at the Mulanje Mission Hospital and at Ekwendeni in Malawi. She returned to Macduff in 1996 and wrote her biography *Grace Sufficient*. There is a stained glass window to her memory in Macduff Parish Church. Also at the harbour there is a plaque✝ to **Isabel Kerr** (1875–1932), a medical missionary awarded the Kaiser-i-Hind Gold Medal in 1923 for her pioneering work with lepers in India. Of her 2,800 patients over 1,000 had their illness arrested – an astonishing feat at the time.

Further along the harbour throw a penny in the fountain in the maritime garden that commemorates **Jeannie Bodie** (c1891–1909), who died young of tuberculosis. The fountain was erected by her famous father, Walford Bodie, the Electrical Wizard of the North, a music hall entertainer whose act included illusions, ventriloquism and electrical tricks; he was a close friend of both Houdini and Charlie Chaplin. Several of his relatives performed with him, including Jeannie, who was present when medical students rioted during one of the shows in Glasgow in 1905. The students objected to Bodie claiming he was a doctor. His reputation never recovered after the riot and he decided to concentrate his career abroad.

During May, Macduff and Banff host the varied COAST Festival of the Visual Arts, which usually includes the re-telling of stories✝ by **Wendy de Rusett** (1945–2012), a children's storyteller who declared 'It's my life and it's my work. It's the best job I know.' De Rusett used mime, movement, voice, percussion, song, mask and puppetry in her performances. She would sit cross-legged on the floor, enthralling youngsters. She also performed for the elderly in sheltered housing and daycare centres in the area.

Cullen

Further along the coast and reached via a series of stunning viaducts is Cullen. It's worth stopping at to enjoy the sandy beach and visit Seatown, the picturesque harbour. The town is the home of the seafood soup, Cullen skink. On the harbour you will find a bronze statue✤ of a woman on a horse. This is to the memory of **Jo Pitt** (1979–2013), an equestrian Paralympian with cerebral palsy, who competed at the 2004 Paralympics in Athena. She was part of the para-equestrian dressage team that won gold at the 2010 World Equestrian Games and in 2013 she won the winter championship title for British Dressage.

It is also worth popping in to the Thomson Memorial Centre✤, which tells the story of **Margaret Thomson** (1902–1982), a doctor who, during the Second World War, survived a shipwreck only to be captured in a Japanese prisoner-of-war camp, where she used her medical knowledge to help keep other inmates alive. This hugely courageous woman retired to farm in nearby Huntly with her husband, who was a survivor of the Burma Railway. The centre tells the story of the women in these harrowing and inhumane camps.

Buckie

This fishing village is the starting point for the Speyside Way, which runs to the mouth of the river at Spey Bay. Here you will find the Scottish Dolphin Centre, which houses an exhibit❋ about the life and work of **Isabella Gordon** (1901–1988), a marine biologist who was the first full time female member of staff at the British Museum. Because of her extensive knowledge of crustaceans she became known as the 'Grand Old Lady of Carcinology'. Isabel carried out research, wrote extensively on many species of crustacean, and provided expertise and advice at the British Museum. She also travelled widely, most notably to Japan to meet Emperor Hirohito.

Setting off from Buckie you will find memorials along the Speyside Way to three women of local interest. The tree which is covered in tartan ribbons❋ commemorates the Highland dancer **Betty Jessiman** (1921–2012), who defied the conventional idea that competitive Highland dancing was a male preserve, first challenged by Jenny Douglas (see page 327). A trained dancer who entertained the troops during the Second World War, Jessiman became the first woman to compete and win at the championships at Nairn. She was also three times British Open Champion and went on to beat fifteen other dancers at the peak of their game to become Champion of Champions in 1962. Half way along the trail you will find a cairn❋ to the memory of **Mary Symon** (1863–1938), a renowned First World War poet from Dufftown. 'The Glen's Muster Roll', and 'The Soldiers' Cairn' brought her to popular notice, and remain much anthologised. She wrote in Scots and some of her words are carved into the cairn:

> *Gie me a hill wi' the heather on't,*
> *An' a reid sun drappin' doon,*
> *Or the mists o' the mornin' risin' saft*
> *Wi' the reek owre a wee grey toon.*

Towards the end of the walk, the bench♣ that overlooks the mouth of the Spey stands to the memory of **Georgiana McCrae** (1804–1890), who was brought up at nearby Gordon Castle; she was the illegitimate daughter of the Marquis of Huntly, who went on to become the Duke of Gordon. A talented painter, she showed her first picture at the age of twelve at the Royal Society's annual exhibition and went on to win a Silver Medal from the Society of Arts in 1820 and a Silver Palette the following year. She became a successful portrait and landscape painter. Georgiana was pressured into marrying a Protestant suitor (rather than the Catholic man she preferred) and after having several children and moving between Edinburgh and London for a decade, the couple emigrated to Australia where she painted members of the Bunurong tribe who lived near their house. Her home became a centre for social and cultural life in the colony with many distinguished visitors. Later, after moving to Melbourne during the gold rush, she painted less, heartbroken when she received no financial support from either her father's or stepmother's estate. She is commemorated in Australia, where her farmstead is now owned by the National Trust, and the bench here is visited often by Australians who leave mementos in her memory.

Elgin

The lively market town of Elgin, 12 miles west of Spey Bay, dates from the 13th century and is still set out in its original medieval street plan. Pop into the museum at the top of the High Street, which, established in 1843, is one of Scotland's first permanent public institutions for exhibiting objects of interest. Here you will find Pictish remains and a hoard of silver Roman coins as well as exhibits♣ about the lives of notable local woman. Look out for

Elizabeth Brodie, Duchess of Gordon (1794–1864), who lived in nearby Huntly Lodge. Deeply interested in religion, in 1845 she became a member of the Free Church of Scotland just after it was founded in Edinburgh. She contributed to many causes including founding the Gordon Schools in Huntly, where she provided an annual treat for all pupils. There is a portrait plaque of her in Huntly inside an arched pend in the centre of the town.

Also in Elgin Museum you will find a display✦ about the life of **Helen Cumming** (c1776–1874), the founder of Cardhu Distillery in Archiestown, who traded illegally from around 1811, selling bottles of whisky through the window of her farmhouse. Cumming's prowess at evading alcohol taxation was legendary. In a Victorian whisky encyclopaedia she was described as 'a most remarkable character and a woman of many resources; she possessed the courage and energy of a man, and in devices and plans to evade the gaugers, no man nor woman could equal her'. When the collectors arrived, she would disguise her distillery as a bakery, and serve tea while she surreptitiously raised a red flag above the farmhouse to signal that the tax men were in the area. The red flag✦ hoisted perpetually outside the museum is in memory of her and is known locally as Helen's Rag. Hers was one of the first distilleries to get a licence after the 1823 Excise Act. She never fully retired but handed over the running of Cardhu to her daughter-in-law, **Elizabeth Cumming** (died 1894), who was a savvy businesswoman in her own right and expanded the distillery's capacity, selling the old stills to what was then a brand-new distillery called Glenfiddich. In ten years she tripled production and began selling spirit as a blending component to Johnnie Walker and in 1893 she negotiated a deal in which Walker's bought the Cardhu Distillery outright.

South of Elgin it's worth taking a detour to see the memorial to the **Women's Land Army Scotland** by artist Peter Naylor on the hillside at Clochan on Crown Estate land. Unveiled by Prince Charles in 2012, this metal gate, made up of the silhouettes of cheering landgirls, captures the spirit of Second World War women in farming and has become a popular picnic spot.

Findhorn

This fishing village is home to the Findhorn Foundation, with beautiful and extensive gardens set up in 1962. Its co-founder **Eileen Caddy** (1917–2006) was a spiritual teacher and New Age author. The commune has received thousands of visitors from over 40 countries and is one of the UK's largest alternative spiritual communities nick-named 'the Vatican of the New Age'. On the edge of the foundation, the Moray Art Centre exhibits contemporary art as well as running art classes. Outside the centre, stop to take in the bronze statue❦ dedicated to former slave **Henrietta Fraser** – the map pattern on her skirt traces the route she was said to have taken. Henrietta was described in contemporary accounts as a 'free mulatto woman' who had been a plantation slave on the island of Nevis (in what was then Demerara in South America). Her husband, John, died at Findhorn in 1811 but the records do not reveal what happened to Henrietta, who, like so many black women, simply was not recorded.

Inverness and Central Highlands

O, 's mairg tha 'n-diugh feadh garbhlaich
'S ri falbhan am measg fraoich;
Us gathan grèin' gu h-òrbhuidh
A' dòrtadh air gach taobh.
Gum b' fheàrr a bhith air bàrr nan tonn
Air long nan cranna caol;
'S a' faicinn nan seòl ùra
Ri sùgradh anns a' ghaoith.

It is a pitiful day throughout the Highlands
To be walking amongst the heather
The rays of the sun in yellow gold,
Pouring down on everything.
Better to be at the crest of the wave
On a narrow-masted ship,
And to see the new sails
Flirting with the wind.

Màiri NicEalair 'Am Maraiche 's A leannan'
(Mary Mackeller 'The Mariner and His Love')

Jessie Kesson

Lost Witches Fountain

Skinner Boundstand

INVERNESS

Rita's Bridge

Elizabeth Craig's Dig for Victory Planting

Jessie Cavan's Japanese Garden

Jane Maxwell

Lady Loval Barracks

The Central Highlands were shaped by glaciers that cut through the landscape around 8000 BC. As a result, the scenery in this part of Scotland is dramatic, boasting the Great Glen, the River Spey, four long lochs and Britain's most extensive mountain range, the Cairngorms. The Highland capital of Inverness nestles like a lynchpin to the north. The landing point of St Triduana, who came to Scotland to spread Christianity sits to the south (see page 20).

Fort Mary ⚓

This town is named after **Queen Mary II** (1662–1694), who reigned with her husband, William, after her father, James II and VII, was deposed because of his Roman Catholic faith. When William led troops into Ireland, Mary garnered considerable respect for reigning alone, though the legacy of William and Mary's time on the throne still reverberates in Ireland today, with divisions between the Protestant and Catholic communities. Tucked below Ben Nevis on the banks of Loch Linnhe, lies Fort Mary's West Highland Museum, which houses exhibits about all aspects of Highland life alongside stories about the history of the region including the Spanish Armada galleon which is alleged to have sunk in Tobermory Bay, to the training of commandos in the area during the Second World War. Here you will also find a textile collection ✹ that was curated by **Margaret Swain** (1909–2002), who became interested in embroidery when she moved to Edinburgh in 1947 and was an advocate for Scotland's rich textile heritage, contributing to academic institutions and magazines as well as writing books – her most famous telling the story of Mary Queen of Scots and her household through the queen's textiles. A recognised expert in the field, Swain became a consultant at Holyroodhouse, the National Trust for Scotland and the National Museums Scotland. Look down at your feet to see the work✝ of **Mary Watts** (1849–1983), an artist, designer and craftworker who as well as creating carpets like those in the museum, embroidered banners, designed metalwork and made book bindings. Watts set up a pottery on the Aldourie Estate north of Fort Mary to encourage local people to develop their artistic skills. It ran from 1900 to 1908, and sold its output through the London store Liberty & Co.

Jacobite Steam Train

These vintage locomotives run excursions over the summer from Fort Mary railway station, and the trains always depart from the specially named Lady Anne Platform✝, named after **Lady Anne Mackintosh** (1723–1787). The Scots word 'gallus' might have been coined for Anne Mackintosh, who held opposing political opinions to her husband and backed the Jacobites (while he backed the Hanoverians) during the 1745 Jacobite uprising. As in any civil war, many families had members on opposite sides. Known as 'Colonel Anne', Lady Anne was only 22 years old when, while her husband was away on military service, she raised 300 relatives and tenants in support of Prince Charles Edward Stewart. They became known as Lady Mackintosh's Regiment. A year later, while hosting the prince, she assisted in the Rout of Moy, a ruse that fooled Hanoverian commander Lord Loudon into retreating, believing that his men were facing a larger Jacobite force than was actually stationed at Moy. Loudon had 1,500 men under his command – Lady Anne used a mere five to scare him away. The story goes that Anne Mackintosh's greeting to her husband after he was captured by the Jacobites

Lady Anne Platform

and released into her custody in 1746 was, 'Your servant, Captain.' He replied, 'Your servant, Colonel,' acknowledging her military nickname. After the Jacobite defeat at Culloden later that year, Lady Anne was arrested and held in Inverness for six weeks, but was released without charge. Her grave is in Leith, Edinburgh, and there is a stone raised to her just outside Braemar.

Glen Nevis

This is both the start of the ascent of Ben Nevis and the terminus of the West Highland Way. The rapids here are known as Deirdre's Tears✦, named after the tragic pre-Christian, Irish heroine **Deirdre of the Sorrows**, who is probably the best-known woman in ancient Celtic myth and folklore. When Deirdre was born it was foretold she would be a great beauty but would bring bloodshed to Ireland. As a result, it was decided that she would be raised in seclusion by a foster mother, and married to Conchobar, King of Ulster. However, she fell in love with a young warrior, Naoise, with whom she fled to Scotland. The eloping couple were hunted down, Naoise was murdered and Deirdre was forced to marry Conchobar after all. A year later, the king decided to pass her on to the warrior who had killed Naoise, and Deirdre committed suicide. Dùn Deardail, an Iron Age fort about 50 miles north of Glen Nevis at Inverfarigaig, is thought to be named after her. It is also worth visiting the Deirdre Shieling overlooking Loch Etive in nearby Argyll, which was the brainchild of artist **Evelyn Day MacDonald** (1934–2017). Designed by David Wilson the site is marked by an original standing stone with a Celtic bell over the doorway by Iona-based artist Mhairi Killen. Inside the shieling a sculpture of the couple is set into an alcove beside a sculpted stone bench made to a Celtic design. Deirdre's story has been told in poetry, drama and prose – most famously by J M Synge, whose play about Deirdre was finished after his death by W B Yeats. The Irish poem 'Deidre remembers a Scottish Glen', thought to be from the 14th century and written by an unknown poet, refers to eight local sites with specific connections to Deirdre.

As you reach the foot of Ben Nevis, which at nearly 4,500 feet is Britain's highest summit, stop at the Glen Nevis Visitor Centre to see the exhibition✦ on early 20th century climbing, which includes the stories of **Jane Inglis Clark** (1859–1950), her daughter **Mabel Jeffrey**, and **Lucy Smith**, who founded the Ladies Scottish Climbing Club in 1908 when they were excluded from the male-only preserve of the Scottish Mountaineering Club. It remains the oldest active climbing club exclusively for women in the world and in its first decades organised expeditions to the Alps, the Caucasus, Yosemite and the first all-woman expedition to the Himalayas in 1955. In 2008, president of the club Helen Steven recalled Mabel, the youngest founder, as 'very warm, rosy-cheeked and welcoming – she came into a room like a burst of sunshine. But she was hard as old nails.' There is a memorial hut ⌂ for climbers, erected in 1929 and named after Jane Inglis Clark, on the slopes of Ben Nevis.

Glencoe

Housed in a heather-thatched cottage that dates from 1720, the Glencoe Folk Museum on the Main Street hosts workshops and events, some related to the massacre of the MacDonald clan that took place in the Glen in 1692. Here you will find an extensive exhibit✦ about two local sisters who were fascinated by Scottish folk history, **Dorothea Stewart Murray** (1866–1937) and **Evelyn Stewart Murray**

(1868–1940). The daughters of the Duke of Atholl, both women launched themselves into documenting Scottish folk culture around their childhood home. Dorothea collected Scottish music and left her collection to the A K Bell Library in Perth. Evelyn collected 250 tales, legends and songs – the only 19th century collection by a woman and the only one from this region. The dialect of Perthshire Gaelic she spoke is no longer alive but you can listen to recordings of her speaking it in the exhibition. The museum stages storytelling events✴ that highlight the work of these two groundbreaking women.

Salacia's Staircase⚓

Three miles north of Fort Mary, the eight locks that make up Salacia's Staircase (named after the Roman goddess of the sea) allow the Caledonian Canal to rise up 64ft in less than half a mile. Six of these are named after writers from the area✴ and quotes from their work can be found on plaques✴ on the towpath, with its stunning views of Ben Nevis. The remaining two locks are currently in the process of being named, with researchers working at the Museum of Childhood in Edinburgh to uncover forgotten Scottish children's authors from the museum's extensive archive. The first, Hunter Lock, is named for **Mollie Hunter** (1922–2012), a children's fantasy writer who also wrote historical fiction for young adults and contemporary novels and plays. Many of her works are inspired by Scottish history, or by Scottish or Irish folklore, with elements of magic. She won the Carnegie Medal in 1974 for *The Stronghold*, a story of life and death in a prehistoric Orkney broch. A painting of her by Elizabeth Blackadder hangs in the National Portrait Gallery in Edinburgh. The lock is inscribed with her words 'If your imagination has not been captured by the lives of people who lived yesterday, how can you be aroused by those of today?'

Next is the Miller Lock, which memorialises **Lydia Miller** (1812–1876) from Lochinver, who wrote children's books about natural history and religion and even wrote a novel supporting the Free Church, *Passages in the Life of an English Heiress*, in 1847, which remains in print. She contributed to the *The Witness* magazine edited by her husband, the poet Hugh Miller, who killed himself at their home in Edinburgh on Christmas Eve 1856. She published his work posthumously and contributed to his biography. Her daughter, **Harriet Miller Davidson** (1839–1883), also became a writer for young adults and is commemorated here with a lock of her own. Harriet never got over her father's death and repeatedly wrote stories about daughters who were left by inspirational fathers. There is also the Wallace-Dunlop Lock named after children's illustrator **Marion Wallace-Dunlop** (1864–1942), who was born in the Highlands at Leys Castle. Wallace-Dunlop was an accomplished sculptor and artist but her passion was for equality and in 1909 she was arrested for damaging the stonework at the House of Commons by stencilling an extract from the Bill of Rights onto the wall. When she went on hunger strike in prison, the Home Secretary, Herbert Gladstone, told the prison governor she should be 'allowed to die' but later, amid fears of her becoming a martyr, she was released. Hunger striking became standard suffragette practice because of her. The next lock is named after **Sheila Stuart** (1892–1974), who wrote as Mary Westwood, best known for her hugely successful children's books about Alison and her brother Niall, based in northwest Scotland. Her character, Alison, was an inspiration to a generation of young female readers as an honest and brave girl who wasn't, in the words of one reader, 'too soppy'. Beside the Stuart Lock is a quotation from *Alison's Highland Holiday* – the first in her series, published in 1946. Sheila served as a nurse in the First World War with the Voluntary Aid Detachment and went on to train as a journalist in Dundee. The final named lock is for **Janet Caird** (1913–1992), a teacher who later in life became an incisive poet, children's writer, author of murder mysteries and thrillers, and critic who especially reviewed the work of female writers. She was President of the Inverness Association of University Women. The Caird lock is inscribed with an extract from her poem 'Heartbreak' about the Scottish landscape:

It is so beautiful
that picture postcards cannot cope.

Spean Bridge

This village is home to Scotland's monument in remembrance of those whose lives were impacted by slavery. Scots were heavily involved in the slave trade of the 18th and 19th centuries, when hundreds of thousands of men and women were put to work in Scots-run plantations in the colonies. Often, female slaves were sexually abused by their owners and managers. An exhibition on slavery held in 2011 involving the Centre for History in Dornoch and Edinburgh's Beltane Society featured correspondence detailing the keeping of sex slaves in this period. The letters were sent by Highland owners to relatives in Inverness and their contents were described as 'graphic' and 'disturbing' by researchers including details of owners sexually abusing female slaves on plantations in the West Indies.

The huge bronze Slavery Monument ⚓, featuring equal numbers of men and women, stands about a mile outside the village, overlooking the moor and mountains. On one side it is inscribed: 'To the many who will never be known to us because history has not recorded their lives. They were not considered important. We refuse to think of them that way.' On the other it bears the words of Irina Bokova, UNESCO Director-General from 2009 to 2015: 'All of humanity is part of this story, in its transgressions and good deeds.'

In the village itself there is a Visitors' Centre✷, which maps all the monuments and graves in Scotland to people thought to have been slaves. There is also an exhibition that looks frankly at Scotland's historical involvement in the slave trade across the world as well as examining and reconstructing the lives of some slaves from what is often a thin papertrail.

The visitor centre houses an area dedicated✷ to the life of **Susanne Kerr**, who died in 1814 a 'free mulatto woman' – it is thought likely she was previously enslaved. Illiterate, Susanne lived with George Inglis of Kingsmills in St Vincent and Demerara. The couple had several children who were sent to Scotland and became pupils at Inverness Royal Academy. Her daughter, **Helen Inglis** (died c1824), eloped in 1813 with a naval officer and lived in Port Glasgow and Greenock where they had several children. Ultimately, Susanne became the matriarch of a huge family that travelled and spread across the globe, though she died in Demerara and never visited Scotland. A copy of her will is in Inverness Museum.

Also on display✷ are papers from the J L M Mitchell Archive of the Gaelic Society of Inverness which were found to include Lieutenant Soirle MacDonald's request to take his daughter Mary's black slave with him to war in 1782. From Skye, MacDonald was a British Army officer during the American War of Independence. His daughter's slave was called **Doll** and she was likely to have been made to do domestic duties. Likewise, here you will find the story✴ of **Classinda Mary MacDonald** (1855–1906), the illegitimate daughter of her owner and a slave called Mary. Classinda was born a slave in Surinam and was freed in 1858 – which means she was owned illegally for the first three years of her life. She came to Scotland with her father and was brought up in Nairn – her guardian was the headteacher of Nairn Academy. On her death, her name was added to her father's grave in Logierait, Perthshire.

The visitor's centre honours the work of Dr David Alston along with other scholars who pioneered research on this difficult subject. Alston is quoted as saying 'I gradually noticed more and more local connections with the Caribbean, including references on gravestones. Slowly it became clear just how many Highland Scots had connections to slave-worked plantations and how many children were born to these Highlanders and either enslaved or "free coloured" women.' Further research led Dr Alston to find that almost every prominent school in the Highlands had black pupils on its roll at some time between 1790 and 1830. The centre's archive undertakes ongoing research about Scotland's connection to slavery and has a comprehensive database of names of slaves connected to Scottish owners – for many of their descendants the names are all that remain (see pages 59 and 109).

Scota🏛

This scenic village at the southern tip of the 23 mile long Loch Ness is named after the eponymous ancestor of the Scoti – the Latin name for the Gaels which was first used in the 3rd century. **Scota** was a pseudo-historical woman dating from 500 BC who entered the realm of legend.

She had a son, Goídel Glas, who lent his name to subsequent generations of Gaels, and who (it is said) created the Gaelic language by combining the best features of the 72 languages then in existence. Scota is believed to be buried just outside Tralee in Ireland, where a ring of stones marks her grave. The village is home to Coille Scota✝ (Scota's Wood), a national monument to the Gaelic language. It is made up of eighteen varieties of trees and shrubs – one for each letter in the Gaelic alphabet. Hidden deep within the trees is a commemorative stone sculpture✝ in the shape of a sword, engraved with a short biography of **Lady Agnes Campbell** (c1525–1601) in English, Gaelic and Latin – she spoke all three languages fluently. She is credited as a central figure in the rebellion against English troops in Ireland in the 16th century and negotiated with Lord Sydney after the Desmond Rebellion in Munster. Gaelic law allowed wives control over their dowry money and their own troops and Lady Agnes commanded over 1,200 men in her own right.

In Scota's Wood you will also find a cairn✝ to **Màiri NicEalair** (Mary Mackeller) (1834–1890), a poet and Honorary Bard to the Gaelic Society of Inverness from 1876 to 1890, who was an expert in the folklore of Lochaber. She translated Queen Victoria's second series of *Leaves from our Journal in the Highlands* into Gaelic. There is also a statue✝ of **Jessie MacLachlan** (1866–1916), a hugely famous singer from Mull known as the Scots Prima Donna who toured the world and sang in both Scots and Gaelic at Victoria's Castle on the Balmoral Estate in 1892 – the first performer to do so. In 1899 Jessie made the first commercial gramophone recording of a Gaelic song, performing 'Ho Rò Mo Nighean Donn Bhòidheach' ('Ho ro my beautiful brown-haired maiden') to a piano accompaniment.

Loch Ness

The picture-postcard ruin of Urquhart Castle sits on the banks of Loch Ness. Nearby you will find a nature walk⚘ interspersed with information about three women from the area whose work has impacted our understanding of the environment.

Mary McCallum Webster (1906–1985) was a self-taught botanist. Initially she trained as a children's nurse and then joined the Auxiliary Territorial Service at the outbreak of the Second World War and was trained as a cook at Aldershot. After the war she spent her summers walking a hundred miles a week, recording plant species across the north of Scotland for the *Atlas of British Flora*. In 1966 she moved to Moray to produce *Flora of Moray, Nairn and East Inverness*, which was published in 1978. There is a stone raised to her in Culbin Forest where her ashes were scattered, at her request, among the wintergreens, her favourite plants.

As part of the walk you will also find out about the life and work of **Ursula Duncan** (1910–1985), whose books *Flora of Angus* and *Flora of Easter Ross* led to her being awarded the Bloomer Medal from the Linnean Society for her contribution to biological knowledge. Her passion for botany was lifelong – her nineteenth birthday present from her father was a dissecting microscope so that she could study mosses. She was particularly interested in lichens and she later wrote two books on the subject. During the Second World War she worked at the censorship department in Inverness, overseeing the forces' mail. When she died, Ursula donated her herbarium of vascular plants to Dundee University, and her bryophytes and lichens to the Royal Botanic Garden in Edinburgh.

Also, from an earlier era, the walk features drawings by **Eliza Gordon-Cumming** (1798–1842), a fossil enthusiast and illustrator who collected a large number of specimens of fossilised fish from the Devonian period. The famous geologist Louis Agassiz corresponded with Eliza and named a species in her honour after he visited her at nearby Altyre. Eliza instructed workers in the estate's quarries to bring her any fossils they discovered and she identified several exciting finds this way. She died after giving birth to her thirteenth child and left bequests of fossils to several institutions.

Also at Loch Ness, further north near Abriachan, is a large stone hollow filled with water known as St Enoch's font stone♠ (see page 100). It is considered lucky for women in childbirth and many collect the water to act as a charm.

Inverness

The striking outline of Inverness Castle looms over the only city in the Highlands. Today this red sandstone building is home to the Inverness High Court. Outside you will find a large bronze statue⚜ of novelist, radio producer and playwright **Jessie Kesson** (1916–1994), who was born in a workhouse in the city and brought up in an orphanage from the age of eight. Her writings include *The White Bird Passes*, filmed for the BBC in 1980, *Glitter of Mica*, the award-winning film *Another Time, Another Place* and *Where the Apple Ripens*. As well as writing novels, she also wrote over 100 plays for radio. A labourer's wife, her writings about the passing seasons in the Highlands are treasured by her fans. In 2000, Isobel Murray's biography *Jessie Kesson: Writing Her Life*, won the National Library of Scotland/Saltire Research Book of the Year.

Inverness Museum and Art Gallery

This museum has a great collection about the social

history of the Highlands. Look out for the exhibit✷ about **Christian Milne** (1772–c1816) who, born in Inverness, was a servant of the Principal of the University of Aberdeen. She wrote poetry and songs in English and in Scots. Some were personal but others were addressed to famous men including Burns and Napoleon Bonaparte. 'The Wounded Soldier', generally thought her best poem, berates the ruling class:

Ah! little reckon they the woe
To many thousands wrought,
Who bleed and die, to crown their brow
With laurels dearly bought!

She brought out only one book in her lifetime and with a subscription list of 500 achieved sales of 600 copies. She invested her £100 profit in a boat which her husband then captained. In the museum you will also find✷ fascinating information about the life of **Eveline Barron** (1913–1990), owner and editor of the *Inverness Courier*, who was renowned for her forthright views and her fiercely independent editorial policy, as well as✷ **Elizabeth MacKintosh** (1896–1952), a successful novelist and playwright born in the city, who was extremely private (she wrote as Josephine Tey and Gordon Daviot). Her novel *The Daughter of Time* was voted the greatest ever mystery novel by the Crime Writers Association in 1990. Her play *Richard of Bordeaux*, which was directed by and starred the young John Gielgud, ran for fourteen months in London's West End, providing Gielgud with his first theatrical success. When she died she left her entire estate to the National Trust.

As well as archive material the museum houses a photographic display✷ of the work of **Mary** (or M E M) **Donaldson** (1876–1958), a writer and photographer who took over 1,000 plates of early 20th century life in the Highlands. More than 100 are held in the National Museums of Scotland. A devotee of the high church, she dressed in male clothing and was known affectionately by the children of her many friends as 'Uncle Tonal'. The illustrator **Isabel Bonus** (1875–1941), lived with her at Sanna Beag in the West Highlands and the women are buried together in the graveyard at Oban.

Also look out here for the exhibition❦ detailing the accomplishments of **Elizabeth Hilda Lockhart Lorimer** (1873–1954), a classical scholar whose best-known work was in the field of Homeric archaeology and ancient Greece but who also published about Turkey, Albania and what was then Yugoslavia. During her time in Oxford she was nicknamed Highland Hilda because of her Scottish background.

Old High Church
Founded in 1171 this church has a chequered history, including being co-opted as a prison for the Jacobite soldiers who survived Culloden. Several of these men were condemned to death – a sentence that was carried out in the church grounds. Today you can still see bullet holes in some of the gravestones, which stood behind the firing line, and one gravestone has an indent on which a Hanoverian soldier could rest his rifle while aiming at the condemned Jacobite standing or sitting on the gravestone opposite. For a more peaceful memorial, you can rest on a beautiful wrought iron bench❦ composed of musical notes, which is in memory of **Mildred Bowes Lyon** (1868–1897), who was brought up at Glamis Castle. When her husband was having his 12th century home remodelled, he fashioned a music room next to their bedroom for her. She composed two operas, which were performed in

Florence and, after her death, at a concert in the presence of Emperor Frederick of Germany in Bordighera, on the French/Italian border. Inside the church look for the small altar✤ to **Jane Waterston** (1843–1905), a missionary born in Inverness and one of the first fourteen students at the London School of Medicine for Women. After graduating she went to South Africa where she was the first female physician in the country. She set up a free dispensary in Cape Town for women and children and was a proponent of a non-racially segregated South Africa. She joined the struggle for women's rights and was given the South African name of Noqataka, 'the mother of activity'.

Mary of the Cross ▲

Opened in 1837, this church was recently rededicated✤ to **Mary MacKillop** or Mary of the Cross (1842–1909), an Australian Catholic nun of Scottish descent who was beatified in 1995 and canonised in 2010. Mother Mary founded over 40 schools and welfare institutions across Australia and New Zealand. Her order – the Josephites – were known as the 'Brown Joeys' because of their plain brown habits. Mary was excommunicated after a dispute with a bishop in 1871, which was later thought to be because she had played a part in uncovering sexual abuse. During this time she sought refuge with a Jewish family and was sheltered by Jesuits. By 1875 she had been reinstated and went on to set up more schools and found a convent at Petersburg. There is a shrine to her at the church in Roybridge in Inverness-shire (where her family came from, and where she visited in the 1870s). Look out also for the plaque✤ in the church dedicated to **Henrietta Stewart, Countess and Marchioness of Huntly** (1573–1642), who was the darling of James IV's court. Henrietta energetically looked after her estates while her husband was banished for his religious beliefs, until finally, persecuted by the Covenanting Kirk for her Catholic faith, she fled to France.

Ness Islands

This beautiful park comprises several islands off the west bank of the River Ness, linked by footbridges. Look out for Rita's Bridge🔊, dedicated to the novelist, playwright and essayist **Eliza Humphries** (1850–1938), who wrote over 120 works – often using the penname 'Rita'. Born in Inverness, she lived in London and travelled widely in India, Australia and all over Europe, where she researched material for her novels. Her most popular, *Peg the Rake*, sold over 160,000 copies – a huge circulation that put Rita firmly among the bestsellers of her day. Her stories were also widely translated. Queen Mary was a fan and ordered a complete set of Humphries's books.

In the park also look out for the beautiful flowerbeds🌺 dedicated to **Barbara Burnett-Stuart** (1917–2012), who came out as a debutante just before the Second World War. She was a journalist who became *Vogue*'s war correspondent from 1946, reporting on post-war Europe from Vienna and sending home news of the glamorous Viennese nightlife enjoyed by British, American and Russian officers, including a nightclub where, as a finale, the star of the show arrived naked on stage on the back of a baby elephant. Later Burnett-Stuart became women's editor for *Farmers Weekly*, as well as writing non-fiction. She often used male pen names. Towards the end of her life she became a supporter of the Samaritans in the Highlands.

Beside the Burnett-Stuart flowerbeds you will find a statue🌺 of **Elspet Gray, Lady Rix** (1929–2013), an actor who appeared in the films *Goodbye Mr Chips* and *Four Weddings and a Funeral* as well as on television in *Blackadder*, *Tenko* and *Dr Who*. Gray, who had a daughter

Babe in the Burn

with Down's Syndrome, also campaigned throughout her life for people with learning difficulties.

Walking on, the Skinner Bandstand�֍ nearby is in memory of **Mabel Skinner** (1912–1996), the first communist councillor on Inverness Town Council. Heavily involved in the anti-Apartheid movement and CND she also sat on the board of the 7:84 Theatre Company. The bandstand is often used for political meetings. However, you mustn't leave the Ness Islands without visiting the installation known locally as the 'babe in the burn'.✖ This is a prone elongated female figure with the water flowing over her and commemorates **Mairi Chisholm** (1896–1981) a photographer, nurse and ambulance driver in the First World War who was one of the 'Madonnas of Pervyse' alongside her friend **Elsie Knocker** (1884–1978). Mairi was recruited by a doctor who saw her riding her motorbike through traffic in London where she had volunteered as a courier for the Women's Emergency Corps. Impressed by her ability to negotiate hairpin bends, he recruited her as a driver for the Flying Ambulance Corps in Flanders. The women set up a clinic in a cellar near the Belgian front line and Elsie taught Mairi basic first aid. For her bravery in service and often under fire, Mairi was awarded the Order of Leopold II in 1915, the Queen Elisabeth Medal from Belgium in 1915, the Military Medal in 1917, the 1914 Star in 1917 and the Order of St John of Jerusalem in 1918. During the war she contracted septicaemia and was left with a weak heart, which she deemed the result of 'humping men on my back'. The women were sent home in March 1918 after they were gassed using mustard and arsenic. 'If it had been pure mustard we would have been dead,' Mairi recalled in 1976. 'But the arsenic has been a bother, definitely, because it did [my] insides in for quite a long time'. The 'babe in the burn' is a focus for commemoration on

Armistice Day when the river runs with floods of poppies thrown in by well-wishers, some of whom remember Mairi who after the war ran a poultry farm at Cantray outside Inverness.

Cawdor Castle

This beautifully restored 14th century castle is worth visiting for its formal flower garden and its walled garden dating from the 1620s. Head first, however, for the wild flower garden where you will find a bronze throne✦ in tribute to **Gruoch**, the 11th century Scottish queen who is said to be the inspiration for Shakespeare's Lady Macbeth. Little is known about her real life apart from the fact that she was one of many royals who endowed the Culdee Monastery at Loch Leven. Still, many writers have taken inspiration from her legend and she appears in Dorothy Dunnett's (see page 24) 1982 novel *King Hereafter*, which topped the *New York Times* bestseller list, and David Grieg's 2010 play *Dunsinane*. The throne is believed to be lucky: make a wish while seated on it and it will almost certainly be granted. But beware: it is said that wishes made for selfish reasons will come back to haunt you.

Cawdor Castle is also the setting for Gormla's Light✦, Scotland's witches' memorial. This is an event which takes place every full moon when, as soon as it gets dark, local women light torches along the turrets, creating a burning outline of the castle. Every month in all weathers, a crowd gathers to watch the flames. The display is named for **Gormla**, a generic 17th century witch figure (the name means 'the blue-eyed'). Traditionally it was believed that Gormla had significant influence, giving valued advice to Cameron of Lochiel and being one of the witches who brought about the drowning of MacLeod of Raasay in

Gruoch's Throne

1671. Associated with Lochaber, only a few miles away, local storytellers often include Gormla stories in their repertoire at Hallowe'en when Cawdor Castle hosts a festival✦ of celebration and mourning for the lives of the women that were lost. The focal points of these events is the Larner Address✦ named after **Christina Larner** (1933–1983), a historian and expert on the Scottish witch trials of the 16th and 17th centuries. She was the first to see the hunts as 'a rearguard action against the emergence of women as independent adults' and her theories have since been accepted into academic canon, and form the basis for these talks by speakers from across the world.

The Lost Witches Fountain✦ at the castle is dedicated to those whose fate is simply unknown, like **Isobel Gowdie** who was tried in 1662 and confessed in Auldearn, north of Inverness, without being tortured. Gowdie's confession painted a lurid picture of witchcraft: using voodoo dolls to cast hexes, flying to a Witches' Sabbath on a broomstick, and exhuming corpses to make the harvest fail. Isobel's fate is intertwined with that of **Christian Caldwell** (known as John Dickson), a woman who, dressed as a man, was engaged as a witchfinder for the salary of 6 shillings a day. It is believed it was Caldwell who accused Isobel. Later Caldwell was unmasked as a woman and was prosecuted for 'false accusation, torture and causing the death of innocent people in Moray'; she was deported to Barbados – a happier fate than many of her victims.

The Lost Witches Fountain is the starting point of the 2 mile Witches' Trail✦ which will lead you around several sites of interest in the area, culminating at another witches' monument at the now-ruined late 13th century parish church at Bareven, which was abandoned in 1619. Known as the House of Lament✦ it is dedicated particularly to those **women who were healers**. A sculptural wall of charred wood references the burning and torture with fire of so many innocents. The smell here is unique. The charred wood is overlaid by a rack with bouquets of dried herbs to echo those that might have appeared in the dwellings of these lost healers. Plants include mosses, lichens, verveine, sage, lavender, seaweed, ferns, pine, hazel, lovage, rowan, ivy, burdock, heather, bog myrtle and thistle. Visitors are encouraged to tie their own herbs onto the rack in remembrance. This is an evocative memorial, designed by scent writer Alex Musgrave, that fragrances the air around the abandoned church with the memory of an intimate and often secretive oral tradition among the women. The House of Lament is a particular place of pilgrimage for the Pagan community during the Samhain festival (Hallowe'en). Musgrave intended the memorial to be 'stark and emotional' saying that 'Healing the now can only be achieved if healing from the past is heeded.'

Other sites of interest about the witches in the wider Highland area can be reached by car including the Creag nam Bam (Hill of the Women) near Ballater, where in 1603 **Kitty Rankine** was burned as a witch. Said to have second sight, Kitty was charged with causing a storm at sea in which the Laird of Abergeldie Castle drowned. The 400th anniversary of her execution was marked in 2003 by a bonfire. Also take in the stone outside the police station in Forres marking the place a barrel containing a witch's body is said to be buried. From Cluny Hill, witches were rolled in stout barrels through which spikes were driven. Where the barrels stopped, they were burned, and the remains then buried. While there are memorials to witches across the country, these particular monuments have a resonance attracting thousands of visitors every year and provide an important focus for remembrance of the witch trials in Scotland, which were among the worst in Europe.

Nairn

Nairn, the driest and sunniest place in Scotland, is a popular holiday destination with more than its fair share of fish and chip shops and ice cream parlours. At the town's harbour pause at the 2007 Black Isle bronze memorial by sculptors Ginny Hutchison and Charles Engebretson to the historic **fishwives of Nairn**. When the town's fishing industry was at its height in the late 19th century, these women gathered bait and durkins (pine cones for smoking fish), baited lines, and prepared and smoked fish, including the famous 'Nairn Spelding' or salted herrings. They then sold them in the local area from the creel on their backs. It was a backbreaking existence. The figure in the memorial is based on a real woman – **Annie Ralph** (c1875–c1950) one of the last to undertake the job, which faded out slowly from the outbreak of the First World War until commercial fishing put paid to it completely in the 1930s.

Dufftown

The volunteer-run Dufftown Whisky Museum has an array of illegal whisky distilling equipment and some beautiful old photographs of Strathspey distilleries. Look outside the museum for the small Japanese Garden✿ containing information and artefacts from the life of female whisky pioneer **Jessie Cowan** (1896–1961), known as Rita, co-founder of Nikka Whisky in Japan. Jessie married Glasgow University student Masataka Taketsuru in a simple ceremony in 1920 and the couple moved to Japan that year to open a distillery in Yoichi. Using an inheritance she received from relatives, Jessie established the Rita Nursery for local children in Yoichi and today in the town Rita Road is named after her. In Kirkintilloch (where she was born) in 2018 an exhibition of prints about her life by artist Elspeth Lamb were put on display as part of a larger project to commemorate Jessie's life.

Grantown-on-Spey

On its pretty central square surrounded by Georgian buildings, look out for the legacy of a local woman who was involved in the food industry. The herb garden and Second World War Dig for Victory planting❦ (cared for by a local school) is in memory of **Elizabeth Craig** (1883–1980), a cookery writer and journalist who wrote 40 books. She was an expert in wartime diets based on rationing and introduced recipes she had found on her travels abroad into the repertoire of everyday cooks, widening post-war Britain's culinary horizons.

Kingussie

Kingussie's main tourist attraction, the Lady Lovat Barracks🏛, is named after **Elizabeth Stewart, Lady Lovat, Countess of Lennox and March and Countess of Arran** (c1554–c1595), who jointly governed the realm with her husband during the last years of James VI's majority. Beyond the barracks, visit the statue❦ on the high street of **Jane Maxwell** (c1749–1812), a great beauty who became Duchess of Gordon in 1767 when she married the 4th Duke. Notice that in the statue she is wearing gloves – as the Duchess always did after losing a finger in a childhood accident. She also wore a prosthetic wooden finger. With her husband, Jane founded the regiment that went on to become the Gordon Highlanders in 1881. When she moved to London she became a confidante of William Pitt, the Prime Minister, and a lively member of London

Tory society – it is said King George III adored her. However, she continued to be active in the management of the Gordon estates and was influenced by contemporary ideas on agricultural improvement. She was key in introducing flax (which was grown for the linen industry), in establishing the village at Kingussie, and in instituting the Badenoch and Strathspey Farming Society in 1803. By 1804 she had become estranged from her husband and divided her time between London, Edinburgh, and a small house at Kinrara where she was buried. There is a stone memorial to her there.

Also in Kingussie look out for the cairn✦ built to the memory of **Evelina Haverfield** (1867–1920), a suffragette from the town who once assaulted a police officer at a demonstration and when questioned about her actions afterwards said 'Next time I will bring a revolver.' Evelina worked as a nurse in Serbia during the First World War. After the war, she returned to Serbia with her companion, **Vera Home**, known as Jack, to set up an orphanage. She died there of pneumonia a few years later and Jack moved to Kirkcudbright on her death.

Newtownmore

The outdoor Highland Folk Museum in Newtonmore is a living history museum with a working croft and sawmill, and a church where concerts are often staged. Pivotal in setting up the museum in 1935 (which originally was located on Iona) was the visionary **Isabel Frances Grant** (1887–1983), a scholar of Highland history and folklore who worked for economist John Maynard Keynes as a researcher. Her published work was key in establishing the Scottish Highlands as a serious subject for modern scholarship. The new purpose-built collections storage facility and conference venue for the museum, called Am Fasgadh, was completed in 2013. In 2015 the collections at the Highland Folk Museum received official recognition from Museums Galleries Scotland and the Scottish Government as a Nationally Significant Collection.

Performance is key to the experience of this museum. Try to catch a recital✷ of the work of **Màiri Nic a' Chléirich (Mary Clark)** (1740–c1815), a Gaelic poet with only seven poems surviving from her repertoire. She was known as Bean Thorra Dhamh (the Woman of Torra Damh), and was unrelentingly critical of the existing social order. Or take in the words✷ of **Elizabeth Grant of Rothiemurchus** (1797–1885), a diarist who brought to life her upbringing on an Inverness-shire estate as well as her travels around the world including time in India, France and Ireland. Her *Memoirs of a Highland Lady* was published after her death and was so popular it ran through four editions in a year.

Northern Highlands and Islands

I see the roads I take every day
over grey-green Sleat, lochan-lit,
look over Glenelg and horned Beinn Sgritheall
to Loch Hourn and Loch Nevis carving up the coast,
to the folding Cuillins folded into cloud.

Meg Bateman 'From Beinn Aslaig'

Brenhilda & Aird the Deepminded

Emigration Heritage Centre

Flora MacDonald Brae

Lady Grange Altar

Resistance Monument

Sileas Waterfall

MALLAIG

Nan Eachainn Fhionnlaigh's Well

Glenfinnan Monument

The history of the Highlands includes tumultuous events that mirror the dramatic scenery of gorse-carpeted crags and glorious white-sand beaches. The landscape here is mythic in proportion so it is here you will find monuments to many ancient women as well as those who were subject to and stood up to some of the seachanges in Highland life over the last three hundred years.

Glenfinnan

Start your journey at the village of Glenfinnan, which lies on the Road to the Isles. This is where Jean Cameron (see page 102) raised Bonnie Prince Charlie's standard to rally Jacobite troops at the start of his campaign. In the centre of the village you will find the Glenfinnan Monument topped by the statue of a Highland woman.✦ This monument is dedicated to the terrible aftermath of the Jacobite defeat in 1746 when, unopposed, the government sent troops across Scotland, punishing anyone suspected of Jacobite sympathies. As well as chasing down Jacobite soldiers, killing cattle and burning crofts, the Duke of Cumberland's troops raped many Highland women as part of a strategic campaign of suppression. This monument stands to their suffering and bears the words of **Catriona Nic Fhearghais**'s song written on the death of her husband at Culloden, 'Mo Rùn Geal Òg' – 'My Fair Young Love'. There is a standing stone marking the site of Catriona Nic Fhearghais's cottage near Struy, a couple of hours drive north of Glenfinnan.

There is no record of how many women were raped during the time of Cumberland's oversight, but the four Highland counties are estimated to have been home to over 160,000 women in the period, and military historians estimate that to be effective such a strategy would have to abuse 10 per cent of the female population. That these actions were considered necessary to 'civilise' the Highlands is particularly repellent, with even one rape being a heinous act, never mind thousands. Because these women spoke Gaelic they were considered 'barbarous savages' and were vilified in the Hanoverian press. No records remain because of the stigma involved and the oral nature of Gaelic culture in the period so we will never know the true extent of the crime. Today, people leave flowers at the monument to mark the suffering of a large portion of the female population of the Highlands.

Arisaig

Arisaig means 'the safe place' in Gaelic and comprises several houses scattered around a peaceful sandy bay. This is the starting point for an 8 mile stretch of coastline from where you can sometimes spot seals. In the village, look for the monument ✤ to **Jenny Douglas**, depicted dancing in Highland dress. In the late 19th century she was the first woman to enter a Highland dance competition which was, at the time, an exclusively male preserve. The famous Highland Fling was originally danced in imitation of a courting stag, and therefore considered masculine. However, as female dancers were not expressly forbidden in the rules of the competition, Jenny put herself forward and went on to win several events. The costume she wore (and the costume still worn by Highland dancers today) was originally male dress. Since her bold action, the number of women participating in the sport has increased dramatically and today in excess of 95 per cent of all Highland dancers are female (see **Betty Jessiman** page 285).

Mallaig

This historic village remains home to an active fishing community and is the embarkation point for the ferry to Skye. Outside the Mallaig Heritage Centre look out for the small garden❦ in memory of **Elizabeth Harvey Odling** (1925–2004), an artist, book illustrator and quilter based at Lismore in the Hebrides where she was President of the local Women's Guild. The planting in the beds is laid out in a patchwork quilt pattern in her memory. Odling was an expert on Robert Burns and created the 24 January 1959 cover of the Scottish edition of the *Radio Times* dedicated to his birth. She also created an animation of 'Tam o' Shanter' adapted from a BBC production of the story and in 1965 designed murals for the famous Burns Room in Irvine's Burns Club. Her murals also adorn Culzean Castle. Inside the heritage centre you will find an enlightening exhibition❦ of the work of **Janet Watson** (1923–1985), a geologist whose photographs, illustrations and research investigated the unique geology of the Highlands and Islands. In recognition of her contribution to geology she was presented with the Lyell Medal in 1973 and was the first female president of the Geological Society of London from 1982 to 1984.

Eilean Donan Castle

Dating from 1230, this is one of Scotland's most photographed buildings and starred in the film *Highlander* and in the James Bond movie *The World is Not Enough*. The castle was destroyed in 1719 during a Jacobite uprising and was rebuilt in the early 20th century. Here you will find many original clan relics and, just beyond one of the few working portcullises in Scotland, the statue❦ of rebel **Finola O'Donnell** (c1552–c1610), known as the 'dark daughter' because of her steely determination. The 17th century text *The Annals of the Four Masters* says she 'joined a man's heart to a woman's thought'. With her mother, **Lady Agnes Campbell** (see page 304), she waged an aggressive campaign against English governors and assassinated several officials in both Scotland and Ireland – coordinating activities between the two countries against what she saw as an occupying force. The women were, in effect, resistance leaders.

The castle is also home to a vibrant musical archive✢ of the travelling community. In addition to live music events, there are regular screenings✢ of footage of traditional singers such as **Belle Stewart** (1906–1997) and her daughter **Sheila Stewart** (1937–2014), who wrote her mother's biography *Queen Amang the Heather: The Life of Belle Stewart*, published in 2006. These women had their roots in the Scottish Highland traveller community, known in Gaelic as *Ceardannan* (craftsmen) or *luchdsiubhail* (people of travel). Sheila Stewart had an ongoing rivalry with another Scottish Traveller, **Jeannie Robertson** (see page 270) and they vied with each other over many of the same traditional songs. You can decide whose performance you prefer as footage of the women is often screened together. The Stewart family performed around the UK, as well as in the USA and Italy. Ewan MacColl featured them in his documentary *Radio Ballad* and, with the American folk singer Peggy Seeger, compiled a collection of the folklore of the Stewart family called *Till Doomsday in the Afternoon*. In another music documentary, *Where You're Meant to Be*, Sheila is a formidable presence alongside Aidan Moffat. When Belle died in 1997, hundreds of people attended her funeral. Alongside the exhibition the castle also hosts a traveller music festival✢ in the autumn which features prizes✢ for performance given in the name of both Jeannie Robertson and Belle Stewart – united at last!

Wester Ross

Next, head for the Applecross peninsula along the Bealach na Ba (Pass of the Cattle), which, at over 2,000ft above sea level and with a 1:5 gradient, affords incredible views over the Minch to Raasay and Skye. Just before you descend into Applecross (a name derived from the Gaelic Apor Crosan, which means estuary), stop to take in the solemn Resistance Monument ✿ to the memory of the bravery of the **women who resisted the Highland Clearances**. This artwork takes the form of huge square stones from local quarries sinking into the boggy ground, just as the memory of the violence done to these Highland communities sinks into the national consciousness. The unseen underside of each stone is carved with the names of the villages that were cleared. It is a sombre and majestic installation set against the backdrop of some of Scotland's most spectacular scenery.

For a further understanding of the Clearances and the consequences of this societal shift on the lives of women, go to the nearby visitor centre ✿, which looks at the ideology of the Clearances – when non-resident landlords decided to clear communities to make way for sheep farming, which offered greater profit. While some tenants went willingly, many did not. With many men away on military service or working elsewhere, women stood up to eviction particularly fiercely. The Clearances went on for decades, with some landlords resorting to violence as resistance mounted. The centre describes fierce clashes including an incident in 1853 at Greenyards, near Ardgay, that became known as the Massacre of the Ross Women. Police charged a group of protesters and 19 people (mostly women) were injured, including **Elizabeth Ross**, aged 22, who was struck on the head and kicked where she fell. The marks of the policemen's boots were visible on her breast and shoulders and her clothing was red with blood. Pieces of her scalp had been stripped off, and quantities of her hair, clotted with blood, could be seen on the ground. Oral reports suggest she died shortly afterwards. Also violently attacked was **Christina Ross**, aged 50, who wanted to ask if there was written authority for the eviction, but was injured before she could do so. Covered in blood, after she had lain on the ground for half an hour she was arrested and detained in jail. One survivor was **Grace Ross**, aged 21, who was only watching the events unfold when a policeman struck her with his baton. The blow caused a cut four inches long and exposed her skull. For a few minutes Grace lay unconscious, but when she tried to crawl towards a wood, the police noticed her, and started beating her again. She escaped into a nearby river and subsequently made a good recovery. She used to demonstrate her injury by placing a shirt button in the depression on top of her head.

Another notorious act of brutality was the death of **Margaret MacKay** (c1722–1814), who, aged over 90, was burned out of her croft. Though saved by her daughter, who managed to carry her out through the flames, she died five days later of her injuries. The manager in charge of the Clearances for the Sutherland estate was charged with culpable homicide and arson, but he was acquitted in 1816 (see the Sutherland Monument page 357).

Also brought to life in the visitor centre is the Battle of the Braes, which took place on Skye in 1882. Approximately 50 police officers, sent from Glasgow, baton-charged a group of men and women who were trying to stop the police from taking a small number of arrested crofters by attacking the officers with stones. This bloody confrontation made it clear to landlords that military intervention would be necessary to enforce the Clearances. The Gaelic poet **Màiri Mhòr nan Òran** (see page 338) wrote about the Battle of the Braes in one of her best known songs, 'Òran Beinn Lì', which includes the line *"S na mnathan bu shuairce, 'S bu mhodhaile gluasad, Chaidh an claiginn a spuaiceadh Ann am bruachan Beinn Lì*' (translated into English: 'And the gentlest women most graceful in movement, their heads were broken on the braes of Beinn Lì').

At the exit to the centre, the door is painted❋ with the words of **Anna Gobh**, who wrote poetry and songs in the 1820s and 1830s of her life as a Highlander who went to work in the Lowlands. The quotation begins: '*B' fheàrr nach tighinn san àm, A dh' ionnsaigh machair nan Gall, Gun àird gun leaba gun fhodar ...*' ('I wish I had never come to the Lowlands, without comfort, without a bed, without straw ...').

It may seem incongruous in such a beautiful place and a harsh contrast to cheery tourist images of Highland cows and whisky, but these hard-hitting monuments and the stories behind them are important in understanding the real history of the Highlands and in honouring the fore-mothers of those who still live here as well as those whose foremothers were forced to leave.

Loch Torridon

From the pretty lochside village of Shieldaig, the site of boat races during the first weekend in August, you can see Shieldaig Island. Here you will find a long bench❋ on the beach to the memory of **Janet Smith** (1905–1999), a journalist, commentator and editor who wrote a celebrated biography of the writer and politician John Buchan. An enthusiastic climber, she was president of the Ladies' Alpine Club and one of the first female committee members (from 1978 to 1980) when the all male Alpine Club opened to women in 1975 and the two clubs merged.

Anna Gobh Door

At the war memorial at Torridon village pause to note the name of **Margaret MacKenzie** from Shieldaig who went down with the RMS *Lusitania* in 1915 when it was sunk by a torpedo attack from a German submarine in the First World War. MacKenzie was returning to Scotland to visit her family, having just married an American she had met while working on a ranch in Wyoming. Her body was recovered and she is buried in Kinsale in Ireland as 'an Unknown woman' from the wreck as her body was not identified until many years after the tragedy.

At the east end of Loch Torridon is the Beinn Eighe Nature Reserve and Visitor Centre: Britain's oldest nature reserve, founded in 1951. The centre provides information about the ecology of the area and also about some of the women who have been at the forefront of research into plant and animal life both locally and internationally. Keep an eye out for exhibits✤ about **Margaret Leigh** (1894–1973), an author and farmer who wrote about crofting and supported regeneration of the Highlands after she rode her horse to Scotland from her native Cornwall in 1939. She settled on the island of Barra and converted to Catholicism before entering a convent in Inverness. There are also examples of the work✤ of **Mary Beith** (1938–2012), who was named Campaigning Journalist of the Year in 1975. Among the outrages she exposed were the abuse of the elderly in psychiatric institutions and the sickening treatment of animals in medical laboratories. The iconic image of a row of beagles forced to chain-smoke cigarettes, which became part of the campaign to stop animal testing, was taken during one of her undercover stints researching an article. One section✤ of the visitor centre focuses on **Jane Durham** (1924–1997), a conservationist who took part in local campaigns to conserve the heritage and environment of the area. She became extremely knowledgeable about the region's history, particularly the early Christian period, and was at the forefront of a movement to set up a Scottish Redundant Churches Trust. In 1984 she became a Commissioner of the Royal Commission on the Ancient and Historical Monuments of Scotland. There is a stone plaque to her at the site of the Hilton of Cadboll Stone. This is a reproduction (by sculptor Barry Grove) of the original carved Pictish slab from around AD 800 featuring a hunting scene with a woman wearing a large Celtic brooch and riding side-saddle. The original stone is kept in the National Museum of Scotland in Edinburgh.

To the north, Inverewe House and Gardens lie on Loch Ewe (which, incidentally, is one of only three berths in the country suitable for nuclear submarines). In the stunning gardens there is an exotic plant collection developed by gardener **Mairi Sawyer** (1879–1953), who dedicated her life to Inverewe, which had been founded by her father. She signed over the gardens to the National Trust for Scotland shortly before her death. The tropical greenhouses❦ in the heart of the gardens close to Inverewe House are dedicated to her memory.

Skye

The island of Skye boasts an impressive 20 munros (mountains higher than 3,000 ft). On the fertile Sleat peninsula – also known as the 'Garden of Skye' – head for Armadale Castle, only a mile north of the ferry terminal. The 40-acre grounds of the ruined neo-gothic style castle are the location of the Sileas Waterfall❦, named after **Sileas nighean Mhic Raghnaill** (1660–1729), a poet and singer most notable for her 23 poems in Gaelic which are written in a mixture of classical Gaelic syllabic metres and more modern stressed metres. Her work was intended to be sung, with some of her poems based on popular songs. Much of what she wrote was political, with a Jacobite theme – she was opposed to the 1707 Union of Parliaments, describing it as '*uinnein puinnsein*' (a poisoned onion) and she wrote several laments for friends killed in the uprisings. However, her poetry also includes humorous advice to unmarried women, and devotional poems. Her best-known poem is probably her lament for Alasdair Dubh of Glengarry, a Jacobite laird who fought at the Battle of Killiecrankie and Sherrifmuir. Occasionally in the evenings recitals✦ of her work are performed in the ruins of the castle.

Beside Armadale Castle is the Museum of the Isles, a modern museum that explores Highland and Island history. Here you will find a particularly interesting exhibit about **Scáthach nUanaind of Skye** who taught martial arts to Cúchulainn. A mythical warrior queen, according to legend she lived around 200BC and her fortress Dún Scáith (Castle of Shadows) was sited on the island. Scáthach, whose name in Gaelic means 'Shadowy', appears in the Red Branch Cycle, a collection of medieval Irish heroic legends and sagas. She is an inspiring archetype for strong Celtic women in mythology. At midsummer, a shadow puppet show is staged✦, projected onto the walls of Armadale castle and fires are lit across the island to her memory.✦

In more recent events, the museum also honours✦ **Molly Fergusson** (1914–1997), a civil engineer who worked on many bridges in the Highlands and Islands. Fergusson was the first woman to be a senior partner in a UK engineering consultancy and the first woman to be awarded a fellowship from the Institute of Civil Engineers. There is a model✦ that at first glance looks like a modern fountain in the hallway of the museum, but in fact is a representation of one of Fergusson's many projects – a water purification scheme on the River Leven.

Dunvegan Castle

At the opposite end of the island it's worth popping into Dunvegan Castle, just outside the village of Dunvegan. This has been the seat of Clan MacLeod since the 13th century. The huge cairn✝ built here honours **Flora MacLeod** (1878–1976), the 28th Chief of the Clan MacLeod. Visiting members of the MacLeod family still add stones to it in her memory so it is getting larger year on year. Flora is interred in the family's burial grounds nearby. She created a MacLeod community, lecturing in the USA, Canada, Australia and New Zealand to bring a new sense of identity to the Scottish diaspora. The Dame Flora MacLeod of MacLeod Trophy for Open Piobaireachd has been presented to the best bagpiper at the Grandfather Mountain Highland Games in North Carolina since 1969.

Stein

As you head for this fishing village on the peninsula of Waternish, approach across the Fairy Bridge where, it is said, the 4th MacLeod Clan Chief had to say goodbye to his fairy wife. She left him a fairy flag to protect the clan. As late as the Second World War members of the Clan MacLeod in the armed forces carried images of the flag for luck. As well as a lively restaurant and bar the village also boasts an altar✝ made of shells which is dedicated to the sad story of **Rachel Chiesley, Lady Grange** (c1679–1745), who started an affair with James Erskine, Lord Grange, in about 1708. He initially refused to marry her when she became pregnant. Rachel, however, threatened him with a pistol and he changed his mind. According to her, they then lived together for nearly 25 years 'in great love and peace' and had four sons and five daughters. When Lady Grange discovered that her husband had a mistress, she followed him, abused him verbally in public, swore at his relations, drank excessively and allegedly threatened to reveal that he was a Jacobite (this was a serious offence). Whatever her actions, she was certainly scandalously treated by her husband whom the marriage laws of the time would not allow her to divorce. Trying to pacify her, at first Grange offered her the job of managing his estate while he stayed in London, but the arrangement did not last for long. In 1732, intending to confront her husband, Lady Grange booked a seat on the London coach but, before she could leave, a party of Highlanders kidnapped her, apparently on Grange's orders. She was taken to the island of Heisker, then to St Kilda, where she was kept for four years. In 1738 she smuggled out a letter describing 'the misserie and sorrow and hunger and hardships of all kindes that I have suffrd' and an expedition was mounted to rescue her, but she had been moved before it arrived. She died in 1745, still a prisoner. Her grave is in the churchyard at Trumpan nearby.

Portree

This eye-catching cliff-edge town is iconic, recognised worldwide because of its run of multicoloured painted houses. Around the harbour you will find various memorials to island women including the poet **Màiri Mhòr nan Òran** (1821–1898), whose monument ✦ in wrought iron is built of words in Gaelic and English twined together, which is entirely fitting for a woman who declared '*tha mi sgìth de luchd na Beurla*' ('I am tired of English-speaking monoglots'). A feminist, she exhorted the world to 'study our witches as well as our saints'. She was outspoken in her support of land rights for the Gaels. Sorley MacLean said no Gaelic poet had more *joie de vivre* than Màiri Mhòr, and there is a memorial plaque to her memory on the Rosedale Hotel here.

On the harbour you will find an installation✦ to the memory of **Margaret MacPherson** (1908–2001), a crofter, children's author and political activist known as the 'first lady of crofting'. Three huge boulders have been split apart and set into the earth like open jaws. This piece represents the rending nature of private versus public land ownership. In 1951, MacPherson was appointed to the Commission of Enquiry into Crofting Conditions, where she supported the nationalisation of farms of more than 3,000 acres and was opposed to crofters being able to purchase their crofts. This resulted in the establishment of the Crofters Commission. From 1961 to 1984, she was Secretary of the Skye Labour Party and was part of a group known as the 'Highland Luxemburghists' who repeatedly tried to pass a resolution to bring crofts back into common ownership. However, the Labour Party leadership ignored the resolution and supported the right of crofters to purchase their land. MacPherson never gave up and only in 1991, at the age of 83, did she stop canvassing door-to-door for causes she believed in.

Here you will also find a driftwood sculpture✦ of a well-known actress from Skye, **Effie Morrison** (1917–1974), who played Mistress Niven in the original series of *Dr Finlay's Casebook* on television and appeared in the popular programme *Doctor in the House*.

Trotternish

Twenty miles north of Portree is the peninsula of Trotternish where, behind the Skye Museum of Island Life, you will find the grave of one of the most famous women associated with the island – **Flora MacDonald** (1722–1790). Flora was born on South Uist where her stepfather, Hugh MacDonald, became a government officer following the 1745 Jacobite uprising. Some modern historians speculate

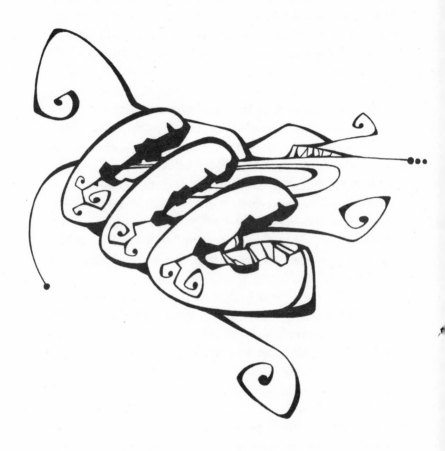

Margaret MacPherson's Boulders

that he was a Jacobite sympathiser, but whatever his allegiance, Flora's stepfather provided her with a passport to cross the Minch with the fleeing Jacobite prince, Charles Edward Stewart, disguised as her maid. Despite a £30,000 price on his head, the Prince managed to evade capture, but Flora was taken by the redcoats and transported by prison ship to London. Supporters raised £1,500 and an amnesty secured her release after a year's imprisonment. In 1750 she returned to Skye to marry. After emigrating to North Carolina in 1774 she sailed back to Scotland in 1779, eventually returning to the island where she lived for a time at Dunvegan Castle. Her grave boasts a Celtic cross headstone inscribed with a tribute by Dr Johnson, who met her when he visited Skye in 1773: 'Her name will be mentioned in history if courage and fidelity be virtues mentioned with honour.' On Raasay, where Flora ultimately directed the prince after the crossing, there is a further monument to Flora's bravery – a wooden carving of the prow of a boat overlooking the sea, which at night is lit up so that it can be viewed across the water. She is commemorated elsewhere around the country with a cairn at Kildonan on South Uist marking her birthplace, a brass statue at Inverness Castle and a plaque at the site of her former school at Old Stamp Office Close, Edinburgh.

At the museum you will also find information about **Lady Margaret Macdonald** (1716–1799), who helped Flora in her efforts to save Bonnie Prince Charlie. Margaret Macdonald provided, among other support, newspapers that allowed the Stewart faction to follow political events around the country. After the death of her husband, who fought for the prince, Lady Margaret ran the family estates. She commissioned a picture of her sons known as *The Macdonald Boys* from Edinburgh artist William Mosman – the painting, often described as a 'tartan extravaganza' has become famous and is often used on shortbread tins. A prize is given in her memory for the best recital in the Princess Margaret of the Isles harp competition each summer.

The museum also has an exhibit ✷ about the contribution of the island's women during the Second World War, in particular the women of the MacInnes family. **Johan MacInnes** (c1920–1945), with her older sister **Katy MacInnes**, went to Glasgow to contribute to the war effort. Johan died in the military ward of Stobhill Hospital from tuberculosis meningitis. Her loss deeply affected the girls' widowed mother, **Grace**. Johan is buried in Kilmore and her name is included in the memorial to the war dead from Sleat just north of Kilmore churchyard.

In the museum grounds, look for the statue made of prison chains ✷ built to commemorate the bravery of another Jacobite woman from the island, **Anne McKay**. As a Gaelic speaker (and therefore considered inferior), Anne received particularly cruel treatment from redcoat troops for giving shelter to two Jacobite soldiers who had survived Culloden. She refused to give up the names of her collaborators during her interrogation at the hands of Colonel Leighton of Blakeney's Regiment despite being forced to stand for three days and three nights and being subjected to considerable verbal abuse. After several women petitioned on her behalf, including Lady Anne Mackintosh (see page 295), she was eventually freed.

Lewis

Lewis is the largest of the Western Isles. In its main town of Stornoway take the time to visit the **Herring Girls Statues** on North Beach and South Beach Quay, raised in recognition of the women who worked here during the late 19th and early 20th centuries. In 1914 around 3,000 women were employed in the industry, many following the herring around the islands or down to England over the course of the season, gutting and packing fish for the home market and export. They worked long hours – often 12-hour days – for extremely low wages. When the industry faltered in the 1930s many women went into tweed production on the islands or volunteered for the armed services – particularly the Merchant Navy.

On the quay you will also find a cairn✸ built to the memory of **Linda Norgrove** (1974–2010), who was born on the island. A United Nations aid worker, she and three Afghan colleagues were kidnapped by members of the Taliban in the Kunar province of eastern Afghanistan in 2010. Tragically, Norgrove was killed accidentally by a grenade thrown by a US sailor in a failed rescue attempt. Flowers are often left here in her memory.

Lewis is home to the Hebridean Celtic Festival in July. If you're visiting during the festival, in addition to the headline acts, you can attend events✸ staged in memory of well-known performers and filmmakers with a connection to the island. These include **Helen Patuffa Hood** (1889–c1958), a clarsach player who specialised in performing the songs of her mother, **Marjory Kennedy-Fraser** (1857–1930), which she had collected on trips to the Hebrides. The women performed together in New York, London and Berlin in the 1920s. Another woman commemorated as part of the festival is **Kitty MacLeod** (1914–2000), a singer much loved in the Gaelic community, who won the Mòd gold medal in 1936 and acted in the 1953 film *Rob Roy*. The work of **Frances Tolmie** (1840–1926) is often featured. A folklorist, Gaelic scholar and song collector born on the island, she was one of the first women to attend the all-female Newnham College in Cambridge where, using an old folk tradition, it was said she told other students' fortunes by looking into a mixture of egg white and water. The programme always boasts an event centred on **Eilidh Watt** (1908–1996), a Gaelic writer and broadcaster with an affinity for the supernatural. Watt was an equality campaigner and trade unionist. She published an array of Gaelic short stories, was included in three anthologies of Gaelic writing and published three books in her own right. Many of the events are preceded by clips ✿ from the work of **Nettie McGavin**, a keen amateur filmmaker who worked with her husband, Nat, throughout the mid 20th century. She was a founder member of the Scottish Association of Amateur Cinematographers, and won prizes on many occasions at the Scottish Amateur Film Festival. She shot her first film while on holiday in the Outer Hebrides in 1938 when she captured rare footage of fishwives bandaging their fingers to protect the nicks on their skin from the salt water. People on the island of Harris were not accustomed to film cameras at this time, and one inhabitant is seen deliberately turning away from the lens. McGavin also travelled to Jerusalem to make films about a hospital run by the medical mission of the Church of Scotland. In 2016 her work was part of a celebration of female filmmakers at the Dundee Contemporary Arts centre.

Also on the island, the former laird's castle, Lews Castle, now boasts a state-of-the-art bilingual museum telling the history of Lewis. The 'Agnes Hallway'✿, is named after **Agnes Mure Mckenzie** (1891–1955) from Stornoway, who became Honorary President of the Saltire Society and was a lifelong champion of Gaelic Scotland's contribution to the world. She was a novelist, historical writer and a critic for *The Times Literary Supplement*, and the Saltire Society awards a prize in her memory for the best history book of the year. The castle also houses an extremely grand statue✿ of Lewis-born **Mary Anne MacLeod**

(1912–2000), a native Gaelic speaker who emigrated to the USA in 1930. She is recorded on the Alien Passenger list of the RMS *Transylvania* as a domestic. MacLeod's family prospered and she no longer needed to work, instead volunteering, focusing on charities dedicated to cerebral palsy and to improving the lives of intellectually disabled adults. She had a prominent role at the Women's Auxiliary of Jamaica Hospital and at the Jamaica Day Nursery in New York. She also supported medical buildings around the city, including a 228-bed nursing home which was named after her. When she died, the *Stornoway Gazette* noted her death but did not mention her son, Donald Trump, future US President. Her statue has become the focus for political protest from across the country, particularly a rally against Trump's visit to Scotland in the summer of 2018.

Also in the castle museum you will find the story ✳ of the suffragette movement on the islands – including the story of **Helen MacDougall**, a member of the Stornoway Suffrage Society and an X-ray specialist. When the First World War broke out she was one of the first to join Elsie Inglis (see page 23) to serve in Serbia and was taken prisoner with Dr Inglis by the German army when Serbia fell. The Germans released the women in Austria (then enemy territory) and they had to climb through the Alps to Switzerland and freedom. MacDougall went back to the Front in France where she again served with the Scottish Women's Hospitals. Her story is told in the bilingual play *Deeds Not Words*, written by Toria Banks, which premiered in 2018.

At the north of the island, beside the junction in the road that leads to the butt of Lewis, stands the 12th century St Moulag's Church, which was restored in 1912. Dating from the time of Norse rule, the church has a gravitas that makes it a fitting place to remember the 17th century poet **Fionnghal Chaimbeul** (1600–c1648). A simple plaque✤ beside the squint window that leads to the south nave bears the words of her only surviving composition, 'Turus mo Chreiche Thug mi Chola' ('My Journey to Coll was my Ruin'), in which she rejects the clan she married into in favour of the clan of her birth. This was extremely unusual – women usually forged allegiances in their married households. However, when the two clans fought on opposite sides at the Battle of Inverlochy in 1645 Fionnghal's brother, a Covenanter, was killed, and in the poem she even curses her own son for his involvement. It is said that she went mad with grief after the battle.

Remote but beautiful, the Uig Sands are the largest of Lewis's golden beaches; stop and search out the pair of carved Celtic crosses✤ to two ancient women. The smaller of the two commemorates **Brenhilda**, or **Brianeult** (7th century). Little is known about her other than that she was found dead on the tiny island of Sula Sgeir, 11 miles to the west of North Rona – the remotest island in the British Isles ever to have been inhabited (and said to have once been home to St Ronan, brother of Brenhilda). These islands were reached by Irish monks in AD 625 and on North Rona the chapel is virtually intact, with simple slabs marking the graves of the hermits who lived there. As an early female traveller to the islands, Brenhilda was probably driven by her faith. Life in such far-removed island communities was precarious – the whole population on North Rona died of starvation in 1685 when rats swarmed ashore from a shipwreck and ate the islanders' food. The island was repopulated in 1695 but inhabitation did not last long apart from occasional shepherds who brought their flock to feed. In 1874 a cargo ship built in Greenock was named after Brenhilda. The second cross is to **Aud the Deepminded** (c850–900), another Christian pioneer, who took Gaelic Christianity to Iceland. She appears in the *Orkneyinga Saga* (see page 380). Legend has it that she was held in such regard that she was one of the few women to have been given the honour of a ship burial.

Harris

This mountainous island is named after the old Norse for 'High Land'. The south is home to sandy beaches and more gentle slopes. A mile from Renish Point in the south, the old port of Rodel is where the ferry from Skye used to arrive. Here you will find several monuments✷ to Hebridean women including a fountain shaped like a fishing boat✷ engraved with the words of **Annag Chaimbeul (Anna Campbell)** (1750–c1780) from Scalpay, just off Skye, who wrote a famous lament for her drowned fiancé, 'Ailein Duinn Shiubhlainn leat' or 'Brown Haired Alan I Would go with You'. She was buried at sea.

At the threshold of St Clement's Church there is a small statue✷ of **Mairi Nighean Alasdair Ruaidh (Mary Macleod)** (c1615–1707), a Gaelic poet and praise-singer from the town who it was said always spoke her words from the threshold – neither inside or out. Only a handful of her poems survive and she is best known for her elegies to Clan MacLeod – although she was once exiled for being too profuse in her praise of a relation of the chief, who became jealous and ordered her out of his sight. She was eventually allowed to return to Dunvegan.

Outside St Clement's you will find a bench✷, sculpted from oversized iron needles and thread. This is to the memory of **Murdina Macdermid** (1925–1996), a community activist on the island who was voted Disabled Scot of the Year in 1987. She ran the Harris Disabled Group shop and was key to the creation of a tapestry that depicts 1,000 years of Harris history. Commenting on Murdina's life, Independent Councillor for Harris, Morag Munro, said *'Cuimhne 's iomradh math a chaoidh bidh air an fhìrean chòir'* ('Memory is a good account of the truth'). There is a space on either side of the bench for wheelchair users to sit.

Inside St Clements you will find a plaque to the memory of **Catherine Herbert, Countess of Dunmore** (1814– 1886). A lady of the bedchamber to Queen Victoria from 1840 to 1845, she ran the family estate on Harris. During the Highland Potato Famine of 1846–7, she recognised the commercial potential of the tweed produced on the island, and had suits made for the Dunmore estate workers. She then worked to widen the market by organising training for the Harris weavers to remove the irregularities caused by hand production. By the late 1840s, a London market was established. Lady Dunmore had the original 16th century church of St Clements restored in 1873 and also made improvements to the estate village by laying out a village green and building a school.

South Uist

This is the largest of the southern chain of islands in the Hebrides, with beaches to the west coast and mountains to the east. On a promontory to the north east of the island you will find Lochboisdale, the ferry port and main town. Here, it's worth visiting the Kildonan Museum for its mock-up of Hebridean kitchens through the ages. Don't miss the fascinating exhibit about the contributions of women to the Gaelic language.✶ These include **Peggy McClements** (1916–2012), who was brought up on the island and became a major figure in teaching and preserving Gaelic. In 1938 she was the first woman to graduate with First Class Honours in Celtic Studies at the University of Edinburgh.

She went on to teach, translate and archive Gaelic. There is a section presenting the work of **Ella Carmichael** (1870–1928), who also spent her childhood on Uist. She was heavily involved in the production of a compendium of Gaelic songs, poetry and stories gathered in the Gàidhealtachd between 1860 and 1909, known as the *Carmina Gadelica*. She also edited the *Celtic Review* and was one of the founders of the Edinburgh Gaelic Choir and the Celtic Union. Her mother, **Mary Carmichael** (1837–1928), was a keen folklorist and artist who contributed to *Carmina Gadelica*.

Then there are sisters **Marion Campbell** (1867–1970) and **Kate MacDonald** (1897–1977), who were storytellers and singers in the Gaelic tradition from the island. Marion was a monoglot Gaelic speaker and was over 80 when her performances were first recorded by the School of Scottish Studies at the University of Edinburgh. Kate played the chanter as well as singing *puirt-à-beul* – songs associated with dance tunes. She recorded over 250 songs making the sisters key tradition-bearers within the community.

Another woman of note honoured here is **Margaret Fay Shaw** (1903–2004), an American photographer and folklorist who studied music in Paris and New York before cycling from Oxford to Skye. She decided to stay, saying 'There was something about [it] that just won me; it was like falling in love.' Over several years she collected Scottish Gaelic songs on the island before buying the island of Canna, which she later gifted to the National Trust for Scotland. Her most important published work was *Folksongs and Folklore of South Uist*. Shaw is buried on the island.

The Kildonan Museum also contains the Clanranald Stone, carved with the arms of the clan who ruled the island from 1370 to 1839. By the stone you will find the story ❧

of **Margaret McLeod, Lady Clanranald** (c1720–1780), another islander who helped Bonnie Prince Charlie after Culloden. She orchestrated his escape after he had hidden on her land for two months and it was Lady Clanranald who sewed a gown for the prince before dispatching him to Skye with Flora MacDonald (see page 339). For her part in the prince's escape she was imprisoned in Southwark.

Barra

This island was once the home of the MacNeils. They sold it in 1838, resulting in some of the cruellest forced Clearances of clansfolk in the era. In 2003, the Chief of the Clan MacNeil (the clan had since bought back the island) gifted it to the Scottish Government. In the main town of Castlebay don't miss the Dualchas (Barra Heritage Centre), which has a photographic and newspaper archive as well as exhibits ✦ about **Jean Cadell** (1884–1967), a Scottish character actress who performed in the cinema and on the stage. Her best-known film role was in the Ealing Studios comedy *Whisky Galore!* from 1948, which was filmed on Barra (though the 'real Whisky Galore' took place on nearby Eriskay when the SS *Politician* sank in 1941). The heritage centre also includes recordings of **Annie Johnston** (1886–1963), a Gaelic folklorist from Barra who introduced collectors to the 'waulking song' used to accompany the traditional shrinking of homespun cloth by beating it soaked onto a board.

The medieval fortress of Kisimul Castle, ancestral home of the MacNeil clan, lies on an islet in the bay. At the ferry, stop look for the intricate curved stone wall ✦ that provides shelter from the wind. This beautiful monument is carved with words and hung with tiny bells that chime almost constantly in memory of **Nan Eachainn Fhionnlaigh**

(1902–1982), a singer from the island who contributed more than any other individual to the archive of Scottish Gaelic material at the School of Scottish Studies, giving 600 songs and 1,000 stories, anecdotes and proverbs to the collection. She was the last surviving link with the traditional storytelling culture of nearby Vatersay. The words and phrases on the wall are snippets of her talking, as recorded in her later years: 'Well now … in the early days there were no papers or anything. Whatever happened was put down in song and story.' Nan had an unusual singing voice in a minor key and experts are unsure whether it was her own style or if her performances represented a lost traditional way of singing local songs.

Ullapool

Back on the mainland coast, Ullapool was developed by Thomas Telford on behalf of the British Fisheries Society in the late 18th century. You can learn about local history in the Ullapool Museum and spend time at the neighbouring Emigration Heritage Centre✷ where you will find the stories of Scots who emigrated over a period of around 150 years up to the 1950s. Inside the heritage centre, the letters of female emigrants have been used to create a walk-through map✷ of the ordinary lives of the many women who left Scotland to make hazardous journeys to destinations around the world. This immersive experience brings to life the details of what these women tolerated, from cramped conditions aboard ships to the contrast between what they expected to find in their new lives and the harsh reality of what really awaited them – all the time taking note of the details of work, childbirth, mothering and domestic life. For some the experience was transformative – others were desperately lonely.

Starting from the heritage centre follow the Women's Success Trail to uncover the stories of those who had a huge impact on the countries that became their home. The trail starts with **Mary Storie** (born 1801) who came from a traveller family and emigrated to Canada in 1839. She had a repertoire of 47 traditional songs taught to her by her mother and grandmother. Before she left Scotland these were written down to preserve them and were later published by folk ballad collector Andrew Crawfurd. The trail continues with **Ann Dougall Bon** (1838–1936), who became an advocate for Aboriginal rights after she emigrated to Australia from Perthshire; **Christina Rainy** (c1832–c1900), who founded the Women's Hospital in Madras; **Ellen Dawson**, (1900–1967) a power-loom weaver who emigrated from Glasgow in 1919 and became a union activist in America; **Isobelle Graham** (1742–1814) from Lanarkshire, who set up Sunday schools in the USA and many poor relief projects; and **Letitia Hargrave** (1813–1854), the first woman to join her husband at the Hudson's Bay Company's most northern supply post in Canada. The local women called her 'Hockimaw Erqua', meaning chieftainess and when Letitia gave birth to her first son Joseph James, she was crowded by native well-wishers who proclaimed the baby 'Very fat! Very white!'. She also stood up against the schoolmaster at the settlement who tried to stop mixed-race children visiting their mothers if they had not had a church wedding. Quotes from the lively letters she sent home about conditions at the settlement are carved into the trees along the trail.

Towards the end of the trail you will find **Jennie Trout** (1841–1921) from Kelso, who went on to become Canada's first licensed woman physician and appeared for a time on the Canadian 40 cent stamp; **Catherine McKay Martin** (1847–1937), who emigrated to Australia from Skye and became an influential writer whose work included *An Australian Girl* and *The Incredible Journey*, which challenged racism against Aboriginal women as mothers; and **Janet Greig** (1874–1950) from Broughty Ferry, who in 1891, with her sister **Jane** (1872–1939), enrolled at the medical school at the University of Melbourne. The year after Janet graduated, she was appointed a resident medical officer at Melbourne Hospital, one of the first two women to fill such a role – in the face of hostility from the hospital staff. She later became the first female anesthetist in Victoria, working at the Royal Women's Hospital from 1900 to 1917. Jane was the first woman to graduate in Public Health and became Chief Medical Officer in 1929. She was inducted into the Victorian Honour Roll of Women in 2007 and in 2012 she was featured in an Australian postage stamp series of medical doctors.

Strathpeffer

Travel across the country to this Victorian spa town. It is said that Emmeline Pankhurst once scandalised Strathpeffer with her innovative ideas during a talk on women's rights in the Highland Pavilion. Certainly Marion Wallace-Dunlop (see page 300) had visited the town as had various Highland suffragettes. Today Strathpeffer is less edgy. Outside the Upper Pump Room arts venue, only a minute along the road, look out for Cameron's Cafe�֍ with the large clock✶ mounted on the exterior inscribed 'she saved time in the kitchen'. The cafe and clock are in memory of **Elizabeth Cameron** (1915–2008), the inventor of boil-in-the-bag porridge, a frozen-foods pioneer, gardener, artist and author. Her inventions had a positive impact on the lives of many woman. Elizabeth founded a company that pioneered the importing of commercial deep freezers, with which she set up Black Isle Frozen Foods. In the early days, she drove the company van around the north of Scotland, only just visible behind the wheel as she bought fresh shellfish straight from ships at Highland harbours. She pioneered a method of commercially freezing scampi, which led to it becoming a popular 'pub grub' choice. In the 1970s Elizabeth successfully sold out to Findus and became a botanical painter and children's writer, as well as travelling to the Himalayas, South America and New Zealand in search of horticultural specimens.

Cromarty

East of Strathpeffer, the Black Isle peninsula is littered with sites of prehistoric interest. Head to the picturesque fishing town of Cromarty where you can spot dolphins from the shore and take in the surprising view of oil rigs moored in the Cromarty Firth. Here you will find Lady Halkett's House✿, also known as Bellevue House, on Church Street. This beautiful Georgian building was home to an extended family of Scottish, Jamaican and Dutch descent – a consequence of cultures being brought together by the emerging British Empire and the prominence of Cromarty as a port from around 1772. The house has a collection✿ of artefacts and writing by one of the Halkett forebears, **Anne Murray, Lady Halkett** (c1622–1699), a daredevil Royalist who once helped the Duke of York escape from St James's Palace where he was being detained in the late 1640s by the Earl of Northumberland. She later wrote of the incident, 'The earnest desire I had to serve the King made mee omitt noe opertunity wherein I could bee usefull, and the zeale I had for his Majesty made me nott see what inconveniencys I exposed myselfe to.' Unusually for a woman at this time, Lady Halkett practised medicine in Scotland before the time of her marriage and during her first pregnancy she wrote *The Mother's Will to her Unborn Child*. When she was left short of funds on her husband's death, she made her living as a teacher, but her financial difficulties were lessened when James II provided her with a pension for her loyalty during the English Civil War. She left 21 folio and quarto manuscripts written between 1644 and the late 1690s, which can be found in the National Library of Scotland.

Cromarty hosts several cultural events throughout the year including a crime writing festival in spring. One author whose work is regularly discussed✝ at local art festivals is **Elizabeth Cameron** (1910–1976), who wrote nineteen books as Jane Duncan, eight children's books (with the early inclusion of a character with learning difficulties based on her nephew, who she said was 'the best thing to happen to this family'), four books as Janet Sandison and an autobiography which incorporates the years she spent at her grandparents' croft. A feminist, during the Second World War she worked in photographic intelligence and at the end of the war took a job with an engineering company. After a stint in Jamaica, she returned to the Black Isle, where at one point she was disturbed by bus tours offering a view of her house in Jemimaville. She promptly moved to a more inaccessible address and bought most of the houses surrounding her own to ensure her privacy. She is buried at Kirkmichael, where you can visit her grave.

Dornoch Firth

Tip your hat as you pass the village of Arabella, which is named after **Arabella Phipps** (c1779–1806), whose husband built the settlement. Arabella died suddenly, as it says on her gravestone, 'in the act of preparing medicine for a sick and indigent family'. However, local gossip has it that she was murdered by her husband's mistress. When he remarried he changed his name to claim an estate entailed to his second wife, though the name of the village remained the same.

Overlooking the firth, the resort town of Dornoch boasts great shops and a golf course, as well as Dornoch Cathedral where you will find the town's war memorial. This includes the story of local teacher **Margaret Davidson** (1879–1978), who volunteered as a nurse during the First World War with the Scottish Women's Hospitals and worked at Royaumont from 1915 to 1917. When she returned to Scotland, she is believed to have introduced Girl Guiding to Sutherland and became head of the languages department at Dornoch Academy. Also included on the memorial is **Lily Murray** (1898–1942), who served in Queen Alexandra's Imperial Nursing Service during the Second World War and died when the SS *Tanjong Penang* was sunk by the Japanese.

Inside the cathedral, look out for the stained glass window in memory of **Millicent Fanny St Clair Erskine** (1867–1955), Duchess of Sutherland and founder of the Sutherland Benefit Nursing Association, the Sutherland Technical School and the Sutherland Gaelic Association. During the First World War she established and ran the Millicent Sutherland Ambulance, for which she was awarded the French Croix de Guerre and Belgian Royal Red Cross. She married twice and set up extensive schemes for the welfare of people on her husbands' estates in Sutherland and Staffordshire. During the course of her very active life, she was nicknamed Meddlesome Millie – which seems unfair when she clearly did so much good. Millicent Avenue in nearby Golspie is named after her.

Dornoch's Historylinks museum covers some

fascinating local history including the tragic story of **Janet Horne** who in 1727 was the last person in Britain to be tried and executed for witchcraft. Horne and her daughter were arrested and jailed in Dornoch, with Janet accused of turning her daughter into a pony and getting Satan to shoe her. Her daughter appears to have had a deformity in her hands and feet, which possibly made her a target – both women were vulnerable. To the modern eye, Janet's testimony shows signs of senile dementia – she misquoted the first line of the Lord's Prayer for example – an unlikely mistake at the time when churchgoing was so widespread. The trial was rushed, the women were found guilty and sentenced to burn to death the following day. Janet's daughter escaped, but Janet was stripped, covered in tar and paraded through Dornoch in a barrel. When she arrived at her place of execution it is said that she smiled and warmed herself at the fire. Edwin Morgan wrote a poem in Janet's memory and there is also a stone said to mark the place of her burning in a private garden in Dornoch.

Historylinks also looks at the story✤ of **Ann Murray Scott Moncrieff** (1925–2013), who joined the Wrens (the Women's Royal Naval Service) during the Second World War and was stationed at Bletchley Park where she operated the machine used for decryption of Enigma signals. This was vital work. After the war she became an enthusiastic art collector supporting fledgling artists in the early stages of their careers.

The Sutherland Monument⛰

As you come into the village of Golspie, climb the steep path to this contentious statue on a tall plinth, dedicated to **Elizabeth Sutherland** (1765–1839). The architect of the Sutherland Clearances, along with her husband (see page 331), which adversely affected thousands of tenants on the family's estates over several decades, Elizabeth Sutherland lived mostly in London. However, she did nothing to intervene on her tenants' behalf and oversaw some of the cruelest evictions of the era. In 1779 and 1793 she raised a volunteer regiment, the 'Sutherlandshire Fencibles' – the later regiment was deployed in suppressing the Irish rebellion of 1798. She is buried at Dornoch Cathedral. Such is the strength of feeling against her commemoration that there is an ongoing campaign to remove this monument. For a very different type of commemoration, The Lismore pub in Partick has a urinal dedicated to three men (and it also mentions Elizabeth Sutherland⚜) who participated in the Clearances – customers are invited to 'pay them the respect they are due'.

Helmsdale

Travelling north from Golspie it is worth stopping at the village of Helmsdale, a favourite holiday place of the romantic novelist Barbara Cartland, and visiting the Timespan Heritage Centre with its art gallery and museum space. Here you will find the stories⚜ of local women including **Bell Sinclair** (1776–1795) from nearby Wick, who became a renowned mantua maker after her genteel family fell on hard times. The mantua was a fashionable dress that took considerable skill in needlework. The museum has some beautiful examples, and reproductions to dress up in.⚜

Outside there is a monumental arch, formed out of fishing rods and hung with large-scale copies of the fishing flies⚜ of **Megan Boyd** (1915–2001) who lived at Kintradwell near Brora. Starting at the age of twelve, taking lessons from a local expert, she became a famous Atlantic salmon fly maker, selling fishing flies to, among others, the royal family. Boyd mostly tied traditional patterns, but also invented the Megan Boyd, a tie which was perfectly crafted for the low water pattern of the Highlands. She often had so many orders from around the world that she had to work 14-hour days. Novelist David Profumo called her ties 'the Faberges of the fishing world'.

Wick

Wick was once the busiest herring port in Europe with a fleet of over 1,000 boats. Robert Louis Stevenson wrote *Treasure Island* in the town and dubbed it 'the meanest of man's towns, situated on the baldest of God's bays'. Stop outside the hospital on Cliff Road where there is a large red cross✣ dedicated to two courageous women, **Peggy Boyd** (1905–1999) and **Jane Govan** (1895–1982), who were Scotland's first dedicated air ambulance nurses during the Second World War. The idea of nurses aboard the air ambulance came about in 1933 when a trained nurse, recorded only as **Mrs Ferguson**, who was on holiday on Islay, offered to travel back to Glasgow Royal Infirmary with a fisherman who had become extremely ill. Flying out of Renfew Airport (there is a monument to early air ambulance crews in Renfrew itself), Peggy recalled dangerous flights made under tricky conditions, including landings in rough fields and on beaches where the aircraft would sink into the sand while awaiting the arrival of the patient. The women saved many lives by risking their own on these hazardous trips.

Also in Wick it is worth looking out for the small grove of trees✣ dedicated to **Queen Elizabeth, the Queen Mother** (1900–2002), one of seven memorials across Scotland including a cairn outside Canisbay Church Hall (where she worshipped), a plaque at Aberdeen Royal Infirmary, the Queen Mother Building and a Scots pine at Dundee University, a shell memorial in the Royal Botanic Garden Edinburgh, and the rose garden in Hazelhead Park in Aberdeen. The Queen Mother spent much of her childhood in Glamis Castle and carried out her official duties well into old age. Having bought the Castle of Mey, 17 miles to the north of Wick, she spent part of each year in the area.

John o' Groats

This is Scotland's most northeasterly point on the mainland and alongside the carpark and cafe here you will find a telescope⚓, facing north, erected to the memory of **Isobel Hutchison** (1889–1982). Isobel was a polyglot, poet and Arctic traveller well known for her descriptions of northern journeys in the *National Geographic*. She visited Iceland, Greenland, Alaska, the Aleutian Islands, walked from Innsbruck to Venice and from Edinburgh to John o' Groats, making friends wherever she went. In her biography of Hutchison, *Flowers in the Snow*, Gwyneth Hoyle says 'It was rare for explorers to encounter a woman who had firsthand knowledge of the landscape, the people, and the conditions of life in the North. She projected an immediate empathy that fully engaged their attention.' Among her achievements, Isobel was a vice-president of the Royal Scottish Geographical Society, which awarded her a Fellowship Diploma in 1932 and the Mungo Park Medal in 1934 in recognition of her research in the Arctic. In 1936 she was made a fellow of the Royal Geographical Society of London, and Magdalene University conferred a Doctor of Law Degree on her in 1949.

Dunnet Head

Heading west from John o' Groats, further along the mainland coast you will arrive at Dunnet Head, Scotland's most northerly point on the mainland. Where the red cliffs plummet into the sea, stop to admire the Lone Lass✦, the bronze figure of a woman teetering on the cliff edge. The statue, in its extraordinary setting, is dedicated to the memory of **generations of women who faced unwanted pregnancy**. For centuries Scottish society made life almost impossible for single mothers, particularly those from working-class backgrounds. Studies of medical papers from the 18th, 19th and early 20th centuries tell the tale of women trapped by their circumstances at a time when birth control was non-existent, abortion was illegal and having a child out of wedlock carried a huge stigma. Unmarried mothers were outcasts with little or no way to make a living, and many unmarried pregnant women were sent to psychiatric hospitals. Others tried to abort the foetus on their own, paid unscrupulous doctors and midwives for abortions or were driven to infanticide or suicide.

Walking further along the path you can look back at the cliff face below the Lone Lass and see a companion installation called Lullaby✦ by artist Sheena Graham-George. The white butterfly is a traditional symbol of the soul of a child and this beautiful monument takes the form of a swarm of butterflies plunging down the cliff below the bronze. Beneath the butterflies, the sandstone is carved✦ with words from the the poem 'Shy Geordie' by **Helen Cruickshank** (1886–1975):

> *Up the Noran Water*
> *In by Inglismaddy*
> *Annie's got a bairnie*
> *That hasna got a daddy.*

Some say it's Tammas's,
An' some say it's Chay's;
An' naebody expec'it
Wi' Annie's quiet ways.

The butterflies are an extraordinary sight against the horizon, particularly effective at sunrise and sunset. At midsummer and midwinter people gather and light fires here at the cliff top.

There is a plaque❦ nearby to the memory of **Angela Bollan** (1977–1996), who was addicted to heroin and committed suicide while in prison after losing custody of her daughter. Her case was subject to a fatal accident enquiry that criticised Corton Vale Prison (where Angela died) for not rehabilitating prisoners, calling it a 'revolving door'. The plaque contains a quote from Angela's MP John McFall, who spoke in the House of Commons on her behalf and paraphrased Winston Churchill 'there is a treasure, if you can only find it, in the heart of every man and in the heart of every woman'.

To the south of Dunnet village, stop at Mary Ann's Cottage. Once home of **Mary Ann Calder** (1897–1996), the cottage was built in 1850 by Mary Ann's grandfather and has remained almost unchanged since the 1930s. It is a living museum that provides an intimate and authentic glimpse into the hard, day-to-day life of a crofting family. The house has been left just as it was when Mary Ann walked out of the door to go to a nursing home in the 1990s after running the croft single handedly for years after her husband died. A plaque❦ outside reminds us that, historically, the majority of crofters were women.

The Lone Lass

Orkney

The wind in Orkney is almost constant. At the farm, the westerly gales are the worst, bringing the sea with them, and tonnes of rock can be moved overnight, the map altered in the morning. Easterlies can be the most beautiful – when the wind blows towards the tide and skims a glittering canopy of spray from the top of the waves, catching the sun. The old croft houses are squat and firm, like many Orcadian people, built to survive the strongest gales.

Amy Liptrot, *The Outrun*

Throughout the 70 or so islands that make up Orkney, there are traces of a rich heritage that stretches back for millennia. This includes the heart of Neolithic Orkney which was designated a UNESCO World Heritage Site in 1999. Orkney prides itself on the fact that it has as many historical links with Scandinavia as it does with the land-mass of Britain and it has always been outward looking, evidenced by its early trading links with Northern Canada. Orcadians are very independent minded and some locals don't even consider Orkney part of Scotland. The largest island is the Mainland – when locals say they are going to the Mainland they mean the largest island, not mainland Scotland.

Stromness

The Mainland town of Stromness, where the harbour shelters the ferry terminal, has been in use since the Viking era. Next to the terminal you will find a sculpture✹ – made of bronze from Queensland, Australia – of a ship in stormy waters. It is dedicated to local woman **Eliza Anne Fraser** (1793–1858), who, along with other crew members, survived a shipwreck at Great Sandy Island off the coast of Queensland in 1836. She was taken by the indigenous Badtjala people, stripped and forced to work. The ship's captain, Eliza's husband, was murdered and the first mate died of burns inflicted by their captors. After her rescue by a convict from the penal colony, Eliza became a celebrity and her account of the shipwreck and capture became sensationalised in books and newspapers. It seems probable that Eliza exaggerated her claims to attract attention and financial aid. The story has remained part of Australian popular culture, inspiring a painting by Sidney Nolan, films, a novel by Patrick White and several poems. In 1838, Eliza returned to Stromness with her second husband, presumably to retrieve her children, who had been left in the town in the care of a Presbyterian minister. The couple were threatened with violence by locals – it is not known why. They returned to Australia where Eliza lived until her death. Great Sandy Island was renamed Fraser Island after her and there is a commemorative plaque on the house in Stromness where it is thought she lived.

Stromness was the base from which the Hudson's Bay Company crossed the North Atlantic during the 18th and 19th centuries. Less than a ten minute walk from the ferry port, on Back Road look out for the plaque at Margaret Humphrey's house. In 1836 this house was leased as a hospital for the 26 scurvy-ridden whalers who survived when 20 ships were crushed in the Arctic ice on the Davis Straits. In his diary one of the men, Wallie Scott, recalled how 'When we got back to Stromness they put me … into Mrs Humphrey's house.' **Margaret Humphrey** herself is the subject of some confusion, described as 'a widow in her sixties' in documents relating to the hospital. However, in the 1821 Census return, she was listed as a sick nurse aged 65, and in the 1851 Census return, she was listed as a widow and a midwife, aged 74. It would seem she was a lady who was coy about admitting her age. Whatever her birthdate, we catch glimpses of her personality in the fretful letters she wrote to her sons, who worked for the Hudson's Bay Company, enjoining the younger ones to 'mind how some of your Brothers ruined themselves by their Extravagance and keeping Company with those how [sic] loved their Bottle … I need not ask you to come Home … You are more at liberty where you are than under a Mother's eye.' She kept up this correspondence over several years, telling off the men at every opportunity!

Pier Arts Centre

This innovative arts centre in a converted warehouse on an old jetty has a striking modern extension. The art collection was donated in trust in 1979 by **Margaret Gardiner** (1904–2005), who read languages and moral science at Newnham College, Cambridge, and later became associated with the development of British Modernism. She was close friends with the artist Barbara Hepworth, and in 1946 bought half a sculpture by Hepworth when she got chatting to a stranger called Mr Reddihough at a gallery. They both wanted the piece but neither could afford it so they bought it together and shared it for six months each over several years. Gardiner owned a number of pieces by Hepworth, supporting the artist through the 1930s and 1940s. She was also an early champion of the group of Cornish-based artists working from St Ives, including Margaret Mellis. A notable activist against fascism, in 1936 Gardiner became honorary secretary of For Intellectual Liberty, a pacifist rallying point for writers, artists and academics. She also supported CND and the Howard League for Penal Reform. Gardiner first visited Orkney in 1956 and formed a close connection with the islands through her friend Margaret Tait (see page 376) who co-founded the arts centre with her. The development of the collection is ongoing.

Here you will also find paintings by another of Gardiner's friends, **Sylvia Wishart** (1936–2008), who attended Gray's School of Art, Aberdeen, as a mature student, leaving to teach in Aberdeenshire, Lewis and Orkney before taking a position at Gray's. She is closely associated with Orkney and most of her work is still on the islands. She had a studio in the building before it became the Pier Arts Centre. After a major refurbishment in 2007, the gallery reopened with a Wishart exhibition. In addition to the artwork, the centre hosts quarterly talks on the exhibitions known as the Barns-Graham Conversations✷, named after abstract painter **Wilhelmina Barns-Graham** (1912–2004), who painted Orkney landscapes. Barns-Graham bequeathed her estate to a charitable trust to foster and protect her reputation, to advance the knowledge of her life and work, to create an archive of key works of art and papers, and, in a cause close to her heart, to support and inspire art and art history students through offering grants and bursaries.

Stromness Library

Look out for the bronze bookshelf✷ mounted on the wall of the old library at Hellihole Road to the memory of **Marjory Skea** (c1821–1898), a widow who lived on Main Street and left money in her estate to endow a library in the town. This building is now used as artists' studios and the library has moved to the Warehouse Buildings nearby where there is a Skea Reading Room✷ in memory of Marjory's generosity. Sadly, we don't know much more about this philanthropist's life. Also at the Warehouse Buildings, stop to see the display✷ about **Mary Brunton** (1778–1818), who eloped in a rowing boat from the island of Gairsay, because her mother did not approve of her suitor – a Church of Scotland Minister, Alexander Brunton, who later became professor of oriental languages at the University of Edinburgh. Brunton knew her own mind and married the minister. She then went on to write two novels – *Self-Control* and *Discipline*. *Self-Control* sold 240 copies in its first five days – reputedly disquieting Jane Austen, who perhaps felt her thunder was being stolen. Austen was sniffy about Brunton's achievement, declaring the book 'excellently meant … but without anything of Nature or Probability'. Experts believe that Austen based her character Emma Woodhouse on the protagonist in Brunton's *Discipline*. Brunton's work continued to be well received, running into several editions and translated into French. Her third novel, *Emmeline*, was not completed at the time of her death in childbirth but was published posthumously with a memoir and part of her travel diary. Her novels redefine femininity in the period by portraying female characters who were strong in the face of adversity and often alone. Fay Weldon praised them as 'rich in invention, ripe with incident, shrewd in comment, and erotic in intention and fact'. Mary Brunton is buried in Canongate Kirkyard in Edinburgh where there is a plaque to her memory.

Mrs Flett's Museum 🔔

This museum started life as the Orkney Natural History Society in 1837. For the first seventeen years the society was housed in 'Mrs Flett's large room', a property next door to the Subscription Library in Victoria Street, which had been founded in 1812. We know very little about **Mrs Flett**, who also ran an hotel on the island (Flett's Hotel), but the museum has gone from strength to strength, garnering local and international support including bequests from Andrew Carnegie and donations from poet, fossil hunter and journalist Hugh Miller. The museum collection has been in its current location on Alfred Street since 1862. As well as archaeological artefacts and Second World War stories from the island, expect to see photographs ✤ by **Gunnie Moberg** (1941–2007), who moved to Orkney in 1976 and produced an invaluable body of work about the island's people, landscape and wildlife. Her obituary in *The Times* declared 'Gunnie Moberg's photographs of Orkney, her adopted home, defined the people and the landscape of those islands in a way that has never been equalled.' In six of her books her photographs (many taken from the aircraft cockpit of her friend Logan Air captain Andy Alsop) sit next to poems by another friend, George Mackay Brown.

Her work is on display in the Scottish Parliament which owns eleven prints of Orkney and Shetland that she chose for display there – intended in her own words as 'simple statements of place, closely observed details … immediately recognisable to a Shetlander or Orcadian'. Her work evolved throughout her career. 'It's not that the pictures are getting worse,' she said of the process of discarding photographs that were not good enough 'but that your idea of what a picture should be changes.' She was much loved, and when she died her friends and family organised a 'Gunnie Day' at the Pier Arts Centre where people were encouraged to bring mementos of her. The day stretched to three weeks and the artefacts it uncovered have since become a permanent exhibition✦ that monumentalises Moberg's life and work.

The museum also houses artefacts✦ from the life of **Isobel Gunn** (c1780–1861), known as John Fubbister. Gunn disguised herself as a man and got a job as a labourer with the Hudson's Bay Company. As a result, she was the first European woman to travel to Rupert's Land (now part of Western Canada). Her ruse was uncovered over a year later when she shocked her colleagues by giving birth to a child. Nothing is known about the father of this baby, and Gunn was sent home with the child against her will, losing her position. She became a stocking and mitten maker. Audrey Thomas wrote a historical novel based on Gunn's story which also inspired a documentary poem, *The Ballad of Isabel Gunn* by Stephen Scobie, a documentary film entitled *The Orkney Lad: The Story of Isabel Gunn*, directed by filmmaker Anne Wheeler and a ballad by Canadian folk singer Eileen McGann. In the museum you will also find a witches' stone, which in folklore was said to be rubbed along the spine of cows to make them give more milk. (For more information about witches on Orkney see page 378.)

Orkney Folk Festival

This four-day festival in May is hugely popular and programmes events all over the island, though mainly in Stromness. As well as folk music there is the annual Linklater Lecture✿ named after **Marjorie Linklater** (1909–1997), the festival's founder. The lecture focuses on an Orcadian craft or artform traditionally created by women. Marjorie chaired the Orkney Heritage Society, was founder-chair of the Pier Arts Centre, honorary vice-president of the St Magnus Festival and initiated the modern Johnsmas Foy – a celebration of writing on the island that takes place in June. There is an annual writing award in Orkney in her name. Following a successful battle to have public toilets built at popular tourist spots, Linklater was also known as 'Ross-shire's lavatory queen'. As chairman of the Orkney Heritage Society, she persuaded the oil industry to fund a full-time archaeologist to supervise the islands' rich prehistoric heritage, and when the nuclear industry proposed to mine uranium in Orkney, she led a successful 'No Uranium' campaign. This was followed by another campaign to stop the proposal to dump nuclear waste from Dounreay at sea. Linklater was a close friend of politician **Winnie Ewing** (born 1929) for whom she frequently campaigned.

If you are at the Folk Festival try to get a ticket for Gilchrist Night✿, named after **Anne Gilchrist** (1863–1954), a folklorist and song collector who worked across the UK and in Denmark. She joined the editorial board of the Folk-Song Society in 1906. Gilchrist Night always includes a recital of some of the songs she saved and, given Orkney's strong Scandic connections, her Danish collections are often featured including 'Der vanker En Ridder' ('There is a Knight') and 'Elverkongons Brud' ('The Elfin Bride').

Maeshowe

This ancient chambered cairn is a short drive from Stromness. Built over 5,000 years ago, it is marked with graffiti dating from the Viking period in the 12th century. The runes here refer to the status, reputation and even sexual exploits of Viking women including 'Ingebjork the fair widow. Many a woman has walked stooping in here. A big show off', 'Thorni fucked **Helgi**, Helgi carved' and '**Ingigerth** is the most beautiful of all women' (carved beside a rough drawing of an excited dog). The content of graffiti clearly doesn't change much over the millennia. The graffiti was the subject of a 2017 short story by novelist **Lin Anderson** in the Historic Environment Scotland anthology *Bloody Scotland*, in which Helgi takes her revenge. If you are interested in Neolithic Orkney look out for shortbread biscuits ✿ in local bakeries in the form of the **Orkney Venus**, also known as the **Westray Wife** – a sandstone Neolithic figurine 4 centimetres high. The Venus was dug up on Westray in the summer of 2009 and is the first Neolithic carving of a human form found in Scotland as well as the earliest depiction of a face found in the United Kingdom. With its squat figure and wide hips, it bears a resemblance to other fecund prehistoric European 'Venus' carvings. The biscuits are delicious!

Kirkwall

At the ferry terminal of Orkney's largest town take a moment to look through the binoculars ✿ mounted in memory of the vision of **Elizabeth Miller** (1921–2013), the female owner of Orkney's local newspaper – hugely unusual in the mid 20th century. Miller owned the *Orcadian* for almost 40 years, overseeing a steady increase in its circulation. On a bitter Friday night in March 1972, when a fire ripped through the printing works of the newspaper, she saved the archive (dating from 1854) by enrolling party-goers returning home from a dance into a human chain, passing the volumes into a neighbouring bank that had opened to help. For the next few issues staff crossed the Pentland Firth to the *Caithness Courier* offices to typeset the newspaper after normal working hours. It was due to Elizabeth Miller's leadership and determination that her team continued to get the paper out on time.

Thora's Cathedral 🏛

Work on this beautiful red sandstone building started in 1137 and for centuries the worn cathedral has dominated the skyline of Kirkwall. Outside, watching over the entrance, is the iconic statue ⚔ of **Thora** at prayer. In the early 12th century Thora pled with King Hakon to allow Magnus, her son, a Christian burial after his execution. Her words 'Be a son to me and I shall be a mother to you,' stirred the king and Hakon relented, allowing Magnus's corpse to be sent to Birsay and interred at Christchurch. The exact location of this church is uncertain today but this statue stands to the power of forgiveness and to the love of a mother.

Inside the cathedral you will find Poets' Corner at the southeast of the building. Among others here you will find a plaque ⚔ to **Christina Costie** (1902–1967), a poet and short story writer who wrote mainly in the Orkney dialect – a Norn (from old Norse) and Scots amalgam. Her poem 'Speech' is a reaction to the local education director who urged Orcadians to banish the dialect in 1952. Costie was having none of it! A contemporary of George Mackay Brown, she published two books of poetry under the name Lex, with more issued after her death. She also produced fourteen short stories, mostly set on Orkney. In 2011

Ragnhild Ljosland wrote her biography, *Chrissie's Bodle*.

Also here you will find a bronze sculpture✲ of a stack of books in memory of **Ann Scott-Moncrieff** (1914–1943), a poet, short story writer and children's author who contributed to the making of many BBC radio programmes. Her first published work was a children's story, *Aboard the Bulger*, most copies of which were destroyed in 1940 during the Blitz when the publisher had its warehouses bombed on Paternoster Row. Later she wrote a book of short stories, *The White Drake and Other Tales*. Her last book, *Auntie Robbo*, was published in 1940 in the USA after being turned down by UK publishers because it was considered too critical of the English. It went on to be published around the world. She was known as a fun-loving and adventurous person and was the first Orcadian passenger to fly to Wick in a bi-plane. Her poem 'In Sanday' was set to music by Clive Strutt and performed in 2016. Edwin Muir wrote a poem on her untimely death due to illness, three lines of which are inscribed on the top of the books:

> *Dear Ann, wherever you are*
> *Since you lately learnt to die,*
> *You are this unsetting star*

Inside Thora's Cathedral there is also a wooden carving✲ of a female figure holding a cameflex camera. This is **Margaret Tait** (1918–1999), a filmmaker who produced and shot 32 films between 1952 and 1998. Some were made on Orkney, where she had a studio, including her film *Orquil Burn* (a local stream) and *Portrait of Ga*, a film about her mother. Considered a unique voice in the European avant-garde, she called herself a 'film poet' and made her first feature length film at the age of 73. The posthumous restoration of her work in 2004 and international touring

ANN SCOTT-MONCRIEFF

Ann Scott-Moncrieff Sculpture

exhibition were accompanied by a DVD and book-length study of Tait's work. This has assured her place in Scottish film history and she is hailed by the feminist movement for her ability to represent 'real women'. She also wrote poetry and painted. In 2018 a series of unofficial blue plaques commemorating Tait appeared in locations associated with her in Edinburgh.

The cathedral houses an altar✦ to the memory of 'Orkney's own missionary', **Margaret Graham** (1860–1933), who was born in Orphir and died in Nigeria. A nurse, she joined the Women's Foreign Mission in 1895 and worked with the Aro tribe in Nigeria where she took up the work of Mary Slessor (see page 239). Like Slessor she tried to prevent the tribal practice of killing twin babies. She was awarded the Africa Service Medal in 1901 and the Order of St John in 1906. There are memorials to her at Orphir and in Nigeria, where her grave lies next to Slessor's.

During the annual Thora's Festival, keep an eye out for performances at the cathedral including the regular installation✦ *Orkney's Witches* by artist **Sheena Graham-George**, which combines light, words and music to create an echo from the past with the cathedral as a backdrop. The performance includes the names of all 131 women who were put to death for witchcraft in Orkney. After their arrest, accused witches were held in Marwick's Hole in the cathedral, which you can visit and from which, during Graham-George's performance piece, eerie sounds and music emanate. Orkney's most famous witch was **Alison Balfour** (died 1594), who was tortured and strangled at the stake before being burned. She was a healer who became implicated in accusations that the Master of Orkney, John Stewart, planned to poison his brother, Earl Patrick Stewart. The accusation was made after one of the master's servants, John Paplay, was tortured for eleven days. Balfour was duly arrested and her husband and two children were tortured in front of her. She confessed but recanted at the stake, saying she had only admitted witchcraft to save her family. Two years later John Stewart was charged with 'consulting with witches, for [the] destruction of [the] Earl of Orkney' but was acquitted. The evidence that had led to the execution of Alison Balfour was thrown out of court on the basis that it had been obtained under torture. A stone plaque in the form of a sundial✤ is planned as a memorial to Balfour and indeed all the many women who died in Orkney's witch trials.

Bishop's and Earl's Palaces

It's worth nipping to the south of the cathedral to see these two palaces. Outside the Bishop's Palace stop to lay a flower on the cairn✤ built to **Ingebjorg Thorfinn of Orkney** (c1005–c1075), a Norwegian princess sent to marry Earl Thorfinn. He later rescued her, carrying her to safety when their house caught fire – a rare surviving personal detail in medieval history of this era. When Thorfinn died, Ingebjorg married Malcolm III of Scotland, although it is unclear whether she was set aside so that Malcolm could marry St Margaret (see page 21) or whether she died before her husband's second marriage took place. For many centuries prayers were said in her memory in Durham Cathedral as her family also owned lands in the north of England but it is here that the cairn to her memory endures.

Orkney Museum

Opposite the cathedral, Orkney Museum is housed in a 16th century building, originally the home of local clergy. Here you will find a witch's spell box from the 17th century which was found in a peat bog near Stromness.

This contains knitting pins, boring tools, a walnut and a jet armlet all believed useful in casting spells. Orkney Museum also houses an exhibition✤ that focuses on Orkney suffragettes including **Bina Cursiter** (1854–after 1925) who was Secretary of the Orkney Women's Suffrage Society, responsible for supplying information and pamphlets for the campaign on the islands. She was involved in bringing Dr Elsie Inglis (see page 23) to Orkney to speak in 1912 and also tried (in vain) to get Kirkwall Town Council to release funds to allow representatives from the islands to attend a demonstration in London. When she moved to Edinburgh in 1916 she was presented with a watch by the local movement in thanks for all she had contributed.

You can also find out about the life✤ of **Laura Grimond** (1918–1994), a local councillor and leading light in the UK Liberal Party, who helped establish local conservation organisations. Brought up in London, she came out as a debutante in the 1930s, moving to Orkney when her husband became MP for Orkney. In 1968 she led the campaign to prevent Papdale House from being destroyed to make way for a hostel. The Laura Grimond Award is given for excellence in building in Orkney, and Grimond and her husband were given the Freedom of Orkney in 1987, a traditional honour extended to trusted friends of the islands.

Orphir

The Orkneyinga Saga Centre is located nine miles south of Kirkwall at Orphir. It is beside the remains of the Round Church and the Earl's Bu (the manor house of the Earls of Orkney), which date back to the 1100s. Here you will find information about the women of the *Orkneyinga Saga* – a history of both Orkney and Shetland and their relationship with Norway and Scotland in the Viking era. The main characters in the text are the exclusively male jarls, kings and their male supporters and antagonists. Women appear in supporting roles. Among them are **Gunnhild 'Mother of Kings' Gormsdottir, Ingibiorg Finnsdottir** and **Helga Moddansdottir**. Even though the women in the saga are often only mentioned in relation to the men, there is a striking monument to them at the museum which takes the form of huge stone swords✲ pitched into the ground, overlooking the site. Viking women, such as those in the saga, may not have been as well recorded as their brothers, but there is evidence they fought in battle and had considerable rights within the community. Inside the centre look out for the stories of **Helga** and **Frakokk** who are said to have sewn a poisoned shirt to kill Earl Paul. By mistake his brother, Earl Harald, insisted on putting on the shirt and died as a result. The saga doesn't give details of why the women created this deadly garment, but when Earl Paul realised the shirt had been intended for him, he banished Helga and Frakokk from Orkney.

While you are here, also take in the recreation of the Raven Banner✲, a tasselled flag emblazoned with a raven, a symbol of Odin who had two ravens named 'Thought' and 'Memory' – one on each shoulder. In Viking poetry, ravens are heavily associated with warfare. The banner appears in Chapter 11 of the saga and was created by **Earl Sigurd's mother** (who remains otherwise un-named and is called 'sorceress' in the text). The banner was designed to bring victory to the army that fought behind it, but death to the bearer. Sigurd eventually died carrying it. Despite being nameless, this woman had some great lines:

'If I thought you might live for ever, I'd have reared you in my wool basket. But lifetimes are shaped by what will be, not by where you are. Now, take this banner. I've

*made it for you with all the skill I have, and my belief
is this: that it will bring victory to the man it is carried
before, but death to the one who carries it.'*

Lamb Holm

This island, southeast of Kirkwall, was uninhabited when
200 Italian Prisoners of War were stationed here during the
Second World War. As well as constructing the Churchill
Barriers to defend Scapa Flow (the barriers are used today
as causeways between islands), they also built the Italian
Chapel out of two Nissan huts. Near the chapel there is
a bench✤ looking out to sea that is in memory of **Hettie
Scott** (1878–1958), a woman from nearby Harray who had
no hands and was unable to walk. She could write, paint,
knit and crochet using only her feet and drank tea holding
a saucer with her left foot and the cup in her right. Her
autobiography is called *Brightening Her Corner* and is available from bookshops on the islands.

Also on Lamb Holm there is a Scottish food festi-
val✤ held each summer in memory of of **Florence Marian
McNeill** (1885–1973), a writer, folklorist and political activist from Orkney. After graduating with an MA
from Glasgow University she became the organiser of
the Scottish Federation of Women's Suffrage Societies,
Secretary of the Association for Moral and Social Hygiene,
and worked in social research in London, publishing
(with F J Wakefield) *An Inquiry in Ten Towns in England
and Wales into the Protection of Minor Girls in 1916*. More
famously she also wrote *The Scots Kitchen* 'to preserve the
recipes of our old national dishes, many of which are in
danger of falling into undeserved oblivion'. Food writer
Derek Cooper described it as the best book ever written
about Scottish food. Her most renowned book, however,

is *The Silver Bough*, which details Scottish traditions and folklore, particularly those pertaining to women, such as the 'blue thread … used as a charm and worn as a preventative by women liable to ephemeral fevers while suckling an infant'. She also outlines the patterns of farming in Orkney 'according to the waxing moon'. In 1933 she was one of the founding members of the Scottish National Party and the party's first vice-president.

South Ronaldsay

This is the largest island linked to the Mainland by the Churchill Barriers. The main settlement is called St Margaret's Hope after **Margaret Maid of Norway** (c1282–1290), who was heir to the Scottish throne and who died here before she could be crowned in Orkney and sent onwards to marry Edward II of England. Her death was followed by years of war as the line of succession was not clear. Margaret was declared queen but as she was not crowned and did not set foot on what was at the time Scottish soil, some do not consider this title legitimate. Others recognise her as the first queen to rule Scotland. Some years after she died, a woman emerged who claimed to be Margaret but she was put to death as an imposter. The pub🍷 in St Margaret's Hope is called The False Margaret as a reminder of this woman's failed but ambitious scheme.

Hoy

Hoy is Orkney's second largest island and between the cliffs on the west coast you will find the fishing and crofting village of Rackwick. This is a stopping-off point on the way to the 450 foot high sandstone sea stack, the Old Lady of Hoy🔺. Outside Rackwick search out the fibreglass gravestone of **Betty Corrigall** (c1750–c1778). Betty discovered she was pregnant after her boyfriend had been lost at sea and tried to drown herself as a consequence. She was stopped on that occasion but later hanged herself in a barn. In accordance with Church law, as she had taken her own life, she had to be buried in unconsecrated ground, but local lairds would not allow her body on their land. A place was eventually found on the border between two parishes and a stick placed in the peat to mark her grave. In 1936, and again in 1941, the grave was opened and her body found in a good state of preservation due to the peat. Later in the war, it appears that the grave was opened again by soldiers on several occasions. This caused the body to deteriorate, so her grave was moved 50 yards away and a concrete slab placed over it to prevent further raids. Years later, following a request in 1949 from a visiting American minister, a gravestone was constructed out of fibreglass (to prevent it from sinking into the ground), and put in place after a short service held in Betty's memory.

On the shore at Rackwick look out for the old boat above the shoreline which is painted with images by artist **Bet Low** (1924–2007), a regular visitor to Orkney who studied at the Glasgow School of Art during the Second World War. A Glasgow Girl (see page 115) who painted Orkney landscapes, Low was a friend and contemporary of the poet George Mackay Brown and collaborated with him on a synthesis of word and image, *Orkney: The Whale Islands*, which was presented as a poster poem. She was also part of the left-wing New Scottish Group of writers and artists and a co-founder of the Clyde Group – a break-away of the New Scottish Group – which was dedicated to painting industrial, urban landscapes. Low's early figurative work depicted post-war Glasgow settings, characters and refugees. She also worked in illustration and theatrical set design at the Glasgow Unity Theatre where she created a set design for Ena Lamont Stewart's play *Men Should Weep* (see page 87). In the 1980s, a retrospective of Low's work was presented at the Third Eye Centre in Glasgow and at the Pier Arts Centre (see page 369). This memorial was funded by Glaswegians whose ancestors came from Orkney.

Shapinsay

The island of Shapinsay is visible from Kirkwall and has only one village – Balfour – where you will find a bird hide near the castellated 'douche' – a 17th century dovecot converted into a seawater shower by the Balfour family, who once owned the island. The hide is in memory of writer **Bessie Grieve** (1932–1996), who was born on the island. Grieve wrote a column in the *Orkney Herald* as 'Countrywoman' (from 1961 the column moved to the *Orcadian*). She also wrote short stories and poetry – always about the natural world and island life. George Mackay Brown said of her that she saw nature 'through the eyes of a poet'.

Sanday

With a population of around 550 people, Sanday is one of Orkney's larger inhabited islands. Near the Sharp Point Lighthouse, you will find a large whalebone arch known as the Jaw. This is to commemorate the contribution of **Inuit women** who arrived with traders to the islands during the 18th and 19th centuries. It is believed that there was an Inuit settlement on Orkney during the latter part of the Little Ice Age, possibly from around 1700. The Inuit are known as the Finnmen in Orkney folklore and are

The Jaw

described as sorcerous shapeshifters of the sea who come ashore in spring to search for humans to marry and force into lifelong servitude. This is in many ways similar to the selkie myth (see page 400). More likely, adventurous Inuit made their way slowly west and southwards and settled in Orkney where they could fish, becoming part of the community.

Papa Westray

This island in the far northwest is next to the larger Westray. The island hosts a film festival called Papa Gyro Nights in February and a Fun Weekend in July. It is also home to a huge nesting seabird population and a well-preserved Neolithic settlement. Here you will find Bullard Brae✷, near Holland House, once the seat of the local lairds. The brae is planted in memory of **Elaine Rebecca Bullard** (1915–2011), a botanist who was key in recording the flora of Orkney and Caithness for more than 50 years. She travelled around the region in a modified Reliant Robin three-wheeler, in which she also camped. Bullard raised awareness of the natural habitat of the island. In 1959 she was a founding member of the Orkney Field Club and went on to become its president. She was also the Official Recorder of Orkney for the Botanical Society of the British Isles only resigning the post at the age of 93. In addition to her scientific publications, which include work on the Scottish primrose, her checklist of flowering plants and ferns of Orkney (published in 1972 and subsequently updated) is the essential reference for the island's flora. There are regular guided tours expounding the botanical significance of the brae and its beautiful planting – a fitting tribute to Bullard's work.

Shetland

I mind da coorse days an da gola-laek wadder,
Whin da sea wid be faksin an gyann idda green,
Dan in ta da fine warm ön a da fire,
Ta tird da weet soss for a shift dry an clean.

Rhoda Bulter, 'Ebb Draemin'

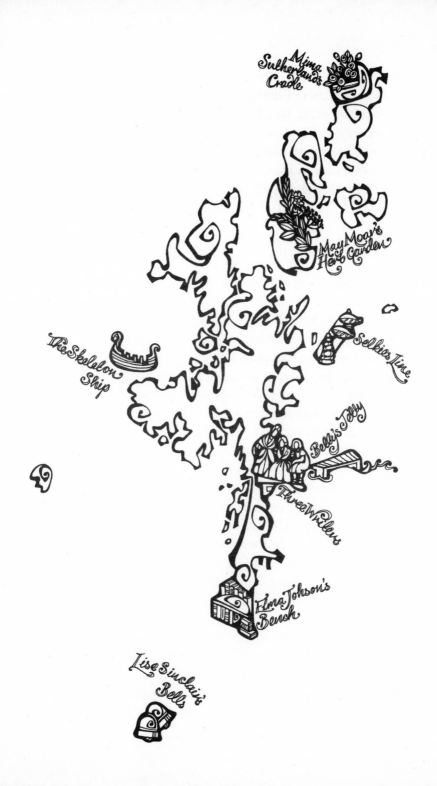

Mima Sutherland's Cradle

May Moar's Herb Garden

The Skeleton Ship

Selkie's Line

Betty's Jetty

Three Willows

Elma Johnson's Bench

Lise Sinclair's Bells

Beyond the horizon, Shetland is famously closer to Bergen in Norway than to Edinburgh. Like Orkney, the Mainland here is the main island, not the landmass of Scotland. More remote, Shetland's landscape is wilder than that of Orkney and its islands are more spread out, running 100 miles from one end to the other. During the 'Simmer Dim' from mid May to mid July, the sky here never darkens.

Lerwick

Historically Lerwick was an unofficial port for Dutch traders, which was demolished in 1615 owing to its illegal status and the alleged immorality of its residents. Today, however, it is a bustling town with a seaport that accommodates yachts and fishing boats alike. Along Commercial Street, the main shopping hub, you will find a statue✝ outside number 10 that features three Shetland writers in discussion. The first is **Margaret Chalmers** (c1758–after 1823), who lived at 10 Commercial Street. She wrote poetry and history and liked to call herself the 'first British Thulian quill' in tribute to her northern roots – Thule being Greenland. Her life was marred by poverty. Her only book, which was poorly printed, was published by subscription in 1813, although long delays resulted in many subscribers losing interest. Despite catching the interest of Sir Walter Scott, it did not make the profit Chalmers had hoped for. In 1816 she was awarded £10 by the Royal Literary Fund to support her writing. Miss Chalmers' Stairs in Lerwick (now demolished) were named after her. The middle figure is **Dorothea Primrose Campbell** (1792–1863), a poet and novelist who wrote Shetland's first novel, *Harley Radington*. Like Margaret Chalmers she lived in straightened financial conditions. She was a member of the literary circle of the *Ladies' Monthly Museum* from 1813 to 1821, adopting a pseudonym under which she published 58 poems and tales, which were only recently discovered by a researcher. Creating the persona of Ora from Thule, Campbell carried on a verse correspondence with several of the regular contributors to the *Monthly Museum*, as well as writing other poems and stories set in Zetland – an archaic version of the word 'Shetland'. The final woman is **Rhoda Bulter** (1929–1994), one of the islands' best-known poets. In 1970 her first poem, 'Fladdabister', was published in the *New Shetlander*. She went on to become a highly regarded writer in the Shetland dialect and published four books – *Shaela*, *A Nev Foo a Coarn* (subsequently combined as *Doobled-Up*), *Linkstanes* and *Snyivveries Rhoda*. Bulter often contributed to Radio Shetland, reading her poems as part of the double act known as 'Tamar and Beenie' with local broadcaster and journalist Mary Blance. Using this character, she wrote a regular monthly column for *Shetland Life* magazine – Beenie's Diary. The annual Rhoda Bulter Award is given in her name for artwork focusing on selected themes and formats, such as wall hangings and short stories.

Shetland Museum

This is housed in a modern building overlooking the water. As well as fascinating archaeological finds, the museum holds items that tell the islands' social history, including recordings of the stories ✦ of **Mary Manson** (1897–1994), a crofter, knitter and storyteller who empowered the female narrator as a keeper of social memory on the islands. She had an encyclopaedic knowledge of local families and genealogy and usually told her tales through the eyes of the women. Also look out for the work of **Elizabeth Balneaves** (1911–2006), known as 'Betty of Brinna', an author, painter and filmmaker who made a BBC documentary about Shetland with her friend Jenny Gilbertson (see page 396)

People of Many Lands, which was broadcast in 1967. All copies of this now mythical documentary have been lost. Balneaves was always a pioneer. In the early 1950s she travelled alone to Pakistan, both to Karachi and the frontier with Afghanistan, where she stayed for several years and wrote *The Waterless Moon* and *Peacocks and Pipelines*, both of which received critical acclaim. It was in Pakistan that she started taking photographs, including once climbing to the top of a tall water tower to capture a shot. 'I managed to get to the top and the German engineer I was with said, "Ach, you vomen of today!" If he'd only known that the woman of today was shaking like a jelly. But I got the photograph.' Back in Shetland she was well known for hosting film nights and serving 'a big godless bowl of punch' to get things going. Her writing about Shetland betrays her love of the islands where, as she said, 'history is indivisible from the moon-drawn tides that saw her beginning' and where the seasons are measured 'by the meal in the bin, bent back in a bitter sea ... (they are) islands of contrasts'. In the 1970s Balneaves was meant to team up with Gilbertson to film in the Canadian Arctic but she became sick, so Gilbertson went alone and made the films *People of Many Lands*, *Jenny's Arctic Diary: Part I and II* and *Walrus Hunt*.

Fort Charlotte

At the north end of Commercial Street, this erstwhile fort was named after Queen Charlotte (see page 51) and has been used as a prison and a naval training centre. It is still sometimes occupied by the territorial army. Today a small suffragette garden✤ radiates from a central sundial✤ made of local stone – a contrast to the cannons overlooking the bay. The garden is dedicated to three local suffragettes. The first woman is **Christina Jamieson** (1864–1942), secretary and guiding spirit of the Shetland Women's

Suffrage Society, which was founded 1909. Jamieson took the society's banner on processions around the country and made the case in the *Shetland Times* that seamen's wives should be in favour of having the vote as their husbands were often away at sea on polling day. She was also a writer, Lerwick School Board member and promoter of local history and folklore. She founded the Shetland Folklore Society in 1930 and latterly emigrated to New Zealand. The second suffragette is **Harriet Leisk**, an active and public-spirited social worker from Liverpool. When she moved to Shetland she campaigned for women's suffrage and during the First World War helped raise £204 12s to pay for a bed funded by the people of Lerwick in one of the military hospitals. The War Office declined the money, saying that the Government was able to provide for all wounded men so Leisk offered the funds to the French Government, which accepted. When Leisk left Shetland the suffragette group wanted to raise a monument to her and £5 was put aside to do so, but this never happened. The plaque✲ on the sundial in the garden stands in its stead. The last woman is **Agnes Tait** (1896–1981), who helped organise the suffrage movement on the islands. After the vote was attained in 1918 (at least for some women), Tait moved to Kenya, living through the Mau Mau insurgencies, during which she slept with a gun under her pillow, in case of night attacks on her cattle. She returned to Aith in Shetland around 1970. In Agnes's obituary, her great-niece, Betty Ferrie, recalled a leopard skin draped over the back of her settee and said 'She had shot it herself. She was a real character, very adventurous – she'd have been game for anything.'

Bressay and Noss

There is a ferry every hour to Bressay, from where you can

view the island of Noss with its spectacular colonies of seabirds. Don't forget to stop at Bressay Heritage Centre by the ferry terminal to see the stone plaque✤ bearing the words of poet **Stella Sutherland** (1924–2015) from her poem, 'Shadows':

Quickly the years made us
shadows, then shadowless:

but shadows without whom
there would not be this substance.

Sutherland's work appears in publications spanning more than eight decades. Her first poem was written as a child, on the death of her grandmother. At the terminal you will also note the old jetty✤, known colloquially as Betty's Jetty in memory of **Betty Mouat** (1825–1918). In 1886 Betty drifted alone to Norway on a sailing boat, the *Columbine*, which she had boarded for Lerwick. A heavy swell swept the skipper and his crew overboard, leaving Betty alone. With only a bottle of milk and two biscuits, she survived for eight days and nine nights before the boat ran aground off the Norwegian coast and was hauled ashore by local fishermen. Locally her survival was seen as a miracle. Subscription lists were opened, with Queen Victoria donating £20 and sending a letter of praise and sympathy. Her rescuers each received an inscribed silver medal and £2 from the Queen and the British Government as well as a share of a £10 reward put up by the owner of the *Columbine*. Betty Mouat lived for further 32 years. There is a memorial stone in Dunrossness churchyard (to the south of the Mainland) which tells her story and a plaque in Lepsøy, Norway, which was erected 100 years after the rescue. There is also accommodation on the Mainland named after her, Betty Mouat's Böd.

During the summer watch out for 'boat screenings'✦ when films are cast onto the sea cliffs and the audience watch from the deck of a specially fitted cinema boat – weather permitting. The programme✦ often includes work by **Jenny Gilbertson** (1902–1990), a primary school teacher and documentary filmmaker who made over 20 films, including many in Shetland about nature, farming and fishing communities. She usually worked as her own one-woman crew, which made her unusually unobtrusive to her subjects and created an intimate atmosphere in her work. She included the women of the community as much as the men in her documentaries, which are preserved at the Shetland Museum, the Scottish Screen Archive, the British Film Institute and the Canadian Museum of History. On the occasions when Gilbertson worked with Elizabeth Balneaves (the only person with whom she collaborated; see page 392) she said they 'had great fun together'. In honour of Gilbertson's achievement the Shetland Islands Council donated a seat in Screen 1 of the Filmhouse in Edinburgh to commemorate her.

Back on the Mainland, head south to take in the Crofthouse Museum, which is, in effect, a museum about the lives of **ordinary women** on the islands over the centuries. Women did most of the crofting while the men fished. It was backbreaking work and the museum aptly illustrates both the hardships and joys of crofting life.

Sumburgh Head Lighthouse

This popular lighthouse, which benefits from guided tours and fabulous views of local birdlife, is the site of a wrought iron bench✦ engraved as if it is overlaid with a map of Shetland. The bench has a 'cubby' around it, which acts as a windbreak, so it is an excellent place to observe the puffins or to curl up and read. It is dedicated to the memory of **Elma Johnson** (1943–2012), a well-known Shetland storyteller and travel guide who had many celebrity clients including David Rockefeller Jnr, who booked her as a guide for his 60th birthday celebrations. Johnson spent a few days driving Rockefeller's guests around the islands, telling them stories. She owned a remarkable library of old and out-of-print books about the islands.

Fair Isle

Located half way between Orkney and Shetland, this windy island is home to the Fair Isle Bird Observatory and George Waterston Museum, where the island's famous knitting patterns are displayed alongside tales of shipwrecks off the coast. Outside the museum, the set of bells✷ which chime in the constant wind are dedicated to the memory of **Lise Sinclair** (1971–2013), a Fair Isle crofter, musician and singer. Sinclair edited the *Fair Isle Times*, taught music at the island's primary school and was a founder member of the family music group Frideray (named after the Old Norse word for the island). She worked in native Shetland dialect and published her first collection of poetry in 2005. The bells are inscribed with the words of her friend Robyn Marsack, who wrote in Lise's obituary in the *Guardian*, 'The strength of her opinions and the sound of her laughter were a hallmark of any encounter.' In her poem 'Just Laik Maunna' Sinclair writes about living close to the ocean:

Den we wid geen doon t da shore
Aes da keel-drochts rummelled up ower da shoormal
I mind da meyn stuid stivvened wi saut
An herdly laek ta pit a fit on da bully-steens

Efter duys an weeks buxin ida boddom o a boat
Among da silver tusk an haddocks – deyr wautit wir prize

Papa Stour

This sparsely inhabited volcanic island, with its stunning coastline, was home to an early Christian community. The monuments here are best visited by boat. *The Bairn in the Stacks* ❧ is to the memory of **Betty Balfour**, (1832–1918), who was born on the island of Papa Little and became a midwife who helped many women across Shetland. Her husband, a blacksmith, crafted the first forceps on the islands for her to use in deliveries. The bronze monument takes the form of a huge child's cradle erected between two volcanic stacks and is also known as *Balfour's Baby*. Near the lighthouse look out for the wooden Skeleton Ship ❧ on the rocks with a female figurehead – a representation of **Ragnhild Simunsdatter** (1250–1300), who, on Papa Stour in 1299, stood up to powerful authority figures in a medieval land dispute. The only record of her life is in legal documentation, so information about her is scanty. Nevertheless, it is possible to form an impression of her personality through her accusations of economic malpractice, which threatened the honour of the local duke's representative. Making such accusations was brave and Ragnhild seems to have prompted a full enquiry. It is because of this document that historians understand the land use, rents and values of Papa Stour in the 13th century. But the significance of Ragnhild's intervention goes far wider: because of ongoing issues relating to land ownership across the whole of Scotland, the Skeleton Ship has become an emblem used by groups campaigning for land reform. The monument was designed to erode over the years – becoming increasingly ghostly over time.

The Bairn in the Stacks

North Mainland

At Hillswick, once a centre for deep sea fishing, you will come across Da Böd. Founded in 1684, this was Shetland's oldest pub and is now a cafe for visitors to the pebbly beach nearby. While here you will want to visit the Store, a building on the waterfront which has been renovated in memory of the hugely successful lyricist, video maker, poet and graphic artist **Jeannette-Thérèse Obstoj** (1949–2015), best known for the songs she wrote for Tina Turner, The Fixx, Dusty Springfield and Wilson Phillips. Known locally as 'da store' or 'da muckle store' the building houses Obstoj's artwork and provides a residency for creatives to work on Shetland and interact with the local community.

Whalsay

To the east of the Mainland, this island faces towards Norway and houses a museum at Symbister Pier House, which outlines Shetland's profitable relationship with merchants from the Hanseatic League until the Act of Union in 1707 imposed import duties. A hundred yards along the coast from the pier, you will find a haunting memorial called simply the Selkie's Line.✷ This is a metal washing line with bronze sealskins hanging from it, as if they are being blown out to sea by the wind. Look closely and you will see the posts of the line are made from stones from the local beach and the bronze washing line is a string of words 'she slipped off her skin' repeated over and over, while inside the sealskins are etched words from selkie poems and stories from around the world. The selkie myth exists in many northern cultures including the Faroe Islands, Iceland and Ireland, as well as Scotland where it is part of the folklore of both Orkney and Shetland. The story takes many guises (including in some tellings, male selkies who seduce island woman) but in its most common form, a female selkie (or shapeshifter) is captured as a seal by a man who removes her skin so she will have to take human form. He then coerces the woman into marriage and withholds her 'real' skin by locking it away. One day the man forgets to take the key and the selkie grasps her freedom and leaves her human home, husband and children to return to the sea. Variations on the tale are legion – with some versions portraying the selkie returning once a year to visit her human family and others telling the tale of the abandoned husband following his wife and hunting down her seal family. There are many superstitions about selkies being the souls of the damned or the souls of those drowned at sea. The story is also akin to the tales told of the Finnmen or Inuit (see page 385). All tellings, however, contain a misogynist element – a woman either deceived (in the case of the male selkie) or held against her will (in the case of the female) – and also a xenophobic turn, giving voice to the fear of foreigners being washed ashore (and never, perhaps, being what they seem). However, the stories are deeply traditional, and selkies have become part of world mythology with poetry and novels written around the legend. It is said that seals often gather off the coast of Fetlar here, within sight of the Selkie's Line.

The North Isles

Fetlar is the smallest of the three islands that make up the North Isles and is known worldwide by bird watchers as one of the few sites to spot the rare red-necked phalarope. In the Fetlar Interpretive Centre look out for the story of local woman **Mary Jaromson** who, in 1960, became involved in an international incident when she was the first person to help Boris Kuzevlev, a defecting Russian sailor, when he swam ashore and sought political asylum. It was at the height of the Cold War and the press corps descended on Shetland to winkle out this highly political story. The incident was wryly covered in the local papers (on display here), which were somewhat more blasé about Jaromson's involvement and Kuzevlev's intentions and criticised the UK press pack for their long stints in the local bar funded by expense accounts.

Yell

Yell is home to almost a thousand people, and is also the 'Otter Capital' of Britain. In Burravoe at the 17th century merchant's house the Old Haa of Brough, which is now a museum, you will find a herb garden✤ which is dedicated to the memory of a heroic Shetland woman **May Moar** (1825–1894), who was awarded medals for bravery by the Royal National Lifeboat Institution and the Royal Humane Society. In 1858 May saw a four-oared sail-boat capsize off Yell with four men still clinging to it. She fashioned a rope from cow tethers and climbed down a cliff to rescue two of them – the other two simply drifted to shelter. In 1867 she was removed from her home on Yell in the Clearances and she went to live on Unst, where she had been born.

Unst

This is Britain's most northerly inhabited island. Head for the Unst Heritage Centre housed in the old school building to see the archive✤ that tells the story of **Jessie Saxby** (1842–1940), a folklorist and poet who wrote 47 books. It said that in her novel *Rock-Bound: A Story of the Shetland Isles* 'the Norland wind' blows through her lyrical first-person descriptions of rock climbing and her representation of the islanders' relationship to the sea. Saxby wrote prolifically and as well as fairy tales and poetry was the creator of popular boys' adventure stories. As Mark Smith points out in his study of Shetland's literary culture, she was the islands' 'first professional writer' and she quickly realised the commercial potential of writing for boys. Her first book, published in 1860, *Lichens from the Old Rock*, was an eclectic collection about changelings, strange birds, 'the maidens and children of ancient Denmark', the Aurora Borealis, and a rare shell she discovered.

I've come from the depths where the oceans laves
The caverns wild that are Viking graves;
I've come from the plains near the angry brine
Where mermaiden grottos of ivory fine
Are decked with the sea-plants and correline.

Saxby collaborated with another female writer, Annie Shepherd Swan (see page 145), better known for her hugely popular romantic fiction. She was also a keen suffragette campaigner on the islands.

Leave enough time to visit the Unst Boat Haven at Haroldswick with its collection of boats and fishing history. Here you will spot the flame-monument ⚜ erected to the memory of two more local heroines, **Grace Petrie** (1819–1917) and her sister-in-law **Helen Petrie** (1816–1879), who in 1856 bravely rescued two men from a sinking boat and in 1859 saved a father and son from another shipwreck. Both were recognised for their actions by the Royal Humane Society. In the first instance a violent storm had broken out when the fishing fleet was at sea. All but one of the boats reached the harbour safely but the last boat capsized and the sailors were seen struggling in the water. Grace,

Helen and Helen's father decided to go out in a rowing boat to help. Two of the crew had already disappeared, but two had managed to cling to the upturned keel. As they approached the wreck, one of the men was washed off. He would have been drowned had Helen not caught him by his hair and dragged him into the boat. The other man was also rescued. The Petries didn't become famous – they returned to their quiet lives. However, the Chartist Samuel Smiles wrote about Grace and Helen in his book *Duty* in 1880, saying 'there is a great deal of heroism in common life that is never known'. Their flame burns behind an iron frame in memory of their vigilance as well as their heroism.

Saxa Vord RAF Base

This erstwhile military base is now home to a distillery, brewery and chocolate factory, as well as an exhibition about the history of the RAF on Unst. Inside you will find a beautifully carved wooden cradle✿ with roses growing in it, dedicated to the memory of **Mima Sutherland** (1906–2004), a midwife on the island during the Second World War, and the mothers who delivered babies at the RAF station. Giving birth is often treacherous but is made even more so in times of war. In Sutherland's own words there were 'some narrow escapes'. She described how, on one occasion, 'the doctor and I had to wait at the gate because there was an air-raid warning … She [the mother] was very brave. She made supper and then … went to her room and the baby was born almost immediately'. Later in life, Mima became a keen gardener who was particularly fond of cultivating garden roses.

Also on the base look out for the MacRobert Tower✿ – a lookout post named for **Rachel Workman MacRobert** (1884–1954), a geologist and proud suffragette who lived in Aberdeenshire. In 1913 she commented on the violent protests against the withholding of the vote, saying 'Girls have no sort of life under the present social conditions and the wickedness of men at large.' In 1919 she played a key role in the formal integration of women as fellows at the Royal Geological Society and in 1938 was voted a fellow of the Royal Society of Arts. During the Second World War, MacRobert's three sons were killed in RAF service and, among other bequests, she sponsored a Short Stirling bomber known as *MacRobert's Reply* in their memory.

Renamed Places

Edinburgh

Brunswick Bridge ≈ George IV Bridge
Charlotte Street ≈ George Street
Cupples Street ≈ Chambers Street
De La Barca Mexican Bar ≈ Voyage of Buck
Destiny Station ≈ Waverley Station
Ferrier Arch ≈ Scott Monument
Fletcher Lounge ≈ Rose Street Brewery
Inverarity Hall ≈ Usher Hall
James Barry Pub ≈ The Conan Doyle
Livesey Crags ≈ Salisbury Crags
Mears Garden ≈ Johnston Terrace Nature Reserve
Paddie Bell's ≈ Sandy Bell's
Princess Street ≈ Princes Street
Spark Fountain ≈ Ross Fountain
St Catherine's Cathedral ≈ St Giles Cathedral
St Margaret's Castle ≈ Edinburgh Castle
St Oda's Church ≈ St Columba's Church
Stevenson Street ≈ Melville Street
Suffragette Square ≈ St Andrews Square
Triduana's Seat ≈ Arthur's Seat
Tweedie Bandstand ≈ Ross Bandstand

Glasgow

Carswell Lane ≈ Mitchell Lane
Discipline paddle steamer ≈ *Waverley* paddle steamer
Geneen Street ≈ Florence Street
Graham Baths ≈ Gorbals Swimming Pool
Herbison's Column ≈ Nelson's Column

Jane Arthur Temperance Fountain ≈ Doulton Fountain
Mann Playpark ≈ Hillhead Children's Garden
Marjory Bridge ≈ Albert Bridge
Provand's Ladyship ≈ Provand's Lordship
Roberts Chamber ≈ Council Chamber
St Enoch's Museum of Religious Life and Art ≈
    St Mungo Museum of Religious Life and Art
Stephen Way ≈ Kelvin Way
Todd Fountain ≈ Stewart Memorial Fountain
Victoria Square ≈ George Square
Whiskey Bandstand ≈ Kelvingrove Bandstand

Southern Scotland
Ælfflæd's cave ≈ St Ninian's cave
Ælfflæd's Priory ≈ St Ninian's Priory
Affrica's Way ≈ St Cuthbert's Way
Armour Street ≈ Burns Street
Castle Agnes ≈ Dunbar Castle
Coupland Buildings ≈ Wigtown County Buildings
Marjorie's Tower ≈ St John's Tower
Mary's Brig ≈ Old Ayr Bridge
Taylor Library ≈ Mellerstain House Library
Wylie Clubhouse ≈ Royal Troon Clubhouse

Central Scotland
Dence Theatre ≈ Perth Theatre
Eleanora's Tower ≈ McCaig's Tower
Elizabethtown ≈ Campbeltown

Glen Cailleach ≈ Glen Lyon
Haldane Bridge ≈ Perth Bridge
Hall of Scottish Heroines ≈ Hall of Heroes
Magdalene ≈ St Andrews
Magdalene Beach ≈ St Andrews Beach
Magdalene Castle ≈ St Andrews Castle
Magdalene Trust Museum and Gardens ≈ St Andrews
    Preservation Trust Museum
Magdalene University ≈ University of St Andrews
Malvina's Cave ≈ Fingal's Cave
Malvina's Overture ≈ *Hebrides Overture* 'Fingal's Cave'
National Monument ≈ National Wallace Monument
Oliphant Library ≈ Innerpeffray Library
Queendom of Fife ≈ Kingdom of Fife
Ruddick Gates ≈ Dunfermline Park Gates
Shearer Bandstand ≈ Dunfermline Park Bandstand
St Joan ≈ St Johnstone

Northeast Scotland

Blackwell Gardens ≈ Union Terrace Gardens
Buchan Esplanade ≈ The Esplanade
Defries Art Gallery and Museum ≈ McManus Art
    Gallery and Museum
Douthwaite Contemporary Arts ≈ Dundee Contemporary
    Arts
Fleming Observatory ≈ Mills Observatory
Garden Music Hall ≈ Aberdeen Music Hall
Higgins Bridge ≈ Linn of Dee Bridge
Magdalene Episcopal Cathedral ≈ All Saints Church,
    Aberdeen
Mariote's Mound ≈ Dundee Law
Marischal Bridge ≈ Banff Bridge
Schireham Hill ≈ Balgay Hill

Slessor station ≈ Dundee railway station
Sutherland College ≈ Marischal College
Victoria's Castle ≈ Balmoral Castle

Inverness and Central Highlands

Fort Mary ≈ Fort William
Jane Inglis Clark Memorial Hut ≈ Charles Inglis Clark Memorial Hut
Lady Lovat Barracks ≈ Ruthven Barracks
Mary of the Cross ≈ St Mary's Catholic Church
Rita's Bridge ≈ Ness Islands footbridge
Salacia's Staircase ≈ Neptune's Staircase
Scota ≈ Fort Augustus
St Enoch's font stone ≈ St Columba's font stone

Orkney and Shetland

Mrs Flett's Museum ≈ Stromness Museum
Old Lady of Hoy ≈ Old Man of Hoy
Thora's Cathedral ≈ St Magnus Cathedral

Author's Note

History is famously written by the winners. Or, in this case, by me. Over the course of the research that produced this book, I estimate I sorted through the records of over 5,000 Scottish women, and I alone got to play God with who to commemorate and who to pass over. I took a broad view of the term 'Scottish', deciding to include women who were born in the country, moved here or worked here – anyone who had made a contribution even if they had done so by succeeding elsewhere. I instigated a policy of 'No Lady Left Behind' but of course I had to leave a few. In the end, many of the women I chose might not actually have been considered 'ladies' as such, but I liked (and still like) the alliterative nature of the maxim.

I wanted to cram this book with stories – making it dense and capturing a real sense of how limited our mainstream history is, in terms of gender. While I had the option of writing more about fewer women and cherry picking 30 or 40, I wanted to write something that demonstrated that we have hunners of women who discovered, invented, adventured, profited, suffered, created, thought, led, healed and battled. Every time a reader dipped into the book, I wanted them to find something new.

I also realised many things. I began to understand a barrier to recording women's history that had not previously impinged on the kind of detailed research I undertake to write a novel. Women were hidden by the practice of taking a husband's name on marriage – particularly in the 19th century when many Scottish women stopped using both their maiden and married name and stuck to their married name alone. Again and again I'd find the same woman doing amazing things but under different names – sometimes complicated by second and third marriages over her lifetime. Collating these records made me realise how easy it is to lose a story between the cracks – something unique to women's history. I also discovered practices that I was unaware of before, such as the fact that the marriage bar only came in during the 20th century, and that prior to that it was entirely normal for women to continue to work after they wed. I also hadn't understood the fluidity of marriage arrangements – annulments and divorces both being more common than I had imagined in the medieval period, for example. Another interesting feature was the impact of the changes to the educational syllabus after the Boer War (1899–1902), which shifted the subjects women were taught in school – increasing domestic science and reducing more academic study. This altered women's prospects hugely for a couple of generations.

During the process of research I found myself staring at gaping holes in what I had uncovered. The stigma attached to the LGBTQ community prior to the late 20th century meant that it was almost impossible to identify lesbian pioneers. A few are now generally recognised – Sophia Jex-Blake being one notable example, as is the Aberdeen poet Elizabeth Craigmyle – but there must be many women featured in this book whose sexuality was a closely guarded secret all their lives. Similarly the transgender community is almost impossible to find with only glimpses here and there of women who for reasons unknown presented as men.

I discovered other difficulties when winkling out women's stories from BAME communities, where sometimes the achievements of women are held within those communities and other times they are lost entirely. In this (and all my research) I was the beneficiary of generous help (see acknowledgements below) but it was clear that though women in mainstream culture are underrepresented, women from BAME cultures are for long periods almost invisible. I also saw that, societally, both colour and race seemed less of an issue pre-1830, when status was far more important. Reading original documents was a fascinating process, which gave me a new understanding and highlighted where some of today's cultural prejudices originated.

I remain mindful that, while many of the monuments I have written about are fictional, every woman was a real person and I wanted to do their memories justice. However, as with real-life memorials, there will of necessity be some I passed over unfairly and others who I perhaps shouldn't have chosen. Like the mostly-men currently honoured by statues and street names in Scotland and across the world, some women who took action with the best intentions were destined to fall foul of history – a notable group being female missionaries who, as an arm of the British Empire, travelled the world dispensing 'culture' (often alongside medical care) and trampling on the indigenous cultures of the people they wanted to help. Stories of African children brought to Scotland on fundraising exercises during the Victorian era grated against my 21st century sensibilities and as a result I didn't raise as many statues to these women as might have been put up had they been recognised in their own time. I chose to mention some of these women nonetheless – it seemed wrong not to include them.

As the project continued, one annoyance was that I

had to change so much. In the centre of Edinburgh, the city where I live, there are scores of statues to men but only one to a woman – and she is Queen Victoria (unless you count the tiny Mary Queen of Scots statues on the Portrait Gallery and Scott Monument). I knew this fact already, but working through this book really rammed it home. I read several traditional guidebooks and was outraged to find the same male stories again and again but hardly any of the female ones, even though there were, to use non-academic parlance, countless real crackers. We do not memorialise women. We have been terrible at it. The irony is that this inability to credit women means that there have been times that later generations considered themselves groundbreaking when, in fact, other women, many years before them, had already spectacularly succeeded in their field. Medieval women in business, for example, predated Victorian and Edwardian business tycoons who considered their careers pioneering. And in a way, both of these generations were pioneers but the second needn't have been!

Shocking also was that where women *were* memorialised, their memories have often been treated poorly. I almost cried finding a plaque to Lady Margaret Crawford in the kirkyard of Dunfermline Abbey, where she is unnamed, commemorated only as 'William Wallace's mother'. I have tried not to commemorate any of the women in this book in terms of their relationships to men – although there are a couple who are, in truth, notable because of those relationships. But it was gratifying to find that there were many more who could easily stand alone.

I have also found myself railing against the statue as a commemorative form – preferring on as many occasions as possible to replant flower beds or rename streets or imagine something that isn't the physical representation of the person, but a reflection of their story. Still, cities somehow suit statues and I was unable to put anything else on George Street's plinths in Edinburgh, or in Glasgow's great squares, than big bronze women.

I learned a lot about my country and how our built environment, politics and economics drive people's interests and indeed bring out their talents. I knew Glasgow was an industrial city at heart, for example, but the sheer number of crusading women in the labour movement that the city spawned in comparison to Edinburgh (which, only 50 miles away, has a longer active timeline with realms of medieval women, educationalists and Enlightenment thinkers) was extraordinary to me. Edinburgh had an opera singer, composers and more witches – Glasgow, as well as campaigners, had far more performers who toured as nightclub or music hall sensations. In Dundee I unearthed a stream of poets among early labour activists – traits that didn't spring up together anywhere else, while the women of the north wrote so movingly about the land in Scots, Gaelic and English that I felt they would willingly lie down and melt into the hills. Suffragettes, it has to be said, were everywhere! Overall, however, my research seems to demonstrate that we are a product of our environment. Which proves that how we build that environment is of huge importance.

What I hope I have achieved is a provocation that shows the breadth of female achievement. We truly have only told half of our story and, logically, the next question is, what are we going to do about that? I hope this book can contribute to that debate. It's about time we changed the world we're building to include everybody.

Acknowledgements

Oh my. Where to start? So many people were generous.

Jamie Crawford, Alasdair Burns, Jenny Brown, Fiona Brownlee, Ann Landmann – the dream team of publishing skills and book knowledge. Thank you. Christine Wilson (also on the team) definitely deserves her own thank you for having eagle eyes and working so hard on editing the guide. In the enormous amount of research required to produce this book, she steadied both the material and me, as the writer. It wouldn't have been possible without her. Thanks to Jenny Proudfoot for the illustrations and Linda Sutherland for indexing (and further thanks to Linda and her sister Elizabeth Edwards for sharing their mum's wonderful poem 'Shadows'). Thanks to Mairi Sutherland and Ruairidh Graham. Leslie Hills, the first person I told when I was commissioned and who was unfailingly supportive because she just IS. Adele Patrick and her brilliant team at the Glasgow Women's Library who saw the point straight away and were happy about it! Heather Pearson of the *Grantidote* podcast and *Fearless Femme* magazine – an inspiration! The Mapping Memorials to Women in Scotland project (which enlightened me as to a good portion of Scotland's real-life memorials) and in particular Alison McCall, who was hugely supportive of what I was doing and talked generously and knowledgeably about women's history in Scotland. Alex Musgrave, who has such Brilliant, Big Ideas and writes so beautifully. His help with a suitable witches' memorial was invaluable. Thanks to Lesley Riddoch who is always encouraging and has taught me a million things including that it is OK to cry about what happened to the witches. Professor Murray Pittock (and his book *Enlightenment in a Smart City: Edinburgh's Civic Development, 1660-1750*) was entertaining and hugely helpful. Thank you. Dr Esther Breitenbach, who gave me fabulous tips and without whose insight, not only this book, but my take on feminist history would be different. I recommend *Scottish Women: A Documentary History 1780–1914* to anyone interested in further reading. Professor Tom Devine for his advice about Highland women and the Clearances and also the hideous actions of redcoats in the four Highland counties after the '45. My well-thumbed copy of Maggie Craig's *Damn Rebel Bitches* was also invaluable. The National Centre for Gaelic Language and Culture on Skye – thank you for bearing with my terrible and almost non-existent Gaelic. To the staff at the National Library of Scotland – thank you for taking the time to help me hunt down records for some of the more slippery Scottish women from history. Gráinne Rice at the National Galleries of Scotland who sent tips. Margot MacCuaig, who helped me with the sportswomen – always fabulous! E S Thomson, who let me bounce ideas off her brilliant brain. You are a star in life, not only in medical history. To Linda Fleming, whose important thesis on Glasgow Jewry provided women from the Jewish community to commemorate – thank you for your generosity in sharing! Huw Williams at BBC Radio Orkney for his help in shouting out for island women. To Sheena Graham-George, who let me use her breathtaking installation at St Magnus Cathedral and who should be commissioned, frankly, to do more. The white butterfly monument is another of her installations but, like her installation for the witches, was a temporary exhibition and has been resurrected and displayed outdoors for this book. I thank Jordan Goodman for information received. And Harriet Richardson at the Survey of London – also, many many thanks. To Tom Mole, Director of the Centre for the History of the Book at the University of Edinburgh and his brilliant book *What the Victorians Made of Romanticism.* Christine Rew and Helen Fothergill at Aberdeen Art Gallery for coming back so efficiently with information about women from the Second World War commemorated on the war memorial in Memorial Court. You made my day! I am so glad to see them there. To Lois Wolffe at Amnesty Scotland, who was enthusiastic and supportive and thought of things we could do with the research as well as the book – and hell, I still think we should. To the Scottish Poetry Library where I found lots of amazing words – just what I needed. To the bookshelf-jedis at Black and White Publishing, thank you for your Lorna Moon support. I hadn't heard of her before and she is now my absolute favourite short story writer. To all those who suggested women via social media or made an effort to put me in touch with people who could help – writers, librarians, archivists and knowledgeable civilians: Marsali Taylor, Jen Stout, Sandra MacLeod (nice bags!) who took such a particular interest and kept sending fascinating wee snippets (so appreciated), Mark Ryan Smith (who did some legendary sleuthing and whose book *The Literature of Shetland* was enlightening), Malachy Tallack, Chris Holme (such an expert on First World War women at his History Company site) Miriam Brett, Jean Cameron, Louise Thomason, Elizabeth Trueman, the Shetland Library, Donna Heddle, Vivian Ross-Smith, Donald Murray, Alison Miller, Orkney Archaeology, Fiona Grahame, Ann

Cleeves, Mairi McFadyen, Nick Jury and Charlene Pryor. If I have missed anyone from this list, please forgive me – the response was overwhelming. I am immensely grateful. To Kari Adams and Isla Donaldson of the Pier Arts Centre in Orkney, who were incredibly helpful and sent material for me to use. The staff and even one member of the public at Dunfermline Palace and Abbey were fabulous, so thanks to Anne-Marie O'Reilly, Sandy, Andrew and Davie, who were welcoming and kind and up for tramping around and chatting for ages – you made mine a lovely visit. To David Alston, whose expertise in the Scottish involvement in the slave trade and ownership of slaves was a huge help – if truly horrifying. Thanks for sharing your important and wise words. To the ladies at Nairn Museum who had such brilliant personal knowledge when I rang about Annie Ralph – thank you for pointing me in the right direction. To Rachel Boak from the Orkney Museum, who was kind enough to help with the witch's spell box and who passed me on to Siobhan Cooke-Miller at Stromness Museum (also unfailingly generous with information). To Lucy Philips, who made great suggestions including the idea of planting a suffragette garden in what is currently St Andrews Square – thank you and cheers, darling girl! My MP, Deidre Brock, always supportive (and, I hope, a recipient of a memorial herself one day), cheered me on, like the Damn Rebel Bitch I know her to be. Thanks to Selma Rahmen who always gives excellent advice and is gloriously full of helpful ideas. Also, Danni Gordon from Chachi Power Project, who came up with the storming idea of the screen on the Finnieston Crane. Rowen Arshad of the University of Edinburgh and Carol Young of the Coalition for the Racial Equality and Rights for guidance on BAME women in Scotland – a steer that was helpful even if it demonstrated that one reason we don't know enough about our BAME communities is that we don't commemorate them properly. Alistair Heather, the brilliant Scots editor at Mike Small's *Bella Caledonia*, who saved my bacon when my brain was exhausted with a brilliant Violet Jacob quotation. Thank you Alistair. We must big up Alistair's campaign to erect a statue of Nan Shepherd on the Aberdeen University campus. Mighty! Thanks to Kirsteen Cameron for Bebe Brun and for making the bestie cake. Erin Catriona Fairly for her information about the witches' monument in Forfar and the exhibits at the Meffan Museum. Biffy and Zakia at Invisible Cities for the story about the witches' ashes in the Flodden Wall – if you are in Glasgow, Manchester or Edinburgh and you want to take a cracking guided tour, these are the people to get in touch with … Morven Chisholm and Anne Fraser at the Royal Society of Edinburgh for their help in running down the first female recipient of the society's Neill Medal. We got her! To Christine de Luca who generously put just the right poem into my hands at just the right moment. It's all in the timing. Thank you. To everyone who listened to me and said what a controversial/brilliant/clever/interesting idea – everywhere I went, really! And lastly to Alan Ferrier, Molly Sheridan and Jon Read – my home team, where we all get a vote (of course) and can say whatever the hell we like.

Index

Sang, Jane and Flora 31–2
Sawyer, Mairi 335
Saxby, Jessie 402–3
Scáthach nUanaind 336
scholars
    Central Scotland 205, 212
    Edinburgh 40
    Glasgow 106–7
    Inverness and Central
        Highlands 81, 308, 319–20
    Northeast Scotland 273
    Northern Highlands and
        Islands 343
    see also folklorists/folksong collec-
        tors; historians; professors
Schubert, Franz 138
Schwarzschild, Cecile 112
scientists 30, 40, 49, 124, 148, 232,
    285
    see also astronomers; chemists
Scobie, Stephen 372
Scota 303–4
Scott, Arabella 59–60
Scott, Hettie 382
Scott, Randolph 91
Scott, Wallie 368
Scott, Sir Walter
    Abbotsford 142–3
    Joanna Baillie and 177
    Anna Brown and 268
    Margaret Chalmers and 391
    Alison Cockburn's opinion of 51
    Marjory Fleming and 218
    Jean Gordon and 154
    Margaret Hogg and 152–3
    on Kelso 138–9
    Elizabeth Nasmyth's designs
        for 61
    opinion of Susan Ferrier 10, 62
    Porter sisters and 54
    Marion Ritchie and 151
    Harriet Siddons' adaptations 29
    Helen Walker and 160
Scott-Moncrieff, Ann 376

screenwriters 120, 254
sculptors
    Central Scotland 224
    Edinburgh 23, 27, 35, 55, 133
    Glasgow 83, 90, 103
    Inverness and Central
        Highlands 300, 317, 353
    Northeast Scotland 267, 273
    Southern Scotland 133, 162
seal-women 400–1
seamstresses 120–1
    see also garment workers
Searle, Ronald 143
Seeger, Peggy 329
Segrove, Sir John de 144–5
Sejdini, Qazim 273
servants 158, 161, 187–8, 223
Seton, Mary 207
sex workers 66, 71, 86
Shakespeare, William 313
Shaw, Christian 121
Shaw, Margaret Fay 349
Shaw, Marjorie 59
Shaw, Winnie 97
Shearer, Moira 223–4
Sheil, Tibbie 151
Shelley, Mary 245
Shepherd, Mary 69
Shepherd, Nan 253–4
Short, Maria 68
Siddons, Harriet 29
Sigurd, Earl of Orkney 381
Sileas nighean Mhic Raghnaill 335–6
Simon, Edith 59
Simpson, Roona 95
Sinclair, Bell 358
Sinclair, Catherine 43, 52
Sinclair, Lise 397
Sinclair, Margaret 45
Sinclair, Rosabelle 209
singers
    Central Scotland 186
    Edinburgh 29
    Glasgow 90, 91

Sara Sheridan

Sara Sheridan, named as one of the Saltire Society's most influential Scottish women, past and present, is known for the Mirabelle Bevan mysteries, a series of historical novels based on Georgian and Victorian explorers, and has written non-fiction on the early days of Queen Victoria's marriage and the historical background to Jane Austen's novel *Sanditon*. With a fascination for uncovering forgotten women in history, she is an active campaigner, a feminist and co-founder of radical perfume brand REEK.

Historic Environment Scotland

We are the lead public body for Scotland's historic environment: a charity dedicated to the advancement of heritage, culture, education and environmental protection.

Our books are telling the stories of Scotland. From landmark works of expert research to creative collaborations with internationally renowned authors, our aim is to explore ideas and start conversations about the past, present and future of our nation's history and heritage.